THE ROLLING STONES

A to Z

by SUE WEINER
and LISA HOWARD

GROVE PRESS, INC./NEW YORK

First Evergreen Edition published in 1983

Library of Congress Cataloging in Publication Data

Weiner, Sue
 The Rolling Stones A to Z.
 1. Rolling Stones — Dictionaries, indexes, etc.
 I. Howard, Lisa.   II. Title.
ML421.R6W44   1983   784.5′4′00922   83–48291
ISBN 0-394-62000-3

Manufactured in the United States of America

GROVE PRESS, INC., 196 West Houston Street, New York, N.Y. 10014

10 9 8 7 6 5 4 3 2 1

THE ROLLING STONES A TO Z

Foreword

In 1964 when I listened to the radio constantly, obsessed with terror that some Beatles Bulletin might miss me over the airwaves, I heard New York disc jockey Murray the K ("the fifth Beatle") speak to John Lennon (one of the four Beatles) on a show taped in London. John told Murray about a song that he and Paul McCartney (another quarter of the Beatles—the cute quarter) had written called "I Wanna Be Your Man," for a British group called The Rolling Stones. One of them described the Rolling Stones. They were so long-haired and dirty that it was not to be believed—I mean, so long-haired and dirty that it was *scary,* they said. But if you were brave and wanted to see the Stones for yourself—these guys had yet to be seen or heard of outside of England—you could write away for a picture. Murray gave the name Andrew Loog Oldham (what kind of a name was Loog? I wondered) and a London address. I bought an airmail stamp and told my parents if anything arrived for me from England, not to *dare* open it.

Three weeks later, fresh from Nick the postman, I saw my first picture of the Rolling Stones. They weren't dirty, but they weren't wearing matching suits either (a rarity in those days). And their hair was only about a quarter of an inch longer than the Beatles. But the picture was *autographed*—not printed-up-autographed—*really autographed!* I could tell 'cause they all used different pens (Mick used magic marker). As Cheap Trick sang, "Heaven Tonight." And in May 1964, the Stones made a fan for life.

The Stones were never my *favorite* band (the Yardbirds were), but significant life events of an entire generation—and now subsequent generations—coincided with them. Personal events, too. Brian Jones is dead. I never knew anyone who died before, or at least *felt* I knew him; I spent the July 4th weekend locked in my room crying. Altamont. The Stones sure knew how to end the sixties. I saw the Stones a lot that decade; it helped that my best friend's father's third cousin was Allen Klein. I can't forget the film *Performance* because it was the only time I ever went to the movies *alone*—absolutely everyone I knew in 1970 heard that the film was "disgusting," but I had to see Mick. Because of the Stones I missed, "the reunion of the decade," a few years ago when Frank Sinatra brought Dean Martin onstage at a Muscular Dystrophy Telethon to hug former comedy partner Jerry Lewis. Since Martin's insulting comments about the Stones during their first American TV appearance on *The Hollywood Palace* variety show which he hosted, I've been unable to even *look* at the man. I don't know how Lewis and Martin get along today, but I've held my grudge for 19 years. I also missed it when the Stones played on a flatbed truck *outside my very own apartment building* in 1975 because I was working in an office two miles uptown. But the god of rock 'n' roll was smiling: I was introduced to my favorite musician and all-time idol, Jeff Beck, that night. Another important day in Stones history for me, you bet.

The list goes on.

The Stones keep rollin'.

The most significant aspect of the present-day Stones, I believe, is that they represent rock 'n' roll for all non-rock 'n' roll media. *Playbill,* the monthly Broadway theater program, described the "leader of the cat pack" in the hit musical *Cats* as "Jagger-like"; in the film *Nightwing,* about vampire bats destroying a village, the father of a teenage American Indian girl defends her purity with the words, "Hell, she doesn't even know who Mick Jagger is"; comedian Robin Williams does an impersonation, complete with accent, of Lawrence Welk introducing "the lovely Lennon sisters who will sing '(I Can't Get No) Satisfaction'"; and in the TV show *Remington Steele,* private investigator Laura Holt, played by Stephanie Zimbalist, returns dead drunk from an undercover assignment, and stumbles into her office slurring the lyrics to the self-same song. *Savvy,* "The Magazine for Executive Women," entitles an article about the baby-boom generation's ability to afford today's home mortgage rates "Gimme Shelter."

There are no worlds left to conquer.

In an Italian restaurant in 1981, Sue Weiner and I sat near a family whose members were loudly arguing as to who would get the tickets should the family be fortunate enough to win the right to buy tickets in the lottery held for the Stones' New York Madison Square Garden dates later that year. Mom and Dad wanted the tickets, but Sis and Junior insisted they should be theirs. In twenty years, the Rolling Stones have released more than 30 albums and destroyed the nuclear family. Can we ever again believe that "Father Knows Best" when he's battling the kids for a chance to see Keith Richards?

But most of all, I like the way the Stones grew up. Charlie is a well-dressed, well-respected musician, a jazz drummer who just happens to play in a rock 'n' roll band. Bill is a cultured man of the world, solo recording artist, soundtrack scorer, and published photographer. And he's *still* (ignore all rumors) a Rolling Stone. Ron looks like what people dream British rock stars look like. He gets older and better and better. He's an accomplished artist and tries to spread the rock 'n' roll word. I believe him.

Mick is probably THE MOST FAMOUS MAN IN THE WORLD, as singer, lover, jet-setter, fashion plate, and "personality." "What can a poor boy do . . . ?"

Brian—R. I. P.

Mick T.—wherever.

And—oh, yeah,—the other one.

Even in silhouette, Keith's is the image that has come to define "rock 'n' roll." His stance sounds the music, and without him there's silence. It was a very happy day when someone who knows told me, "Keith dresses like that *all* the time." He keeps the faith. In his book *Guitar Heros,* John Tobler quotes an anonymous scribe with the words, "When Keith Richards enters a room, rock 'n' roll comes in with him." It's no wonder, then, that he staggers a lot—for all of rock 'n' roll ain't the easiest burden in the world to carry.

I've spent six years selling—and many more than that reading—rock 'n' roll books, a lot of which, naturally, are about the Stones. But this is my favorite. Its heart is in the right place. Read it cover to cover (you can use it just to look things up later)—it's written right, and it's *not* only rock 'n' roll! But you'll like it.

Karen Rose, Rock Read
New York, 1983

HOW TO USE THIS BOOK

The main entries for all members of the Rolling Stones past and present—Mick Jagger, Brian Jones, Keith Richards, Mick Taylor, Charlie Watts, Ron Wood, and Bill Wyman—are listed alphabetically by last name. However, with the exception of Mick Taylor, they are usually referred to throughout THE ROLLING STONES A TO Z by first name only. Other leading characters in the Stones story who often appear with only one name are:

Andrew—Andrew Oldham
Oldham—Andrew Oldham
Bianca—Bianca Jagger
Anita—Anita Pallenberg
Marianne—Marianne Faithfull
Astrid—Astrid Wyman
Jo—Jo Howard

On Rolling Stones ALBUM listings, all songs are written by Jagger/Richards, unless otherwise noted in parentheses after the song title. (On solo Stone efforts, the songs are written by the given solo Stone, unless otherwise noted in parentheses after the song title.) Additional non-Stone musicians are listed below the song titles along with other album data. The "s" or "no s" notation at the end of an album entry refers to the ever-changing spelling of Keith Richard/Richards' last name on the LP covers and disc labels. When American and British LPs differ in any way, even though they may have the same title (ie: AFTERMATH), they are listed separately in order of release date.

Some albums released by various record labels after the Stones' recording contracts expired with them are compilation albums with material culled from more than one Stones LP. Since no one producer is credited for these, we have noted "Compilation Album" under the listing for "Producer."

On individual Rolling Stones *songs*, Mick is lead singer unless otherwise noted. (On solo Stone efforts, the solo Stone is lead singer unless otherwise noted.) When a song's author is listed as "Trad," it is a traditional song in the public domain, not credited to anyone. The release date for a song is its first appearance, be that on a single, EP, or album. When a song appears on several LPs, the albums are listed in chronological order. When a song appears on a single we list the tune it is backed with (b/w) if it is the A-side, and its more famous counterpart if it's the "flip." Also listed under each song are non-Stone musicians performing on it and other vital statistics.

An EP is an extended play record, containing more than two songs, though usually the size of a single.

Solo albums by members of the Rolling Stones are listed in full detail only if the artist was a Rolling Stone at the time of the album's recording. That's to say, all Bill Wyman solo LPs are completely detailed, whereas early pre-Stone Ron Wood works aren't. That's also to say, if you're not a Stone you don't count.

When a Rolling Stone appears as a guest performer or producer on another artist's LP or song, the work is listed under the LP or song *title*, not under the artist's name. (Example: Mick Jagger guests on Leslie West's THE GREAT FATSBY. This is listed under THE GREAT FATSBY, not Leslie West.) Mick Taylor plays on almost every other album ever released, and you'll find him under those titles.

Welcome to Stonedom. Hope you enjoy your "Magical Mystery Tour" . . . Ooops!

ACKNOWLEDGEMENTS

For Karen Rose and Bill German

And thanks to all who came to our
rescue, emotional and otherwise
(A to Z, of course):
David Allen who made it gorgeous and
not only because he went to the same
art college as Charlie Watts
Colin Burns/Rolling Stones Records,
U.K.
Art Collins/Rolling Stones Records,
U.S.
Christine Freeman
Goldie Friede
Bill German/BEGGARS BANQUET
Jodie Gould
The Guys from DINER
The whole Howard family
Mick Jagger
Fred Jeffery/Rockit Records
Brian Jones
Fred Jordan for the fact that you're
reading this now!
Jayne Law
Ginny Lohle/Star File
Barbara O'Shea
Neal Preston
Keith Richards
Helen & Larry Rose
Karen Rose
Phyllis Rosney
Nick Schaffner
Bella Sussman
Robin Titone
Gary Victor who saved us at every
last minute
Charlie Watts
Frank Weiner
Pearl & Richard Weiner
Ron Wood
and
Bill Wyman

THE ROLLING STONES

A to Z

by SUE WEINER
and LISA HOWARD

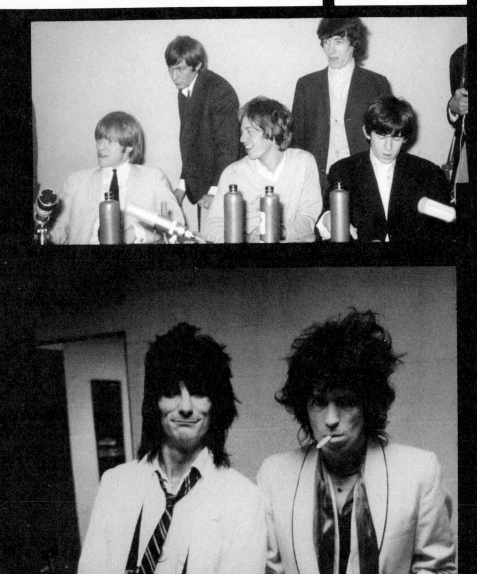

A

A & M RECORDS
Record company with which Bill has a solo recording contract.

A.B.C. TEASHOP
Bakery next door to the Ealing Club where Bill's hair was first combed Stones-style. It was then he knew he belonged.

ABKCO RECORDS
Allen Klein's record company, to which the Stones were signed in America. ABKCO, in turn, contracted them to London Records. (See Klein, Allen.)

A. N. OTHER
Supergroup formed for "The Rolling Stones' Rock and Roll Circus" comprised of Keith on bass, John Lennon on rhythm guitar and vocals, Eric Clapton on lead guitar, and Mitch Mitchell on drums. They performed "Yer Blues."

ADLER, LOU
American record producer who, as "Lou-in Adler," is credited with the title concept of FLOWERS.

"ADONAIS"
Poem by Percy Bysshe Shelley, part of which was read by Mick in memory of Brian Jones at the free Hyde Park Concert given by the Stones on July 5, 1969.

ADVENTURES OF VALENTINE VOX THE VENTRILOQUIST, THE
1974 Chris Jagger album featuring Dave Edmunds and Peter Frampton, though all Stones remained unturned for this effort.

AFTEL, MANDY
Author of *Death of a Rolling Stone: The Brian Jones Story.*

"AFTER MUDDY AND CHARLIE"
Song recorded by the Stones in Jamaica during the GOATS HEAD SOUP sessions, but never released.

AFTERMATH (U.K.)
Artist: The Rolling Stones
Producer: Andrew Loog Oldham
Release date: April 1966
Record label: Decca
Tracks: 14
"Mother's Little Helper"
"Stupid Girl"
"Lady Jane"
"Under My Thumb"
"Doncha Bother Me"
"Goin' Home"

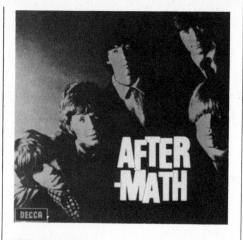

"Flight 505"
"High and Dry"
"Out of Time"
"It's Not Easy"
"I Am Waiting"
"Take It or Leave It"
"Think"
"What to Do"
• 4th U.K. LP.
• Jack Nitzsche—percussion, piano, organ, harpsichord.
• "The Sixth Stone," Ian Stewart —piano, organ, harpsichord.
• Studio—RCA Studios, Hollywood.
• Engineer—Dave Hassinger.
• Arranged by The Rolling Stones.

- Photography—Guy Webster, Jerrold Schatzberg.
- Cover design—Sandy Beach (aka Andrew Oldham).
- Liner notes by Dave Hassinger who compliments the Stones on being real "professionals" and "a gas to work with."
- "Lighting" by Mick Jagger.
- This is the first Stones album to be entirely written by Jagger and Richards.
- The title AFTERMATH might refer to the people and things remaining at the "aftermath" of World War Three.
- AFTERMATH was to have been the soundtrack for the never-filmed Stones feature, *Back, Behind, and in Front*.
- No "s" in Keith's last name.

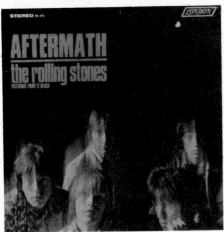

AFTERMATH (U.S.)
Artist: The Rolling Stones
Producer: Andrew Loog Oldham
Release date: June 1966
Record label: London
Tracks: 11
"Paint It, Black"
"Stupid Girl"
"Lady Jane"
"Under My Thumb"
"Doncha Bother Me"
"Think"
"Flight 505"
"High and Dry"
"It's Not Easy"
"I Am Waiting"
"Goin' Home"
- 7th U.S. LP.
- Photography—David Bailey, Jerrold Schatzberg.
- Cover design—Steve Inglis.
- All other details are the same as AFTERMATH (U.K.).

"AIN'T TOO PROUD TO BEG"
Written by: Holland/Whitfield
Recorded by: The Rolling Stones
Release date: October 1974
Record label: Rolling Stones Records
Album: IT'S ONLY ROCK 'N' ROLL
Single: B/w "Dance LIttle Sister" (U.S. 10/74)
- Billy Preston—piano, clavinet
- Ed Leach—cowbell

ALABAMA
German film (1969) about death which features the song "2000 Light Years from Home."

ALBERT, HOWARD AND RON
Engineers who also mixed and served as production assistants on MONKEY GRIP; engineers and production assistants on STONE ALONE.

ALEXANDER, LARRY
Assistant engineer of STILL LIFE.

ALEXANDRA PALACE, LONDON
Site of June 1964 "Rolling Stones Fan Club Presents All Night Rave," a show which lasted from 9 P.M. to 6:30 A.M. and featured John Lee Hooker, John Mayall, and many others in addition to our heroes.

"ALL ABOUT YOU"
Written by: Jagger/Richards
Recorded by: The Rolling Stones
Lead singer: Keith
Release date: June 1980
Record label: Rolling Stones Records
Album: EMOTIONAL RESCUE

"ALL DOWN THE LINE"
Written by: Jagger/Richards
Recorded by: The Rolling Stones
Release date: May 1972
Record label: Rolling Stones Records
Albums: EXILE ON MAIN ST.
TIME WAITS FOR NO ONE
Single: Flip of "Happy" (U.S. 6/72)
- Bill Plummer—upright bass.
- Jimmy Miller—percussion.
- Kathi McDonald—backup vocals.

"ALL I WANT IS MY BABY"/"EACH AND EVERY DAY"
1965 Bobby Jameson single produced by Andrew Oldham with musical direction by Keith. Both sides are Jagger/Richards compositions.

"ALL SOLD OUT"
Written by: Jagger/Richards
Recorded by: The Rolling Stones
Release date: January 1967
Record label: Decca/London
Albums: BETWEEN THE BUTTONS (U.K.)
BETWEEN THE BUTTONS (U.S.)

"ALL YOU NEED IS CASH"
Eric Idle's 1978 satirical "documentary" TV show about the fictionalized band, The Rutles, which featured Mick and Ron in cameo appearances.

"ALL YOU NEED IS LOVE"
Beatles song on which Mick and Keith sing backup vocals. Mick and Marianne Faithfull joined the festivities when the Beatles performed this song live to the world via the "Our World" telecast in 1967.

ALLIK, LENNE
Creator of cover concept for MORE HOT ROCKS.

ALLRIGHT ON THE NIGHT
1973 Tucky Buzzard album produced by Bill.

ALTAMONT
The Stones wanted to put on a free concert in California similiar to Woodstock because they wanted to thank their fans for the success of their 1969 U.S. tour and because they were filming the tour and needed a climax for the movie's ending. They got more than they ever bargained for. 300,000 people attended the one-day outdoor concert held on December 6, l969, at Altamont Speedway in Livermore, California. Among those opening the show were Crosby, Stills, Nash, and Young; Santana; the Flying Burrito Brothers; and the Jefferson Airplane.

The performers could sense that the audience's mood wasn't the laid-back, let's-have-fun feel of the Woodstock generation. Tension was in the air and the audience was just waiting for something to happen. And the Hell's Angels (who the Grateful Dead had suggested act as "police" in exchange for free beer) only added to rather than cooled down the crowd's uneasiness. When the Airplane were on stage, Marty Balin was knocked out by a Hell's Angel and Grace Slick's pleadings for the audience to keep cool went unheaded. It was dark when the Stones came on, opening with "Jumpin' Jack Flash"; but even though the crowd had been waiting for them, the Stones too were unable to stop the scattered outbreaks of violence around them. Mick tried to calm the crowd down by talking to them; Keith showed that even an angry crowd of 300,000 couldn't scare him. He threatened to stop playing if they didn't stop fighting. Between the performances of "Love in Vain" and "Under My Thumb," unbeknownst to the Stones and most of the audience, Meridith Hunter aimed a gun at the stage; doing what he felt was his job, a Hell's Angel stabbed him to death. (He was later acquitted.) Altamont appeared to be the symbolic ending to the peace-loving sixties, and it furthered the Stones' violent image. Keith put it best in his understated way: "Altamont was something that the Stones could have well done without."

AMERICAN EMBASSY, LONDON
Mick took part in the 1968 storming of this embassy in protest of the Viet Nam war.

AMERICAN SUCCESS COMPANY, THE
Original title of the 1983-released film, *Success*.

AMYL NITRATE
Drug which Keith does not take.

Also, the name of the marimba player on "Sweet Black Angel."

"AND THE ROLLING STONES MET PHIL AND GENE"
Song recorded by the Stones in February 1964, but never released. The names in the title refer to Phil Spector and Gene Pitney.

ANITA
See Pallenberg, Anita.

"ANDREW'S BLUES"
Song recorded by the Stones at the "Not Fade Away" sessions, February 1964, but also never released. Mick and Phil Spector sing, with Graham Nash (of the Hollies) and Gene Pitney singing backup.

ANDREWS, PAT
A Cheltenham girlfriend of Brian's

who, in October 1961, at the age of 16, gave birth to Brian's second child (he sold his records to buy her flowers in the hospital). During Pat's pregnancy, she and Brian lived at her sister's home, but soon Brian moved to London. On Easter Sunday, 1962, Pat and Infant Jones #2 joined Brian in London, where she worked in a laundry and Brian wandered from job to job. Pat and Brian's relationship ended when, rumor had it, Mick began a brief affair with Ms. Andrews.

"ANGIE"
Written by: Jagger/Richards
Recorded by: The Rolling Stones
Release date: August 1973
Record label: Rolling Stones Records
Albums: GOATS HEAD SOUP
      MADE IN THE SHADE
      BY INVITATION ONLY
      TIME WAITS FOR NO ONE
Single: B/w "Silver Train" (U.S./U.K. 8/73)
• Nicky Hopkins—piano.
• Nicky Harrison—string arrangement.
• Rumored to be about Angie Bowie (the former Mrs. David).
• Rumored that above rumor was started by Angie Bowie.

ANNENBERG, WALTER
Former U.S. ambassador to Britain. In 1975 he reportedly arranged for Keith to be able to enter the U.S. for the Stones tour providing that Keith pass a blood test drug-free.

ANNIE
Mick was offered, but turned down, a role in the film version of the play of the comic.

AN ANTHOLOGY OF BRITISH BLUES VOL. 1
1968 Immediate Records compilation LP featuring "Snake Drive," and "Tribute to Elmore," both credited to Eric Clapton, but listing Mick and Bill as musicians on the two tracks in the liner notes. (See BLUES ANYTIME VOL.1)

AN ANTHOLOGY OF BRITISH BLUES VOL. 2
1969 Immediate Records compilation LP featuring "West Coast Idea." (See BLUES ANYTIME VOL. 1.)

"APACHE WOMAN"
Written by: Bill Wyman
Recorded by: Bill Wyman
Release date: February 1976
Record label: Rolling Stones Records
Album: STONE ALONE
Single: B/w "Soul Satisfying" (U.S./ U.K. 9/76)
• Dallas Taylor—drums.
• Danny Kortchmar—guitar.
• Hubie Heard—organ.
• Albhy Galuten—synthesizer.

• Ruth and Bonnie Pointer—backup vocals.
• Guille Garcia—percussion.

APOCALYPSE, NOW
1980 Viet Nam war film in which "Satisfaction" can be heard.

APPICE, CARMINE
Drummer with Vanilla Fudge, Cactus, Beck Bogert & Appice, and Rod Stewart. He performs on Ron's "Priceless."

APPLE
The brand of computer which Bill uses to chronicle the history of the Stones.

APPLEBY, JOHN
"Beat" character and author of *38 Priory Street and All That Jazz*, whom Brian met at Cheltenham's El Flam club and adopted as a father figure. Appleby's interest in music and, of all things, buses, influenced Brian in the career we all know about, and also in his short stint as a bus conductor.

APRIL WINE
Group advertised as appearing at El Mocambo, a Toronto club, the night the Stones played there in 1977. Since April Wine's manager was friends with Peter Rudge, the Stones' tour manager, he let them use the band's name as a cover for the Stones.

ARANBEE POP SYMPHONY ORCHESTRA, THE
Group which recorded the TODAY'S POP SYMPHONY LP.

ARCHBISHOP OF CANTERBURY
In 1965, Charlie bought a sixteenth-century Sussex mansion which was built as a hunting lodge for the Archbishop.

ARDEN, DON
Promoter of the Rolling Stones' first U.K. concert and, later, the manager of the Small Faces. Arden eventually bought Immediate Records from Andrew Oldham. He now presides over Jet Records and, most recently, became Ozzy Osbourne's father-in-law.

ARNOLD, P.P.
American vocalist and former Ike and Tina Turner backup Ikette, who moved to the U.K. and was signed by Andrew Oldham to Immediate Records. Her backup group was the Nice, who were also signed to Immediate. Arnold sang with Mick at Mick and Bianca's wedding reception.

ARNOLD, SHIRLEY
Personal secretary to the Stones for nine years after Keith picked her out of an audience and asked her to answer the Stones' fan mail. Mick, Bianca, the Wattses, and Mick Taylor attended her farewell party when she left the Stones in 1972 to work with the Faces. She didn't return with Woody, however.

ARONOWITZ, AL
N.Y. newspaper columnist for whom Brian wrote the song, "(Thank You) For Being There."

"AROUND AND AROUND"
Written by: Chuck Berry
Recorded by: The Rolling Stones
Release date: August 1964
Record label: Decca/London/Rolling Stones Records
Albums: 12 x 5
  PROMOTIONAL ALBUM
  STONE AGE
  LOVE YOU LIVE (live in Toronto)

EP: FIVE BY FIVE (U.K. 8/64)
• Ian Stewart—piano.
• This song was also performed by Little Boy Blue and the Blue Boys on the demo tape they sent to Alexis Korner.

ARRESTS
"Being busted…it's no pleasure, but it certainly isn't boring. And I think boring is the worst thing of all…."
    —Keith Richards
Quite simply, the Stones and members thereof, except for Charlie, have been arrested more times than any other rock 'n' roll band. When a few times a decade a new band comes along with some strong musical statement, they are hailed as "the Stones of the seventies . . . eighties . . ." whenever. No one has taken their place. The reason that *the Stones* have remained "the Stones of the seventies . . . eighties . . ." whenever, is that along with their music, they have always retained that outlaw (a lot stronger than "bad boy") image which Andrew Oldham so prophetically created for them. Especially Keith, who in the mid-seventies noted, "For a time we were in danger of becoming respectable." *Danger* is correct, because even though the Stones are now the age of their teen fans' parents, it's this sense of menace that keeps them

eternally young and rebellious, and "the Stones of . . . forever." As long as they can afford the bail. . . .

The following Rolling Stones and Stones-related arrests are listed in chronological order:

Liverpool, England
In August 1964, Mick was fined for speeding and driving without a license and insurance. His lawyer defended Mick by claiming that he was on his way to visit "two fans who had been injured in a car crash." Mick was fined twenty-three pounds.

Staffordshire, England
In November 1964, Mick was fined sixteen pounds for reckless driving and insulting a policeman.

Francis Service Station
In March 1965, Bill, Mick, and Brian were arrested for "insulting behavior," "obscene language," and "urinating in public" at this gas station in Stratford. Customer Eric Lavender and Charles Keely, gas station attendant, reported the trio to the police after the Stones had stopped at the station following a concert. They were brought to Forest Gate Police Station. The trial was held in June 1965 and Judge Albert Moorey fined the three Stones three pounds

each, plus fifteen guineas costs between them, for insulting behavior. The other charges were dropped.

Redlands Bust
On February 12, 1967, at 7:55 P.M., Sussex police, headed by Chief Inspector Dineley, knocked at the door of Keith's country home, disrupting a small party he was having, and produced a search warrant, claiming that drugs were being used on the premises. The police ransacked the house in search of the drugs, discovering four pep pills in a green velvet jacket that Mick claimed was his (it was, in actuality, Marianne Faithfull's); a naked woman, "Miss X.," wrapped only in a fur rug (also Marianne); and heroin in the possession of Robert Fraser. Mick, Keith, and Fraser were arrested, though a "Mr. X.," also in possession of drugs, was not.

On May 10, 1967, at Chichester Magistrates Court, Mick, Keith, and Fraser were allowed bail of £100 each. "Mr. X." had fled the country. (Ironically, on the day of the hearing, Brian was busted in his home for possession of cocaine, Methedrine, and cannabis. [See London Courtfield Bust—next entry.])

From June 27 to 29, Mick, Keith, and Fraser were on trial at West Sussex Quarter Sessions, with Judge Leslie Block presiding. Mick had to spend the night of his trial, before sentencing, at Lewes Prison. After Keith's case was heard, it took the jury little more than five minutes to reach their verdict. Judge Block, who felt that Keith and Mick were "scum and filth," sentenced them. Mick was found guilty of illegal possession of pep pills, fined £100, and sentenced to three months in jail. Keith was found guilty of allowing people to smoke hashish in his home, fined £500, and sentenced to one year in jail. Robert Fraser was found guilty of possession of heroin, fined £200, and sentenced to six months in jail. Keith was sent to Wormwood Scrubs for the night, and Mick and Fraser went to Brixton Jail.

The next day, June 30, witnessed a strong public outcry, an editorial in the *London Times,* the Who releasing two Stones songs to keep their name in the public eye, and protests outside the courthouse. Public opinion truly rallied around the Stones, with all concurring that the government wanted to make examples out of the Stones by giving them such strict sentencing on flimsy charges. A doctor testified that he gave Mick a prescription for the pills, which Mick had purchased legally in Italy. Another fact brought out at the trial by Keith was that the Stones felt they had been set up by *The News* of the World, in retaliation for Mick's

threatening to sue the paper for libel in response to their article stating that he took drugs. "The vanishing 'Mr. X.'" had supposedly tipped off the paper, who in turn called the police when they heard drugs were being taken at Keith's party. Keith and Mick were released on bail of £7,000 each at the High Court.

A month later, on July 31, 1967, Lord Parker, the Lord Chief Justice at London Appeal Court, dismissed the charges against Keith, giving Mick a conditional discharge. Only Robert Fraser went to jail. On August 18, the Stones released "We Love You" to thank the public for their support.

London (Courtfield Bust)
On May 10, 1967, the same day Mick and Keith had their Redlands hearing, Scotland Yard busted Brian and Prince Stanislaus Klossowski de Rola for unlawful possession of drugs at Brian's flat at Courtfield Road. Brian was given £250 bail and had to report to Marlborough Street Magistrates Court the next day. In October of 1967, Brian was sentenced to nine months in prison for possession of cannabis and had to spend the night at Wormwood Scrubs. He was released the following day on £750 bail. In December, his prison sentence was set aside by Lord Parker, and Brian was fined £3,000 and given three years probation, which entailed seeing a parole officer once every two weeks.

Brian had been warned of the bust, and the Stones felt that it was done because the police "were out to get the Stones." Mick attended Brian's appeal in December, which made Brian feel good since he desperately needed the support of the other Stones. Brian was terrified of going to jail and took the entire experience much more seriously than Mick and Keith did. Doctors testified that Brian could never survive locked away in jail, and many of his friends felt that the police harassment that continued to follow Brian was partly responsible for his eventual death.

Barcelona, Spain
After the Redlands bust, the Stones wanted to get away from England, so Mick, Keith, and Brian planned to holiday in Morocco. Mick and Marianne Faithfull were going to meet the others there, and Brian, Anita, Keith, and two traveling companions, Tom Keylock and Debra Dickson, opted for a long drive in Keith's Bentley. Along the way, Brian overdosed and was left in a hospital in Toulon, France, and Keith, Anita, Tom, and Debra were arrested in Barcelona for disorderly conduct. They were held at the police station for six hours, but no

charges were filed against them.

London (Imperial Hotel Bust)
In May 1968, in a residential hotel room on Kings Road, Brian was again busted when the police found hash in a ball of yarn in his apartment. Brian appeared at Marlborough Street Magistrates Court and his bail was set at £2,000. Mick and Keith attended the hearing, lending their moral support to Brian, who was so upset after the bust that he was admitted to Priory Nursing Home the next day.

Brian's court case was set for June at Inner Court Sessions, and the trial was held in September. Brian was found guilty of unauthorized possession of cannabis, even though he claimed the ball of yarn hadn't been his. He had to pay £50 and £105 in court fees. People in the Stones' organization feared that because this was Brian's second drug arrest he would have a difficult time entering America and this would seriously hinder the Stones' touring possibilities.

London (Chelsea, Cheyne Walk)
It seemed that once a year—in May—at least one Stone was busted. In 1969 it was Mick's turn. On the day that he announced his plans to star in *Ned Kelly,* the police busted Mick and Marianne Faithfull for possession of cannabis at their Chelsea home. They were released on £50 bail each. In December Mick was found guilty and fined £200 and had to pay £53 court fees; Marianne was acquitted of the charges. Along with the sentencing came an eighteen-month U.S. visa ban. At the trial Mick accused Detective Sgt. Robin Constable of asking for a payoff. Constable subsequently sued Mick for libel.

Rome, Italy
In August 1970, Mick was ordered by a judge in Rome to pay a £1,200 fine for allegedly punching a photographer.

Nice Airport, France
In June 1971, Shirley Watts was arrested at Nice Airport for assault when she allegedly hit an airport official and swore at customs officials. She was released on bail and sentenced *in absentia* to six months in jail with a fine of £30. In August she appealed and was given a fifteen-day suspended sentence.

Warwick Airport, Rhode Island, U.S.
In the summer of 1972, when Andy Dickerman, a photographer for the *Providence Journal and Bulletin,* accused the Stones of assault at Rhode Island's airport during their 1972 U.S. tour, Keith and Stanley Moore (in charge of Stones security during the tour) were charged with simple assault.

Mick, Marshall Chess, and Robert Frank were charged with obstruction of police.

Chelmsford, England
In November of 1972 at Chelmsford Magistrates Court, Bill was fined £20 for speeding and was temporarily banned from driving.

Jamaica
In December of 1972, Anita was alone in Jamaica when she was arrested and put in prison for possession of marijuana. She claims she was beaten and raped while in jail. Keith, in England, wanted to go to Jamaica to help, but it was feared that he might be arrested if he set foot in the country. Anita felt the government had arrested her because of her friendship with the Jamaican religious cult, the Rastafarians. It was rumored that Anita was let out of jail after a bribe was paid.

Nellcote, France
While living in Villefranche, France, Keith and Anita were busted in December of 1972 when police found hashish, cocaine, and heroin at Nellcote, a rented villa. Police in Nice also had found drugs aboard their yacht, Mandrax. Reports from France at first

stated that Mick, Charlie, Bill, and Mick Taylor were also involved in the arrest, but they were only questioned by Judge André Lasfarque and never charged. Keith and Anita were formally charged with violating drug laws. The Nice police reported that they had secretly been investigating Keith for the prior thirteen months until they had enough evidence against him. Keith and Anita were in Jamaica when the warrants for their arrest were issued. In October 1973, Keith and Anita were fined £1,350 each and given one-year suspended sentences. In 1974, after Keith lost the appeal, he was banned from entering France for the next two years.

London (Cheyne Walk)
Keith returned to London after the Nellcote bust, and his Cheyne Walk home was raided in June 1973. Keith, Anita, and Prince Stanislaus Klossowski de Rola were busted for possession of cannabis, heroin, mandrax, and on the non-drug side, artillery. Bail was set at £500, and the trial was set for July 31. But, unfortunately, that day there was a serious fire at Redlands and the trial was postponed until September. At Marlborough Street Magistrates Court,

Keith was found guilty of all charges and fined £200. Anita was given a conditional discharge for possession of mandrax, and the Prince was found not guilty.

As at the Redlands trial, it was reported that in their eagerness to get the Stones the police overlooked most of the serious drugs in the house during their search.

London (Wick)
After Keith was busted in his Cheyne Walk home he was afraid to live there because he felt the police might come back. Ron Wood offered him the use of the guest cottage on the grounds of his home, Wick, and Keith moved in there. The police, however, tracked him down in April 1975, and went to Wick to bust him. To their surprise Keith wasn't there, but Krissie Wood and a friend were arrested instead when the police found heroin on the premises. Years later they were acquitted.

Fordyce, Arkansas, U.S.
In July 1975, during the Stones U.S. tour, Keith, Ron, Jim Callaghan (head of security), and a friend decided to drive through Arkansas to get a real

feel of America, which they did when the police stopped their car in Fordyce and found Keith's knife. Keith was charged with possession of a weapon and reckless driving. Ron was held but not charged. Both were freed on bail, and reportedly the case was settled without convictions because the police failed to fingerprint Keith.

Toronto Bust
When Keith and Anita arrived at the Toronto Airport from London in February 1977, Anita was busted after hashish, heroin, and a Tic Tac were found among her twenty-eight pieces of luggage. She, Keith, and son, Marlon, proceeded to check into the Harbour Castle Hotel, where the rest of the Stones and entourage had been waiting several days for their arrival. They had been booked into various suites, for security reasons, and decided to move into the one registered under the name "Redlands." On February 27, the Royal Canadian Mounted Police raided their suite while Keith was asleep and seized twenty-two grams of 32 percent pure heroin, five grams of cocaine, and narcotics paraphernalia. Keith admitted that all of the drugs were his and that he had been addicted to heroin for over four years. He was arrested by the Brampton police and released on a $1,000 bail deposit, after his passport was seized. On March 8, bail was set at $25,000 and his passport was returned. Because of the amount of drugs found, police felt that Keith had plans to traffic the drugs, and the maximum sentence he could receive for such an offense is life in prison. The mood among the Stones was very bleak; even Keith was frightened. As soon as the band finished their El Mocambo dates, the rest of the Stones —along with Margaret Trudeau, the wife of Canada's prime minister—left Keith in Toronto.

On March 14, Anita was fined $400 for possession of hashish, and in April Keith and Anita were given visas so Keith could leave Canada—on the condition that he return for the trial. Keith and Anita flew directly to the States, where Keith underwent a three-day detoxification treatment and continued daily therapy.
At his trial in October, Keith received a one-year suspended sentence and was placed on a year's probation after pleading guilty to a reduced charge of possession of heroin. (The charge of possession *with the intent to traffic* was dropped.) Judge Lloyd Graburn handed down the decision with the condition that Keith keep a clean criminal record, continue drug rehabilitation treatment at Stevens Psychiatric Center, report to his probation officer twice, and give

a benefit concert for the blind. The prosecuter, Paul Kennedy, felt that "if you get a member of the Rolling Stones off heroin, you've done some good." The Mounties, however, felt that Keith got off too easily and should have spent some time in prison. The decision was appealed by the government, and in June 1979, the Ontario Court of Appeals unanimously rejected the government's petition. Keith didn't attend the appeals trial, but his written statement was read in court: "I can truthfully say that the prospect of my ever using drugs in the future is totally alien to my thinking."

Stafford, U.K.
Again the month of May proved to be ripe for the Stones vs. the police. After a concert in May 1977, Keith smashed his Bentley into the center highway divider on the M1 in Stafford. The police found a silver cylinder containing cocaine on the car floor, and LSD in Keith's jacket pocket when he was searched at the police station. Luckily no one was hurt (other passengers included son, Marlon, two women, and a male companion). On the day of the hearing Keith was two and a half hours late claiming he had to wait for his trousers to be washed. Magistrate Margaret Durbridge remarked to Keith: "I find it extraordinary, Mr. Richards, that a man of your stature has only one pair of pants." The trial itself was held in Aylesbury, attended by Mick and John Phillips, and took three days. Ron and Ian Stewart were among those testifying on Keith's behalf. The jury found Keith not guilty of LSD possession, but he was convicted of coke possession and fined £750, plus a £250 court fee.

St. Maarten
In February 1980, Ron and his girlfriend, Jo, were busted while they were vacationing on the island of St. Maarten. The police, who had been tipped off about the drug possession, found five grams of coke in the couple's rented apartment. Ron and Jo spent five days in jail, but no charges were filed against them and they were deported to America. Ron claimed that two men had tried to sell him the coke, and when he refused to buy it from them, they left it in the apartment, informing the police that it was there.

ART OF CHRIS FARLOWE, THE
Chris Farlowe album produced by Mick in November 1966. The LP contains the Jagger/Richards compositions, "Paint It, Black," "Out of Time," "I'm Free," and "Ride On Baby," in addition to ten other songs.

ARTWOODS, THE
A band which Ron's big brother Art formed in 1964, after singing with Alexis Korner's Blues Incorporated and various other bands. The five-piece group, which lasted until 1967 and recorded an album called ART GALLERY, also included Keef Hartley and, most notably, Jon Lord, who went on to form that quiet little band, Deep Purple.

"AS TEARS GO BY"
Written by: Jagger/Richards/Oldham
Recorded by: The Rolling Stones
Release date: November 1965
Record label: London/Decca
Albums: DECEMBER'S CHILDREN
         BIG HITS (U.K.)
         BIG HITS (U.S.)
         STONE AGE
         HOT ROCKS
         ROLLED GOLD
         SLOW ROLLERS (Italian version)
Singles: B/w "Gotta Get Away" (U.S. 12/65)
        Flip of "19th Nervous Breakdown" (U.K. 2/66)
• Arranged by Mike Leander and Keith.
• This song was originally written to help launch Marianne Faithfull's career. She had a top-ten hit with it in the U.K. in 1964. The Stones had their top-ten hit with the song in the U.S. in early 1966.
• The version that appears on SLOW ROLLERS is the Italian single, "Con Le Mie Lacrime."
• The Stones version was frequently compared unfavorably to the Beatles' "Yesterday," because of its acoustic guitar and string quartet sound.

ASHBY, HAL
American filmmaker and director of *Let's Spend the Night Together.* Mick is planning to work with him on the film version of Gore Vidal's book, *Kalki.*

ASK RUFUS
1977 Rufus LP on which Ron plays.

ASSASSINATION OF MICK JAGGER, THE
Title of a film David Bailey wanted to make in 1966.

ATLANTIC RECORDS
Major record company and part of Warner Communications, Inc., which has distributed Rolling Stones Records in the U.S. and Canada since RSR's inception in 1971.

ATLANTIC STUDIOS
New York studio where the Stones mixed some tracks for TATTOO YOU.

AUCKLAND, AUSTRALIA
After the Stones' February 1973 concert here, the local recreation center auctioned off—piece by piece—the sixteen cotton sheets and pillowcases used by the band, raising over $1,000.

AVORY, MICK
Replacement Stones drummer for Tony Chapman. Later, drummer of the Kinks.

BACK, BEHIND, AND IN FRONT
Title of Stones' first intended full-length movie, to be co-produced by Andrew Oldham and Allen Klein. Filming was to start in April 1966, and though Oldham had a basic plot for the film, nothing ever happened. Don't watch for it at a theater near you!

"BABY, YOU'RE A RICH MAN"
Beatles song on which Brian plays saxophone.

"BACK STREET GIRL"
Written by: Jagger/Richards
Recorded by: The Rolling Stones
Release date: January 1967
Record label: Decca/London
Albums: BETWEEN THE BUTTONS (U.K.)
       FLOWERS
       SLOW ROLLERS
• Nicky Scott recorded this song as a 1967 single produced by Mick and Andrew Oldham.

BACK TO THE ROOTS
1971 John Mayall album featuring Mick Taylor.

BAILEY, DAVID
Official photographer to Swinging Sixties London, he photographed the Stones for the following album covers: THE ROLLING STONES NO. 2, 12 x 5, THE ROLLING STONES, NOW!, OUT OF OUR HEADS (U.S.), GET YER YA-YA'S OUT, and GOATS HEAD SOUP, for which he also did the album design. One of Bailey's photos of the Stones was used on a Times Square, N.Y. billboard advertising DECEMBER'S CHILDREN. Mick was best man at Bailey's

wedding to French actress Catherine Deneuve. In 1966, Bailey planned to make a film titled *The Assassination of Mick Jagger,* but this never got off the ground.

BAKER, ROY THOMAS
Producer of albums by Queen, the Cars, Foreigner, and many more, who produced GIMME SOME NECK.

BALDRY, LONG JOHN
Six-foot-seven-inch-tall British singer who as a fringe member of Alexis Korner's Blues Incorporated used to come on stage at the end of the set with Mick and Paul Jones to sing "I've Got My Mojo Working." Upon Cyril Davies' death, Baldry took over the All-Stars, of which he had been a member, changing the band's name to

the Hoochie Coochie Men, a lineup which included singer Rod Stewart until its breakup in 1965. He and Stewart joined Steampacket, another band which lasted for about a year. By 1966 Baldry led a band called Bluesology, which featured pianist Reg Dwight (who later changed his name to Elton John) and singer Marsha Hunt (see Marsha Hunt entry). It was this band that opened for the Stones on their eighth British tour in September/October 1966.

BALL, ERNIE
Manufacturer of the guitar strings used by Keith and Ron. Alan Rogan claims that Ball is the only supplier who will custom-print the "profane" guitar picks used by the Stones.

"BAMBA, LA"
One of the songs on the demo tape sent to Alexis Korner by Little Boy Blue and the Blue Boys.

BARBARELLA
Sci-fi film by Roger Vadim starring Jane Fonda, with Anita Pallenberg. Keith would occasionally join Anita during the filming in Rome, summer 1967.

BARCLAY, EDDIE
Record company executive who was both the boss and fiancé of Bianca, and who made the fatal mistake of introducing her to Mick at a party following the Stones concert at the Olympia in Paris, September 1970.

BARE WIRES
1968 album by John Mayall's Blues Breakers featuring Mick Taylor.

BARNES STUDIO
Mick Taylor first played with the Stones in this British studio when they were recording.

BASIE, COUNT
Jazz great who performed at Mick's twenty-ninth birthday party at the St. Regis Hotel, New York.

BATTERED ORNAMENTS
British psychedelic-era band—led by Peter Brown, composer of most of Cream's lyrics—who were infamous for their infinite jams and who opened for the Stones at Hyde Park in 1969.

BATTLE OF NW6
1970 Keef Hartley LP featuring Mick Taylor.

BAUD, ABBÉ LUCIEN
St. Tropez religious instructor who tutored Mick in Catholicism for four weeks before his marriage.

BEACH, SANDY
One of Andrew Oldham's aliases.

BEACH BOYS, THE
American institution who appeared in the film, the *T.A.M.I. Show.*

BEAN, GEORGE
Decca recording artist who released "It Should Be You," the very first Jagger/Richards composition.

BEARD, THE
In 1972 Mick agreed to play the starring role of Billy the Kid in the film version of this controversial play by Michael McClure. Joey Heatherton was signed to play opposite Mick as Jean Harlow. Donald Cammell was to direct, and Sanford Lieberson to produce the film, but it never got past the planning stages.

"BEAST OF BURDEN"
Written by: Jagger/Richards
Recorded by: The Rolling Stones
Release date: June 1978
Record label: Rolling Stones Records
Albums: SOME GIRLS
SUCKING IN THE SEVENTIES
Singles: B/w "When the Whip Comes Down" (U.S. 11/78)
Flip of "Going to A Go Go" (U.S./U.K. 82) (live)

BEATLES, THE
That *other* band. The Stones were always pitted against them as the bad guys in "good vs. bad," "clean vs. dirty" battles contrived by the British press.

BEATON, SIR CECIL
Legendary British photographer who met Mick, Keith, Brian, and lady friends in Marrakesh in early 1967 and began photographing them. His portrait of Mick was sold in auction at Sotheby's for £220 in 1973.

BECK, JEFF
England's all-time flash guitar hero, Jeff led the group bearing his name, which was the nest for Ron Wood between Ron's leaving the Birds and joining the Faces, 1967-69. Beck was a contender in the Stones' "Great Guitarists Hunt" after Mick Taylor's departure, though rumor has always had it that Beck rejected the Stones, feeling that the rhythm section was not "funky" enough for his tastes. He did, however, record two unreleased tracks in February 1975 with Keith and Robert A. Johnson. Asked to participate in the New Barbarians tour in 1979, Beck uttered his favorite word, "No!"

BECK OLA
1969 album by the Jeff Beck Group featuring Ron on bass.

BECKENHAM GRAMMAR SCHOOL
School attended by Bill, where he did best in math.

BECKWITH, BOB
A member of Little Boy Blue and the Blue Boys.

"BEFORE THEY MAKE ME RUN"
Written by: Jagger/Richards
Recorded by: The Rolling Stones
Lead singer: Keith
Release date: June 1978
Record label: Rolling Stones Records
Album: SOME GIRLS
• Engineered by Dave Jordan—the only track on SOME GIRLS not engineered by Chris Kimsey.

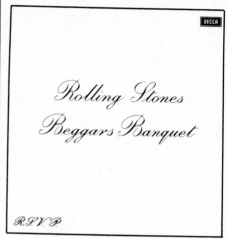

BEGGARS BANQUET
Artist: The Rolling Stones
Producer: Jimmy Miller
Release date: November 1968
Record label: London/Decca
Tracks: 10
"Sympathy for the Devil"
"No Expectations"
"Dear Doctor"
"Parachute Woman"
"Jig-Saw Puzzle"
"Street Fighting Man"
"Prodigal Son" (Rev. Robert Wilkins)
"Stray Cat Blues"
"Factory Girl"
"Salt of the Earth"
• 12th U.S. LP.
• 8th U.K. LP.
• Nicky Hopkins and "many friends" are credited with playing on the album. Rumor has it that the "many friends" include Dave Mason and Eric Clapton.
• Studio—Olympic Studios, London.
• Engineers—Glyn Johns, Eddie and Gene.
• Photos—Michael Joseph.
• Album design—Tom Wilkes.
• Christopher Gibbs suggested the LP's title.
• Both Decca and London refused to release BEGGARS BANQUET with its original sleeve, a Barry Feinstein photo of a graffitied toilet wall. In September of that year, the Stones took out a full-page ad in *Melody Maker,* showing the album cover and advising fans to write to Decca if they wanted the record. Mick's idea was that the album and sleeve be shipped in a brown paper bag with the words, "Unfit for Children" stamped on the

Nine years later, in June 1981, Keith went backstage after one of Berry's shows at the Ritz in New York. Not recognizing Berry's "Do Not Disturb" vibes, Keith approached him from the rear to say hello. Berry turned, swung, and got Keith in the eye. Keith quietly left the scene of the crime. Later that summer at the same venue, Ron came on stage to jam with Berry. Chuck introduced Ron to the audience as "Keith Richards of the Rolling Stones" and apologized for hitting him earlier that year.

outside. Decca said no to this, and the album wound up with a white cover, almost identical to the Beatles' "white album" which had been released a month earlier.
• BEGGARS BANQUET is the favorite Rolling Stones LP of Mick, Keith, Brian, and Mick Taylor.
• No "s" on album sleeve; "s" on actual disc label.

BEGGARS BANQUET
Rolling Stones fanzine which recently celebrated its fifth anniversary. It's published by Bill German.

BELL SOUND
London studio where parts of THEIR SATANIC MAJESTIES REQUEST was recorded.

BELLE, MADELAINE
Backup vocalist on "You Can't Always Get What You Want."

BELLI, MELVIN
Prominent U.S. lawyer who offered to fight Filmways on behalf of the Stones. (See Altamont.)

BENNETT, DOUG
Assistant engineer on GOATS HEAD SOUP.

BELVEDERE NURSING HOME
Paris hospital where Jade Jagger was born on October 21, 1971.

BELUSHI, JOHN
Late comedian who served as Master of Ceremonies at Keith's benefit concert for the blind held at Oskawa Hall in Toronto on April 22, 1979. The New Barbarians and the Stones performed.

BERGMAN, JO
Stones secretary who in 1967 was forced to hunt for London office space incognito due to the troubles the Stones were having with British law enforcement at the time.

BERLINE, BYRON
Fiddler on "Country Honk" and pianist on "Live with Me"; also plays fiddle on MONKEY GRIP.

BERRY, CHUCK
Called the "creator of rock 'n' roll," Berry was an early favorite of Mick's and Keith's, especially Keith. It was the imported American Chuck Berry records that Mick was carrying when the future Glimmer Twins were reunited on the Southern Line in 1960 that made the two realize their common interests in R & B and American music.
The Rolling Stones have recorded the following Chuck Berry songs:
"Around and Around"
"Bye Bye Johnny"
"Carol"
"Come On"
"Don't Lie to Me"
"Little Queenie"
"Talkin' 'Bout You"
"You Can't Catch Me"
In 1972, Keith joined Berry onstage at a Berry concert and was promptly booted off. Though rumors have it that The Master was annoyed at Keith's upstaging him, Berry claimed that he didn't recognize Keith. In his idol's honor, Keith has noted that Berry is the only one who could ever pull such a stunt and live to tell the tale.

BERRY, DAVE

Backed by the Cruisers, this British singer opened for the Stones on their second (January 1964) and sixth (March 1965) British tours.

BERRY PARK

Chuck Berry's home/amusement park/country club in Wentzville, Missouri. After Berry heard the Stones recording his songs at Chess Studios in 1964, he invited them to visit.

BETWEEN THE BUTTONS (U.K.)

Artist: The Rolling Stones
Producer: Andrew Loog Oldham
Release date: January 1967
Record label: Decca
Tracks: 12
"Yesterday's Papers"
"My Obsession"
"Back Street Girl"
"Connection"
"She Smiled Sweetly"
"Cool, Calm and Collected"
"All Sold Out"
"Please Go Home"
"Who's Been Sleeping Here?"
"Complicated"
"Miss Amanda Jones"
"Something Happened to Me Yesterday"
• 6th U.K. LP.
• Studio—Olympic, London.
• Arranged by the Rolling Stones.
• Cover photo—Gered Mankowitz.
• Back cover drawings by Charlie Watts take the form of a six-frame cartoon showing the Stones' mass audience acceptance vs. the wavering indecisiveness of the industry powers-that-be. Also on the back cover is Charlie's poem "Between the Buttons":
> *To understand this little rhyme*
> *You first must tap your foot in time.*
> *Then the buttons come much nearer*
> *And the Stones you see more clearer.*

In order to find the title and group's name on the cover, you must look at what would ordinarily be the "buttons" of Charlie's jacket. If you squint at these buttons, they appear to be cat's eyes, legend having it that this was the Stones' most "catty" album.

• BETWEEN THE BUTTONS marks the first time the Stones went into the studio and emerged with a finished product.
• No "s" on the album jacket; "s" on the label on the disc itself.

BETWEEN THE BUTTONS (U.S.)

Artist: The Rolling Stones
Producer: Andrew Loog Oldham
Release date: January 1967
Record label: London
Tracks: 12
"Let's Spend the Night Together"
"Yesterday's Papers"
"Ruby Tuesday"
"Connection"
"She Smiled Sweetly"
"Cool, Calm and Collected"
"All Sold Out"
"My Obsession"
"Who's Been Sleeping Here?"
"Complicated"
"Miss Amanda Jones"
"Something Happened to Me Yesterday"
• 9th U.S. LP.
• All other details the same as BETWEEN THE BUTTONS (U.K.).

"BIG BAYOU"/"SWEET SUNSHINE"

1976 solo single by Ron, the A side of which is taken from NOW LOOK.

BIG HITS (HIGH TIDE AND GREEN GRASS) (U.S.)

Artist: The Rolling Stones
Producer: Andrew Loog Oldham
Release date: March 1966
Record label: London
Tracks: 12
"(I Can't Get No) Satisfaction"
"The Last Time"
"As Tears Go By" (Jagger/Richards/Oldham)
"Time Is on My Side" (Meade/Norman)
"It's All Over Now" (B. & S. Womack)
"Tell Me"
"19th Nervous Breakdown"
"Heart of Stone"
"Get Off of My Cloud"
"Not Fade Away" (Petty/Hardin)

"Good Times, Bad Times"
"Play with Fire" (Nanker Phelge)
• 6th U.S. LP.
• Photography—Guy Webster, Gered Mankowitz.
• Cover design—Andrew Loog Oldham.
• The cover photo was scheduled for the never-released COULD *YOU* WALK ON THE WATER? LP.
• The LP contains a photo booklet.
• No "s."

BIG HITS (HIGH TIDE AND GREEN GRASS) (U.K.)

Artist: The Rolling Stones
Producer: Andrew Loog Oldham
Release date: November 1966
Record label: Decca
Tracks: 14
"Have You Seen Your Mother, Baby, Standing in the Shadow?"
"Paint It, Black"
"It's All Over Now" (B. & S. Womack)
"The Last Time"
"Heart of Stone"
"Not Fade Away" (Petty/Hardin)
"Come On" (Berry)
"(I Can't Get No) Satisfaction"
"Get Off of My Cloud"
"As Tears Go By" (Jagger/Richards/Oldham)
"19th Nervous Breakdown"
"Lady Jane"
"Time Is on My Side" (Meade/Norman)
"Little Red Rooster" (Dixon)
• 5th U.K. LP.

BILL NILE'S DELTA JAZZ BAND

Brian was in this band when he lived in Cheltenham.

BILL WYMAN

Artist: Bill Wyman
Producer: Bill Wyman and Chris Kimsey
Release date: 1981
Record label: A & M
Tracks: 10
"Ride On Baby" (B. Wyman/S. Wyman)
"A New Fashion" (B. Wyman/T. Taylor)

"Nuclear Reactions"
"Visions"(B. Wyman/
T. Taylor)
"Jump Up"(B. Wyman/
C. Kimsey)
"Come Back Suzanne"
"Rio de Janeiro"
"Girls"
"Seventeen"
"(Si Si) Je Suis un Rock Star"
• The core of Bill's band is Bill on bass, vocals, and assorted instruments; Terry Taylor on guitars and backup vocals, Dave Mattacks on drums; and Dave Lawson on synthesizer. (See individual songs for additional musician credits.) Bill's also joined by Stray Cats Brian Setzer and Slim Jim Phantom, in addition to his son, Stephen.
• Stuart Epps—backup vocals.
• Chris Kimsey & the Cookham Cookies—backup vocals.
• Engineers—Stuart Epps, Chris Kimsey.
• Assistant engineer—Stuart Eales.
• Tape Mixing—Chris Kimsey at The Sol, except for "Come Back Suzanne," mixed by Stuart Epps.
• Tape Mastering—Chris Kimsey and Ted Jensen.
• Photography—Bill Wyman (assisted by Stephen Wyman).
• Cover concept—Bill Wyman and Michael Ross.
• Illustration—Syd Brak.
• Art direction and design—Michael Ross.

BILLY PRESTON'S LIVE EUROPEAN TOUR
1974 Billy Preston album featuring Mick Taylor on eight tracks.

BIRD
Brand name of Ron's first amplifier, when he was in the Birds.

BIRDS,THE
Ron's first group (originally named the Thunderbirds), they were together for six years but disbanded when the American Byrds became famous in the mid-sixties. They left behind one cut, "Leaving Here," on the HARD-UP HEROES compilation album and a brief appearance in the horror flick, *The Deadly Bees*. When the Birds broke up, Ron decided to phone his casual acquaintance Jeff Beck, who had just left the Yardbirds. The rest is history.

"BITCH"
Written by: Jagger/Richards
Recorded by: The Rolling Stones
Release date: April 1971
Record label: Rolling Stones Records
Albums: STICKY FINGERS
           MADE IN THE SHADE
           TIME WAITS FOR NO ONE
Single: Flip of "Brown Sugar" (U.K. 4/71) (U.S. 5/71)
• Bobby Keys—sax.
• Jimmy Miller—percussion.
• Jim Price—trumpet.
• Most radio stations banned this song.

BLACK AND BLUE
Artist: The Rolling Stones
Producer: The Glimmer Twins
Release date: April 1976
Record label: Rolling Stones Records
Tracks: 8
"Hot Stuff"
"Hand of Fate"
"Cherry Oh Baby" (Donaldson)
"Memory Motel"
"Hey Negrita"
"Melody"
"Fool to Cry"
"Crazy Mama"
• 24th U.S. LP.
• 24th U.K. LP.
• Guest musicians include Nicky Hopkins, Billy Preston, Ian Stewart, and Ollie E. Brown. (See individual songs for credits.) Though released after Ron was crowned an "official" Stone, BLACK AND BLUE was recorded during the band's "Great Guitarists Hunt" of 1975 and features two other top contenders, Harvey Mandel and Wayne Perkins, in addition to Ronnie —and, of course, Keith— on guitar.
• Studio—all but "Melody" recorded at Musicland, Munich, West Germany; "Melody" recorded in the Rolling Stones Mobile in Rotterdam, Holland. Work also done at Casino, Montreux,

Switzerland, with the Mobile.
• Engineers—Keith Harwood, Glyn Johns, Phil McDonald, Lew Hahn.
• Assistant engineers—Jeremy Gee, Dave Richards, Tapani Tapanainen, Steve Dowd, Gene Paul.
• Tape mastering—Lee Hulko.
• Photography—Hiro.
• Layout—Bea Feitler.
• The poster which advertised the LP featured a scantily clad, bruised and bound, black and blue blond woman and caused quite a bit of controversy.
• No "s."

BLACK BOX
Device which transmits an extremely weak electrical signal to a drug addict's brain via electrodes taped behind the ears. These neuroelectric charges restore physiological normality to those going through withdrawal without their having to experience cravings and irritability. Keith has gone through the black box treatment as developed by Dr. Meg Patterson.

BLACK BOX, THE
Assembled by Bill, this was the Stones' choice of material they preferred, and also the title of the album which became METAMORPHOSIS. (See METAMORPHOSIS for Bill's BLACK BOX songlist.)

BLACK FOREST CAKE
Keith's favorite. Does it go with Jack Daniels?

"BLACK LIMOUSINE"
Written by: Jagger/Richards/Wood
Recorded by: The Rolling Stones
Release date: October 1981
Record label: Rolling Stones Records
Album: TATTOO YOU

BLACK UHURU
Reggae band who opened for the Stones on some of the dates of their European 1982 tour.

BLACKHILL ENTERPRISES
Organization which staged the Stones' free Hyde Park Concert on July 5, 1969.

"BLAME IT ON THE STONES"
Song performed by Kris Kristofferson at England's Isle of Wight Festival, 1970. With an audience sing-along, Kristofferson jests about the "middle class" view of why the day's youth was so rebellious.

BLENHEIM PALACE
Winston Churchill's birthplace and the scene of the black-tie promotion party for GOATS HEAD SOUP, September 1973.

BLOCK, JUDGE LESLIE
Judge at Keith, Mick, and Robert Fraser's Redlands bust trial. He felt that the Stones were a bad influence on youth and was quoted as saying he was sorry their sentences weren't stronger.

"BLOOD RED WINE"
Song recorded by Stones in Los Angeles, 1971, but never released.

"BLOWIN' IN THE WIND"
Keith plays acoustic guitar on this Dylan song as performed by Marianne Faithfull.

BLUE LENA
Keith's 1966 blue Bentley. Keith painted the car orange along the way. Mick thinks the color's obscene; Keith finds the car easy to find.

BLUE MONDAY AND THE COCKROACHES
Pseudonym used by the Stones when they gave a surprise concert to start their 1981 U.S. tour in a small club in Worcester, Massachusetts, September 15, 1981.

BLUE OYSTER CULT
Legend has it that producer Sandy Pearlman "conceived" of the band upon hearing "Under My Thumb" and deciding that the world needed a heavy-metal band with the same sado-masochistic undertone as the song.

BLUE, SUGAR
American blues harpist who performs on SOME GIRLS and EMOTIONAL RESCUE and on the twelve-minute version of "Miss You."

"BLUE TURNS TO GREY"
Written by: Jagger/Richards
Recorded by: The Rolling Stones
Release date: November 1965
Record label: London/Decca
Albums: DECEMBER'S CHILDREN
STONE AGE

BLUES ANYTIME VOL. I
1968 Immediate compilation album featuring Mick on harmonica and Bill on bass on three tracks: "Snake Drive," "Tribute to Elmore," and "West Coast Idea." The other musicians on these tracks are Eric Clapton and Jimmy Page on guitars, Ian Stewart on piano, and Chris Winters on drums. All three

songs were written by Clapton and Page.

BLUES BY FIVE
The band Charlie joined after leaving Alexis Korner's Blues Incorporated and before joining the Stones. Brian had passed through the same band earlier. The number of musicians in the group varied and it was sometimes known as Blues by Six.

BLUES FROM LAUREL CANYON
1969 John Mayall album featuring Mick Taylor.

BONEROO HORN SECTION
Peter Graves, Mark Colby, Ken Faulk, and Neal Bonsanti, all of whom played on MONKEY GRIP.

BONGIOVI, BARRY
Assistant engineer on STILL LIFE.

BONSANTI, NEAL
Member of Boneroo Horn Section on MONKEY GRIP.

BOOGIE
Keith's dog, who almost got his master and band arrested at the Glasgow Airport in 1971 when airport officials and the police insisted that the dog ride in a case on board. Keith, Mick, and Anita fought with the police, convincing them that the dog should stay on Keith's lap. The police let the plane take off, never noticing that, in addition to the illegal dog, the Stones had drugs on board.

BOOTH, STANLEY
Memphis-based Stones "biographer" who accompanied the band on their 1969 U.S. tour.

BOOTLEG HIM
1972 Alexis Korner LP featuring Charlie.

BOWIE, DAVID
Among a thousand other things, backup vocalist on "It's Only Rock 'n' Roll."

BOY SCOUTS
Keith joined. Keith quit.

BRADFORD, GEOFF
"Blues purist" guitarist who answered Brian's ad in *Jazz News* and was beginning rehearsals with Brian and singer Andy Wren when Brian brought Ian Stewart to hear them. A short while later, Brian met Mick and company, and a group composed of Bradford, Mick, Brian, and Ian rehearsed. Mick started bringing Keith and Dick Taylor along. Bradford, as purist, hated Chuck Berry and Bo Diddley, so immediately didn't hit it off with Keith. He then found Jimmy Reed, Mick's idol at the time, "too commercial," scoring another point against himself. Finally, it was a personality clash with Brian that saw the last of Geoff Bradford, though it's rumored that more than 13 years later, Bradford auditioned for the (Mick) Taylor-less Stones and failed.

BRADFORD REGISTRY
Office in Yorkshire where Charlie and Shirley were married.

BRASS RING PRODUCTIONS
Promoters of the concerts at the Silverdome, a 75,000-seat arena in Pontiac, Michigan, where the Stones performed two shows during the 1981 U.S. tour. "Festival seating" (no reserved seats) was advertised, and fearing another tragedy such as experienced during the Who concert in Cincinnati in 1979, law students Steve Ianmarino and James Rocchio took the company to court to try to prevent this. They lost the case.

"BREAKIN' MY HEART"
Written by: Ron Wood
Recorded by: Ron Wood
Release date: May 1979
Record label: CBS
Album: GIMME SOME NECK
• Charlie Watts—drums.
• "Pops" Popwell—bass.
• Mick Jagger—backup vocals.

BRIAN JONES PRESENTS THE PIPES OF PAN AT JOUJOUKA
Artist: The Maalimin of Joujouka
Producer: Brian Jones
Release date: November 1971
Record label: Rolling Stones Records
• Studio—live in Joujouka, engineered at Olympic Studios, London.
• Engineer—George Chkiantz.
• The Maalimin of Joujouka, the Master Musicians of Morocco, were recorded by Brian and edited down from hours of tapes recorded at the week-long ceremony celebrating the goat-god, Pan.

• The record was almost ready for release when Brian died, but legalities kept it from coming out until the Rolling Stones started their own label.
• An occasional LP cover titles the album BRIAN JONES PLAYS WITH THE PIPES OF PAN AT JOUJOUKA.

BRICKLAYER'S ARMS
Soho, London, pub where Brian, Mick, Keith, Ian Stewart, Dick Taylor, and Geoff Bradford rehearsed in spring 1962.

BRIDGES, ALVENIA
Stones' publicist.

"BRIGHT LIGHTS, BIG CITY"
Jimmy Reed song recorded by Little Boy Blue and the Blue Boys on the demo tape they sent to Alexis Korner. It was also recorded in early 1963 by the Stones during their first session with Glyn Johns, and it was this second version that Bill chose for THE BLACK BOX compilation.

BRIXTON JAIL
Mick was held at this jail overnight after the Redlands bust sentencing. Robert Fraser also stayed here, and a chef from outside catered in food for the two of them.

BROADWAY
Brand name of Bill's first guitar.

BROOKS, ELKIE
Top British singer and sister of sixties Merseybeat heartthrob Billy J. Kramer, who Brian wanted to work with "if I left the Stones."

BROWN, DAVID
Member of Santana who played in the jam session at Mick and Bianca's wedding.

BROWN, DAVID "DB"
Assistant engineer on STILL LIFE.

BROWN, JAMES
American sixties soul superstar who influenced Mick's stage movements. Brown preceded the Stones in the taping of the *T.A.M.I. Show* in 1964, and although he was the toughest of acts to follow, the Stones were pleased with their performance. In 1981, Brown was scheduled to open the New York shows for the Stones but didn't appear.

BROWN, OLLIE E.
Percussionist on BLACK AND BLUE and LOVE YOU LIVE. Brown accompanied the Stones on their 1975 Tour of the Americas, receiving a straight salary for his work, whereas other performing guests, Billy Preston and not-yet-Stone Ron Wood, received a percentage of the take. Brown also played with the Stones on their 1976 European tour.

"BROWN SUGAR"
Written by: Jagger/Richards
Recorded by: The Rolling Stones
Release date: April 1971
Record label: Rolling Stones Records/ London/Atlantic
Albums: STICKY FINGERS
      HOT ROCKS
      MADE IN THE SHADE
      LOVE YOU LIVE (live in Paris)
Singles: B/w "Bitch" and "Let It Rock"
      (U.K. 4/71)
      B/w "Bitch" (U.S. 5/71)
      B/w "Bitch" and "Let It Rock"
      (U.K. 1/74—Atlantic Gold
      Series)
• Ian Stewart—piano.
• Bobby Keys—saxophone.
• "Brown Sugar" was the first single released on Rolling Stones Records.
• The song was a triple whammy, being condemned as pornographic, racist, *and* sexist.
• "Brown Sugar" is rumored to be about singer Claudia Lennear.
• It is also rumored to be about Mexican heroin.
• An unreleased version of the song was recorded live at a birthday party for Keith at Olympic Studios, London, 1970, with Eric Clapton on slide guitar and Al Kooper on piano.

BROWNE, TARA
Heir to the Guinness fortune and Brian's closest friend, whose accidental driving death was immortalized in the Beatles song "Day in the Life," and which threw Brian into an irreconcilable depression.

BROWNJOHN, ROBERT
Creator of cover and liner design for LET IT BLEED.

BOTNICK, BRUCE
Assistant engineer on LET IT BLEED.

BRAK, SYD
Illustrator of BILL WYMAN LP jacket.

BRUCE, JACK
British bassist of note (Cream, etc.), who formed a short-lived band with Mick Taylor after Mick left the Stones.

BUCHMANN, KARL
Munich, West Germany, concert promoter who was billed £1,200 "amusement tax" after the Stones played a concert in Munich in September 1965. In levying the tax, the government stated that the Rolling Stones created *noise* and not *music*.

BUCKLE, CONRAD
General assistant at Rolling Stones Records in New York.

BUCKMASTER, PAUL
Elton John's arranger, who arranged strings for "Sway" and "Moonlight Mile."

BULL DOGS, THE
Name Stones were registered under at the Hit Factory, while mixing their 1983 album.

BURDEN OF DREAMS
1982 documentary by Les Blank about the making of the film *Fitzcarraldo*. It features both Mick and Jason Robards, who were forced to leave the film, which was being shot in the Peruvian Amazon—Mick to start rehearsals for the 1981 U.S. tour; Robards due to illness. Neither appear in the film *Fitzcarraldo*.

"BURIED ALIVE"
Written by: Ron Wood
Recorded by: Ron Wood
Release date: May 1979
Record label: CBS
Album: GIMME SOME NECK
• Charlie Watts—drums.
• Mick Jagger—backup vocals.
• Keith Richards—guitar, backup vocals.
• "Pops" Popwell—bass.
• Jim Keltner—percussion.

BURN, COLLIN
Director of Rolling Stones Records in London.

BURNS, RICCI
Fashionable London hair salon where stylist Anthony gave Mick his first "short" haircut in July 1974.

BURNS, TITO
Bob Dylan's agent, who became the Stones' agent in August 1965.

BURNSIDE, BRUCE
Cover photographer of 1 2 3 4.

BUSH DOCTOR
1978 Peter Tosh album for which Mick and Keith served as executive producers. Mick is on one of the album's cuts.

BY INVITATION ONLY
1976 Atlantic Records compilation LP featuring the Stones tracks "Angie" and "It's Only Rock 'n' Roll."

"BYE BYE JOHNNY"
Written by: Chuck Berry
Recorded by: The Rolling Stones
Release date: January 1964
Record label: Decca/London
Albums: MORE HOT ROCKS
　　　　　ROCK 'N' ROLLING STONES
EP: THE ROLLING STONES (U.K. 1/64)

CBS RECORDS
Company chosen by the Stones in August 1983 to distribute Rolling Stones Records worldwide commencing in 1985. The four-LP deal guarantees the Stones approximately $20 million, beating out Atlantic's $15 million renewal offer.

CAFÉ DES ARTS, ST. TROPEZ
Restaurant where Mick and Bianca's wedding reception was held. Mick wanted the Stones to play, but since Keith had already passed out, he had to settle for a jam featuring himself, Doris Troy, P.P. Arnold, Stephen Stills, Bobby Keys, Nicky Hopkins, and Michael Shrieve and David Brown of Santana. Opening acts were the Rudies and Terry Reid. A bored bride left before it was over.

CAGNEY, JAMES
Legendary actor whose 1974 American Film Institute tribute in Los Angeles was attended by Mick with John Lennon.

CAINE, MICHAEL
An ex-boyfriend of Bianca's who Mick listed as his favorite actor in a 1964 Rolling Stones fact sheet.

CALDER, TONY
Co-founder of Immediate Records with Andrew Oldham, Calder is now married to Oldham's first wife, Sheila.

CALLAGHAN, JIM
Head of security for the Stones.

CAMMELL, DONALD
Writer and co-director of *Performance*. Anita and Brian met for the first time in his Paris flat.

CAMPBELL, MIKE
Tom Petty and the Heartbreakers guitarist, who, displaying the height of Stones' influence, confessed that it was partly because Petty looked like Brian Jones that he was first interested in joining his band.

"CAN I GET A WITNESS"
Written by: Holland/Dozier/Holland
Recorded by: The Rolling Stones
Release date: April 1964
Record label: Decca/London
Albums: THE ROLLING STONES
　　　　　ENGLAND'S NEWEST HIT
　　　　　MAKERS
• Ian Stewart—piano.

"CAN YOU HEAR THE MUSIC"
Written by: Jagger/Richards
Recorded by: The Rolling Stones
Release date: August 1973
Record label: Rolling Stones Records
Album: GOATS HEAD SOUP
• Nicky Hopkins—piano.

CANDY BISON SKIFFLE GROUP
Art and Ted Wood's band, with which

Ron played his first live gig. Ron was nine years old and played washboard, performing in between two Tommy Steele films at the local movie house.

CANNES FILM FESTIVAL
Brian, Keith, and Anita attended this festival in 1967 to see *A Degree of Murder.* While Brian made his final attempt to reconcile with Anita, Keith stayed alone in his room, deciding to let them fight it out by themselves. In 1983 Bill and Astrid screened their film, *Digital Dreams,* at Cannes.

"CAN'T BELIEVE"
Unreleased song recorded during the BETWEEN THE BUTTONS sessions.

"CAN'T YOU HEAR ME KNOCKING"
Written by: Jagger/Richards
Recorded by: The Rolling Stones
Release date: April 1971
Record label: Rolling Stones Records
Album: STICKY FINGERS
• Bobby Keys—sax.
• Billy Preston—organ.
• Jimmy Miller—percussion.
• Rocky Dijon—congas.

CANTRELL, SCOTT
A seventeen-year-old friend of Anita's who killed himself with Anita's gun in her and Keith's Westchester, New York, home, while Keith was recording in Paris in July 1979. Scott had been drinking, smoking joints, and playing Russian roulette with Anita when the gun went off. Anita was questioned at the police station for twelve hours and scheduled to come back in August on charges of possession of guns (one stolen, one unregistered). She was released on $500 bail. After the August hearing, Anita was let out on probation for handling stolen property. Scott's father sued Anita for at least a million dollars "for loss of my son." In November 1979, Anita was cleared of the charges brought against her by Cantrell's father.

CARL TONES, THE
The group formed in a bathroom of the Carlton Hotel in London during the Stones 1982 European tour. Keith, Ron, Bobby Keys, and J. Geils, Peter Wolf, and Seth Justman of the J. Geils Band jammed together in the bathroom, and the next day T-shirts labeled "The Carl Tones, the originals 4/5/6" were given out to the band members.

CARNEGIE HALL
Prestigious New York concert hall where the Stones played their first New York concert in June 1964. The following day, rock 'n' roll shows were banned there for almost a decade due to riots and crazed teenyboppers.

CARR, ROY
Author of *The Rolling Stones: An Illustrated Record* and co-compiler of ROLLED GOLD.

"CAROL"
Written by: Chuck Berry
Recorded by: The Rolling Stones
Release date: April 1964
Record label: Decca/London
Albums: THE ROLLING STONES
    ENGLAND'S NEWEST HIT MAKERS
    GET YER YA-YA'S OUT (live)
    ROCK 'N' ROLLING STONES
    ROLLED GOLD

CARROLL, JIM
Singer/poet whose debut LP, was supposed to be released on Rolling Stones Records in 1980. Mick, Ron, and Keith, the latter accompanied by both Anita and Patti Hansen, attended his performance at Trax, a New York club, in June 1980. Keith jammed with Carroll on his song "People Who Died."

CARTER, BILL
The Stones' lawyer.

CARTER, DICK
Track director at Altamont.

CASH, JOHNNY
American country-western singer who declined the Stones' invitation to perform at their "Rock and Roll Circus."

"CASINO BOOGIE"
Written by: Jagger/Richards
Recorded by: The Rolling Stones
Release date: May 1972
Record label: Rolling Stones Records
Album: EXILE ON MAIN ST.

CASTILLO, EMILIO
Horn player and arranger on STONE ALONE.

CATSOLIDIS, THOMAS
In October 1964, London's *Daily Ex-*

press reported that this Brussels chef had worked hours of overtime to create a special gourmet sauce for the Stones, who were on tour there. The Stones then asked for a British brand-name bottled sauce with their meal. Catsolidis' reaction: "I feel like committing suicide or murder."

CERTAIN WOMEN
Tentative title for SOME GIRLS.

CHAGALL MÉDITERRANEE—THE MEDITERRANEAN CHAGALL
1981 book which features Bill's photographs of the famed artist—and Bill's neighbor—Marc Chagall. The text is in French by poet André Verdet, and there are plans to translate the book into English. Bill first met Chagall when he moved to the South of France. Chagall criticized Bill for following leaders and wearing his hair long. He got Chagall's approval by informing him of his initial trend-setting status. (See A.B.C. Teashop.)

CHAPMAN, TONY
Early Stones drummer, 1962, in a lineup that included Mick, Keith, Brian, and Ian Stewart. Chapman recorded a demo with the Stones at Curly Clayton Sound Studios, while still holding his job as a traveling salesman. This prevented him from coming to a lot of rehearsals, and the drum stool was taken over at those times by Mick Avory or Steve Harris. As the Stones grew more serious, they realized Tony had to go, but they felt that neither Avory nor Harris were suitable (luckily Ray Davies thought that Avory *was* suitable). Enter Charlie Watts. Ironically, before drumming with the Stones, Chapman was in the Cliftons with Bill. After leaving the Stones, he joined the Preachers, who were managed by Bill.

CHARLES HOBSON AND GREY
London advertising agency where Charlie worked.

CHARLIE IS MY DARLING
One-hour documentary of the Rolling Stones filmed during two days of their 1965 Irish tour. The Stones are seen on and off stage and in conversation. Directed and edited by Peter Whitehead, it was produced by Lorrimer Films.

CHARONE, BARBARA
American journalist employed in London and author of *Keith Richards;* she lived with Keith and Anita after their Toronto drug bust in February 1977.

CHATEAU RECORDERS
Los Angeles studio where parts of 1 2 3 4 were recorded.

CHECKERBOARD CLUB
Chicago club where Ron, Keith, and Mick jammed on stage with Lefty Dizz, Junior Wells, Buddy Guy, and Muddy

Waters and his band in 1981. The event was recorded and filmed.

CHELSEA POLICE STATION
Brian and Prince de Rola were brought here when they were busted at Brian's Courtfield flat in 1967.

CHELTENHAM SPA
Town 100 miles west of London where Brian was born and raised.

CHELTENHAM COUNCIL
Office where Brian worked as an architect's assistant.

CHELTENHAM DISTRICT TRANSFER COMPANY
Where Brian was employed as a conductor on a double-decker bus for three weeks in 1960, until his firing.

CHELTENHAM GRAMMAR SCHOOL
School Brian attended after graduating from Dean Close Grammar School. He was suspended twice, once for leading a revolt against the prefects, and then for organizing a protest against wearing mortarboards. Brian eventually dropped out of the school when his girlfriend became pregnant. (Ironically, in the continuing "what was with Brian and Dylan" saga, it's interesting to note that in 1970 when Dylan received an honorary Doctorate of Music degree from Princeton University, he consented to wear the graduation gown but refused to touch the mortarboard cap.)

CHEROKEE STUDIOS
Paris studio where GIMME SOME NECK was recorded.

CHERRY HILL
Town in New Jersey where Keith and Anita lived while they attended a drug rehabilitation center in 1977. They rented a house in the area, because Keith was allowed to move only within a thirty-mile radius of the clinic. Keith said "no way" to the clinic's plan to film a documentary featuring him.

"CHERRY OH BABY"
Written by: Donaldson
Recorded by: The Rolling Stones
Release date: April 1976
Record label: Rolling Stones Records
Album: BLACK AND BLUE
• Pre-Stone Ron Wood—guitar.
• Nicky Hopkins—organ.

CHESHER, DEBBY
Designer and editor of *Starart.*

CHESS STUDIOS
The Rolling Stones' dream came true when they were able to record at this Chicago studio during their first American tour in June 1964. All of their American blues and rock heroes had recorded there, and the Stones felt they could get the best sound for their music in the same place. While they were recording, Chuck Berry, Muddy Waters, and Willie Dixon visited. The Stones completed "It's All Over Now," and all the material on FIVE BY FIVE, also recording 12 X 5 and some of the songs on THE ROLLING STONES, NOW! there, with Ron Malo engineering.

CHESS, MARSHALL
Son of Leonard Chess, founder of Chess Records. When in 1971 the Stones started their own record label, Rolling Stones Records, the twenty-nine-year-old Chess was employed to head the label along with the band. He traveled on tour with the Stones throughout the seventies, served as executive producer of *Ladies and Gentlemen, The Rolling Stones,* produced *Cocksucker Blues,* and was jailed along with Mick and Keith for assaulting a photographer at Warwick Airport in Rhode Island. He left the Stones in 1976 due to a personal disagreement with Keith.

CHEVRON HOTEL
Sydney, Australia, hotel where Marianne Faithfull collapsed soon after she and Mick entered their room. She was rushed to the hospital and was in a drug-induced coma for five days. Mick continued his role in *Ned Kelly,* but Marianne lost her part in the film.

CHEYNE WALK
Exclusive section of London where both Keith and Mick have town houses. Mick lived in his with both Marianne and Bianca—at different times—but now rents it out.

CHEYNES, THE
Group which opened for the Stones on their second British tour, January 1964. Bill produced the single "Down and Out," for this band which contained Mick Fleetwood.

"CHICAGO INCIDENT, THE"
During the Stones 1966 tour, Brian

was hospitalized for a drug overdose in Chicago and missed two weeks of the Stones midwest concerts.

CHICHESTER MAGISTRATES COURT
Mick and Keith were given bail here and a date was set for their Redlands bust trial.

CHIEFTAINS, THE
Band who opened for the Stones when they played in Ireland during their 1982 European tour.

CHIFFONS, THE
American "girl group" who opened for the Stones during their first U.S. tour, spring 1964.

"CHILD OF THE MOON"
Written by: Jagger/Richards
Recorded by: The Rolling Stones
Record label: London/Decca
Albums: MORE HOT ROCKS
      NO STONE UNTURNED
Single: Flip of "Jumpin' Jack Flash"
    (U.S./U.K. 5/68)

CHINESE EMPEROR, THE
Character Mick plays in a Cable TV Showtime version of the Hans Christian Andersen fairy tale *The Nightingale.* Actress Shelley Duvall convinced Mick to take part in the production, aired in 1983.

CHKIANTZ, GEORGE
Assistant engineer on LET IT BLEED; engineer on BRIAN JONES PRESENTS THE PIPES OF PAN...; and overdub engineer on IT'S ONLY ROCK 'N' ROLL.

"CHRIS CROSS"
Song recorded by the Stones in Jamaica during the GOATS HEAD SOUP sessions but never released.

CHRIS JAGGER
1973 album on which Mick sings backup vocals on the opening track, "Handful of Dust."

"CHRIST CHURCH WISHES 'GOD SPEED' TO THE ROLLING STONES"
Sign outside the church on Main Street in North Brookfield, Massachusetts, while the Stones were "secretly" rehearsing at Long View Farm for their 1981 U.S. tour.

CHURCHILL, TREVOR
Label manager for Rolling Stones Records in London when the company was first formed.

"CITADEL"
Written by: Jagger/Richards
Recorded by: The Rolling Stones
Release date: November 1967
Record label: London/Decca
Album: THEIR SATANIC MAJESTIES
      REQUEST
• Said to be based on *Metropolis,* the 1926 film by Fritz Lang.

CIVIL SERVICE STORE
London store where Brian worked briefly before he was fired for stealing.

CLAPTON, ERIC
Aka God at the height of his guitar-playing popularity, Clapton has crossed paths with the Stones many times:
• In 1964, Brian asked Eric to leave he Yardbirds, saying that he'd leave he Stones if the two could form a band together. Eric refused, though he wound up leaving the Yardbirds shortly thereafter anyway.

• In the summer of 1968, it was rumored that Clapton would join the Stones after the Cream farewell tour that fall. Brian, still in the band, was not functioning up to par, and the Stones hoped another guitarist would help.

• In December 1968, Clapton served as lead guitarist in A. N. Other, for the taping of "The Rolling Stones' Rock and Roll Circus."
• In June 1969, it was said that Clapton might join the Stones as Brian's replacement.
• In 1975, they talked of Clapton as Taylor's replacement.
• Clapton played on the unreleased live version of "Brown Sugar" recorded at a birthday party for Keith. He also gave Keith the name of a good heroin withdrawal doctor.
• In May 1979, at Clapton's and Patti Boyd Harrison's wedding celebration, Mick sang with the almost reunited Beatles (Paul, George, and Ringo) and with the fully reunited Cream (Clapton, Bruce, and Baker).

CLARK, JACKIE
Guitarist on MONKEY GRIP and STONE ALONE.

CLARKE, ARTHUR C.
Author of *2001: A Space Odyssey,* who Brian and Suki Potier visited in Ceylon during Christmas 1968.

CLARKE, STANLEY
World-renowned bassist who played in the New Barbarians. He also opened for the Stones in St. Louis during their 1981 U.S. tour.

"CLAUDINE"
Song dropped from EMOTIONAL RESCUE due to record company fear that Claudine Longet would sue them.

CLAYTON, MERRY
Backup vocalist on "Gimmie Shelter."

CLEARMOUNTAIN, BOB
Tape mixer on TATTOO YOU; also engineered and mixed STILL LIFE.

CLEVELAND, OHIO
The mayor of this city banned all pop concerts after a seventeen-year-old girl fell from the balcony during the Stones show here in the autumn of 1964.

CLEWSON, GEORGE
Employee at IBC Studios, London, who tried unsuccessfully to sell the Stones first tapes, engineered by Glyn Johns in early 1963. When the Stones met Andrew Oldham shortly thereafter, Oldham, unbeknownst to Johns, bought the tapes and also bought the Stones out of their contract with Clewson and Johns for £98.

CLIFF, JIMMY
Through Island Records president, Chris Blackwell, Keith helped this reggae singing star get the lead role in the film *The Harder They Come.*

CLIFTONS, THE
The band Bill was in with Tony Chapman before either of them were in the Stones.

CLINIQUE CALIFORNIE, LA
Hospital in Tangiers where Brian went after he broke his wrist trying to hit Anita, 1966.

CLOCKWORK ORANGE, A
Anthony Burgess' futuristic novel of ultra-violence, which Oldham wanted to film with the Stones. Although Oldham announced that he had bought the rights to the book, they were actually never sold to him.

"CLOSE TOGETHER"
Unreleased song recorded by Mick, Keith, Brian, Tony Chapman, and Ian Stewart in October 1962.

"COCKSUCKER BLUES"
Song written by Jagger and Richards and presented to Decca in 1970 when legalities forced them to deliver the master tape of one hitherto unreleased song to that company. Decca would not release it. It was later retitled "Schoolboy Blues" and incorporated into the stage production of Geoff Robertson's *The Trials of Oz.*

COCKSUCKER BLUES
1972 film of the Stones on tour directed by Robert Frank and Daniel Seymour, produced by Marshall Chess. Although commissioned by the Stones and "loved" by Keith, it was rejected by the band due to its X-rated content. The Stones allowed the film to be shown under very strict conditions with its alternate title, *CS Blues.*

COKE
Drug which Keith does not take.

Diet Coke—zero-calorie version of "the real thing," which features Jerry Hall in its TV commercial.

COLBY, MARK
Member of Boneroo Horn Section on MONKEY GRIP; also plays sax on STONE ALONE.

COLE, CLAY
Host of a New York City–based, sixties rock 'n' roll television show, which in May 1965 presented "The Beatles vs. The Rolling Stones." The Stones appeared live, performing and speaking; the Beatles didn't.

COLGEMS-EMI MUSIC, INC.
Publisher of the Jagger/Richards catalog of songs.

COLLINS, ART
Vice-president of Rolling Stones Records, a job he assumed in October 1980.

COLLINS, MEL
Saxophone player on "Miss You"; also plays horns on "Jump Up."

"COME BACK SUZANNE"
Written by: Bill Wyman
Recorded by: Bill Wyman
Release date: 1981
Record label: A & M
Album: BILL WYMAN
Single: B/w "Seventeen" (U.K. 81)
• Bob Wiczling—drums.
• Mixed by Stuart Epps, being the only song on the LP not mixed by Chris Kimsey.

"COME ON"
Written by: Chuck Berry
Recorded by: The Rolling Stones
Release date: June 1963
Record label: Decca/London
Albums: THANK YOUR LUCKY STARS. 2
      READY, STEADY, GO!
      BIG HITS (U.K.)
      ROCK 'N' ROLLING STONES
      MORE HOT ROCKS
      ROLLED GOLD
Single: B/w "I Want to Be Loved" (U.K. 6/63)
• "Come On" was the Rolling Stones first single, released on June 7, 1963.
• Produced by Andrew Loog Oldham.
• Studio—Olympic, London.
• Engineer—Roger Savage.
• Fearful of covering the same R & B classics as the other up and coming bands of the time (Animals, Yardbirds), the Stones imported this Chuck Berry single which had never been released in the U.K.
• Decca didn't like the original recording, which Oldham produced, but accepted it on the fifth try.
• Bill celebrated the record's release by quitting his day job.
• In retrospect: "It really was shit."
—Mick Jagger

"COME TO REALIZE"
Written by: Ron Wood
Recorded by: Ron Wood
Release date: May 1979
Record label: CBS
Album: GIMME SOME NECK
Single: Flip of "Seven Days" (U.K. 8/79)
• Charlie Watts—drums.
• "Pops" Popwell—bass.
• Ian McLagan—organ.

"COMING DOWN AGAIN"
Written by: Jagger/Richards
Recorded by: The Rolling Stones
Release date: August 1973
Record label: Rolling Stones Records
Album: GOATS HEAD SOUP
• Nicky Hopkins—piano.

COMING HOME
1977 Hal Ashby-directed film in which "Sympathy for the Devil" and "Out of Time" are heard.

COMPASS POINT STUDIOS
Recording studio in the Bahamas, where some of EMOTIONAL RES-

CUE and TATTOO YOU were recorded.

"COMPLICATED"
Written by: Jagger/Richards
Recorded by: The Rolling Stones
Release date: January 1967
Record label: London/Decca
Albums: BETWEEN THE BUTTONS (U.S.)
      BETWEEN THE BUTTONS (U.K.)

COMSTOCK, BOBBY
Performer opening for the Stones on their first U.S. tour, spring 1964.

"CON LE MIE LACRIME"
Italian version of "As Tears Go By," which Mick sings in Italian with a different musical backing track. Decca Dischi Italia released this as a single with "Heart of Stone" as its flip side. It appeared on SLOW ROLLERS in 1981.

"CONFESSIN' THE BLUES"
Written by: McShann/Brown
Recorded by: The Rolling Stones
Release date: August 1964
Record label: Decca/London
Albums: 12 x 5
      STONE AGE
EP: five by five (U.K. 8/64)
• Performed by the Stones to warm up the audience before they started filming their segment of the "Rock and Roll Circus."

"CONGRATULATIONS"
Written by: Jagger/Richards
Recorded by: The Rolling Stones
Release date: September 1964
Record label: London/Decca
Albums: 12 x 5
      NO STONE UNTURNED
Single: Flip of "Time Is on My Side" (U.S. 6/64)

CONN STROBOTUNER
Electronic device used to tune the Stones' guitars during concerts. Because it is too noisy to hear the tuning, the Strobotuner allows guitar roadies to tune *visually.*

"CONNECTION"
Written by: Jagger/Richards
Recorded by: The Rolling Stones
Release date: January 1967
Record label: London/Decca
Albums: BETWEEN THE BUTTONS (U.S.)
      BETWEEN THE BUTTONS (U.K.)

CONSTABLE, DETECTIVE SGT. ROBIN
British police detective who busted Mick and Marianne Faithfull in their Chelsea home in May 1969. Mick claimed that Constable asked for £2,400 to drop the charge of possession of cannabis; the detective sued Mick for libel. Mick was fined £200 for possession.

COODER, RY
American guitarist who Jack Nitzsche brought to the Stones during the BEGGARS BANQUET recording sessions. Through the years Cooder played on "Love in Vain" (mandolin) and "Sister Morphine" (bottleneck guitar). A long-standing feud with Keith, due to Ry's claim to have written the opening chords to "Honky Tonk Women," prevented him from becoming a Stone after either Brian's or Mick Taylor's departure.

"COOL, CALM AND COLLECTED"
Written by: Jagger/Richards
Recorded by: The Rolling Stones
Release date: January 1967
Record label: London/Decca
Albums: BETWEEN THE BUTTONS (U.S.)
BETWEEN THE BUTTONS (U.K.)

COOLEY FLOYD
Tuba player on "No More Foolin'."

COOPER, AUSTIN
Canadian lawyer who handled Keith's
Toronto drug bust.

COOPER, MICHAEL
Photographer and friend of the Stones
who often traveled with them. He
designed and photographed the cover
for THEIR SATANIC MAJESTIES
REQUEST, constructing the set with
the Stones and "Artchie" and photographing it with a 3-D camera
imported from Japan. He snuck a minia-
ture camera into Lewes Prison to photo-
graph Mick's incarceration for possible
use on an album cover, but the film
was confiscated by prison authorities.
After his divorce, Cooper and his son,
Adam, lived with Keith for two years,
before Cooper's death by suicide.

COOPER, RAY
Percussionist on IT'S ONLY ROCK
'N' ROLL.

"COPS AND ROBBERS"
Bo Diddley song chosen by Bill for
THE BLACK BOX compilation.

CORPORATE HEAD, THE
Designers of the FLOWERS LP jacket.

CORRISTON, PETER
Creator of cover concept and designer
of SOME GIRLS jacket; art director
of TATTOO YOU.

CORT
Manufacturer of the zippers used on
the cover of STICKY FINGERS.

COSMIC CHRISTMAS
Original title idea for THEIR SA-
TANIC MAJESTIES REQUEST.

COTCHFORD FARM
Sussex farm, fifty miles southeast of
London, which Brian bought for
£31,500 in November 1968. It was formerly the home of author A. A. Milne,
who had written *Winnie the Pooh* there.
William the Conqueror had also once
lived at Cotchford.

COULD YOU WALK ON THE WATER?
The name of the Stones album sched-
uled to be released in March 1966
containing the following songs:
"19th Nervous Breakdown"
"Sad Day"
"Take It or Leave It"
"Think"
"Mother's Little Helper"
"Goin' Home"

"Sittin' on a Fence"
"Doncha Bother Me"
"Ride On Baby"
"Lookin' Tired"
Decca refused to have anything to do with the title, but the majority of the songs were released on AFTERMATH a month later.

"COUNTRY HONK"
Written by: Jagger/Richards
Recorded by: The Rolling Stones
Release date: November 1969
Record label: Decca/London
Album: LET IT BLEED
• Byron Berline—fiddle.
• Nanette Newman—backup vocals.
• Berline, preferring the natural sound, went outdoors to record his fiddle part. A car drove by during the recording, and its "honk" was retained in the song.

COUNTY KILDARE
Section of Southern Ireland where Mick and Marianne Faithfull lived while Marianne was pregnant.

COVENT GARDEN OPERA HOUSE
Mick, as a patron to the arts, became a "friend of the Covent Garden Opera House" in March 1969.

"CRACKIN' UP"
Written by: McDaniel (Bo Diddley)
Recorded by: The Rolling Stones
Release date: September 1977
Record label: Rolling Stones Records
Album: LOVE YOU LIVE
        (live in Toronto)
• A never-released studio version of this was recorded at the band's first session with Glyn Johns in early 1963.

CRAIGBRAUNINC
Designer/graphic artist for the STICKY FINGERS sleeve.

CRAWDADDY CLUB
Club run by Giorgio Gomelsky and located in the Station Hotel, Richmond, London, where the Stones had a Sunday afternoon residency in early 1963. They received four dollars each at their first performance, but they soon found so large a following that the club had to close its doors early, leaving throngs of disappointed fans out on Kew Road each Sunday, attracting the press (see May, Barry), quite a few celebrities, and of course, Andrew Oldham.
In April 1963, the Stones and the Beatles met for the first time at the Crawdaddy. "We were playing there one Sunday," Bill remembered, "and suddenly looked up and there were four sort of silhouetted guys with black leather overcoats...all dressed exactly the same. And we said to ourselves, 'Shit, that's the Beatles!' and got all nervous."
• Paul Williams, the father of rock

journalism, named his brilliant magazine, *Crawdaddy,* after the club where the Stones got their start.

"CRAZY MAMA"
Written by: Jagger/Richards
Recorded by: The Rolling Stones
Release date: April 1976
Record label: Rolling Stones Records
Albums: BLACK AND BLUE
        TIME WAITS FOR NO ONE
        SUCKING IN THE SEVENTIES
Single: Flip of "Fool to Cry" (U.K. 4/76)
• Pre-Stone Ron Wood—guitar.
• Billy Preston—piano, backup vocals.
• Ollie E. Brown—percussion.

"CRAZY WOMAN"
Written by: Bill Wyman
Recorded by: Bill Wyman
Release date: May 1974
Record label: Rolling Stones Records
Album: MONKEY GRIP
• Dallas Taylor—drums.
• Danny Kootch—guitar.

• Joe Lala—percussion.
• Joey Murcia—guitar.
• Duane Smith—piano.
• George Terry—slide guitar.
• Betty Wright, George McCrae, Gwen McCrae—backup vocals.
• Boneroo Horn Section—Peter Graves, Mark Colby, Ken Faulk, Neal Bonsanti.

CREATION, THE
The band Ron was in (along with his former Bird bandmate, Kim Gardner) for a brief time between being fired from and rehired into the Jeff Beck Group in 1968. Creation member Eddie Phillips was the first guitarist to use a violin bow with his guitar.

CROSBY, STILLS, NASH & YOUNG
Seventies supergroup that was one of the groups which opened for the Stones at Altamont.

CRUSADE
1967 John Mayall's Blues Breakers LP featuring Mick Taylor.

"CRY TO ME"
Written by: Russell
Recorded by: The Rolling Stones
Release date: July 1965
Record label: London/Decca
Albums: OUT OF OUR HEADS (U.S.)
        OUT OF OUR HEADS (U.K.)

CS BLUES
Alternate "acceptable" title for *Cocksucker Blues.*

CURLY CLAYTON SOUND STUDIOS
London recording studio where Mick, Keith, Brian, Tony Chapman, and Ian Stewart recorded "Soon Forgotten," "You Can't Judge a Book," and "Close Together" in late 1962. Curly engineered the tape, which was submitted to Neville Skrimshire at EMI Records. To discover its fate, see the title of the first above-mentioned song.

CURRENT
Stereo "audio magazine" which made its debut in 1972, featuring an interview with Mick, whose picture was on the cover of its first—and last—"issue."

CURRY'S RECORD SHOP
Cheltenham High Street store which Brian worked in.

CUSTOMS' INTERNATIONAL RED LIST
List of travelers who are searched in private rooms when entering or leaving all countries. When Mick discovered he was on this list in 1967, he held a press conference to denounce it and rally for human freedom. British Customs denied that there was such a list.

CUTLER, SAM
Stones' road manager for their 1969 U.S. tour. He hired the Hell's Angels to police Altamont in exchange for $500 worth of beer.

D

DAILY MIRROR
The June 13, 1963, issue of this British newspaper carried the first full-page article about the Stones to appear in a national general interest paper.

DAILY STAR
Bill sued this British newspaper for libel after it ran an "exclusive" interview with him in 1981, quoting him as saying he planned to quit the Stones. Bill said the interview took place five months earlier than the publication date and that it was only intended for use in the music industry newsletter *MIDEM*. Bill claimed he would never have spoken to the *Daily Star,* and sued for damages. The case still isn't settled.

DALLESANDRO, JOE
Andy Warhol superstar actor whose lower body is featured on the cover of STICKY FINGERS.

DALTON, DAVID
Author of several books on the Stones: *The Rolling Stones; The Rolling Stones: The First Twenty Years;* and *The Rolling Stones in Their Own Words,* co-compiled with Mick Farren.

DALY, SHERRY
Secretary of Rolling Stones Mobile Studio.

"DANCE"
Written by: Jagger/Richards/Wood
Recorded by: The Rolling Stones
Release date: June 1980
Record label: Rolling Stones Records
Album: EMOTIONAL RESCUE
• Max Romeo—backup vocals.

"DANCE LITTLE SISTER"
Written by: Jagger/Richards
Recorded by: The Rolling Stones
Release date: October 1974
Record label: Rolling Stones Records
Albums: MADE IN THE SHADE
　　　　IT'S ONLY ROCK 'N' ROLL
Single: Flip of "Ain't Too Proud to Beg" (U.S. 10/74)
• Ian Stewart—piano.

DANCETERIA
New York rock club where the Stones held a press party to celebrate the release of EMOTIONAL RESCUE.

"DANCING WITH MR. D"
Written by: Jagger/Richards
Recorded by: The Rolling Stones
Release date: August 1973
Record label: Rolling Stones Records
Albums: GOATS HEAD SOUP
　　　　TIME WAITS FOR NO ONE
Single: Flip of "Doo Doo Doo Doo Doo (Heartbreaker)" (U.S. 12/73)
• Nicky Hopkins—piano.

"DANDELION"
Written by: Jagger/Richards
Recorded by: The Rolling Stones
Release date: August 1967
Record label: London/Decca
Albums: THROUGH THE PAST, DARKLY (U.K.)
　　　　THROUGH THE PAST, DARKLY (U.S.)
　　　　MORE HOT ROCKS
Single: Flip of "We Love You" (U.S./U.K. 8/67)
• Mick says that the printed lyrics for this song are totally different than what he wrote and what he is singing.

DARK HORSE
1979 ex-Beatle George Harrison LP, featuring Ron.

DARTFORD
Birthplace of both Keith and Mick, located in Kent, fifteen miles outside of London.

DARTFORD GRAMMAR SCHOOL
School Mick attended.

DARTFORD HOSPITAL
Mick worked as a doorman here while attending school.

DARTFORD TECHNICAL SCHOOL
School Keith attended from age eleven until he left at sixteen, when he was expelled for truancy.

DAVE HUNT BLUES BAND
Resident band at the Crawdaddy Club before the Stones. Their guitarist was Ray Davies.

DAVIES, CYRIL
Legendary British bluesman and member of Alexis Korner's Blues Incorpo-

Prince Stanislaus Klossowski De Rola with Brian.

rated who gave Brian tips on harmonica playing. Cyril died of leukemia in 1964, and his friends and fellow musicians held a memorial concert for him at the Flamingo Club in London. Although Brian attended, he didn't perform.

DAVIS, ANGELA
American political activist who was the inspiration for the song "Sweet Black Angel."

DAVIS, JAY
Bass player on "Priceless."

DAVIS, ROB
Member of the road crew credited on STILL LIFE.

DE NAVE, CONNIE
The Stones' first publicist in America.

DE ROLA, PRINCE STANISLAUS KLOSSOWSKI
Friend of both Brian and Keith who had the unfortunate luck to be busted with each of them. He was at Brian's Courtfield flat when Brian was busted and was again found at the scene of the crime when Keith was busted at Cheyne Walk.

DE SALVO, ALBERT
"The Boston Strangler," whose exact words of confession to murder and rape are quoted in "Midnight Rambler."

"DEAD FLOWERS"
Written by: Jagger/Richards
Recorded by: The Rolling Stones
Release date: April 1971
Record label: Rolling Stones Records
Album: STICKY FINGERS
• Ian Stewart—piano.

DEADLY BEES, THE
1967 horror flick in which the Birds made a brief appearance.

DEAN CLOSE SCHOOL
Cheltenham public school where Brian excelled in music and English.

"DEAR DOCTOR"
Written by: Jagger/Richards
Recorded by: The Rolling Stones
Release date: November 1968
Record label: Rolling Stones Records
Albums: BEGGARS BANQUET
       SLOW ROLLERS

DEATH OF A ROLLING STONE: THE BRIAN JONES STORY
Biography written by Mandy Aftel; published by Delilah Communications, Ltd., in 1982.

DECCA RECORDS
British record company which signed the Stones in May 1963. Through Andrew Oldham's clever manipulations the Stones received a royalty rate comparable to that of worldwide stars.

(Oldham did even better than the Stones, but that's a whole 'nother lawsuit.) Decca wasn't happy with the Stones' original recording of their first single, "Come On," but accepted it on the fifth try. The second single the Stones wanted to release, "Poison Ivy," was rejected by Decca, which felt it was too rough for English taste. Placing a sure bet, the Stones gave Decca their version of Lennon and McCartney's "I Wanna Be Your Man." On this fond footing, it seemed that between album cover art, album titles, and, of course, material, the Stones' and Decca's disagreements never stopped. As Keith puts it, "Decca are supposed to be making records, but they might as well be making baked beans." When the Stones' first contract was up in August of 1965, Allen Klein was able to negotiate a more satisfactory deal for them, which also included Decca's promise to finance five films to be made in the next three years. It was still not true love. In July of 1970 the Stones' contract with Decca expired again and the band decided to venture out on its own with Rolling Stones Records. The Stones owed Decca one more song and presented them with "Cocksucker Blues." Decca retained the rights to all Stones songs that they had previously licensed or released, and for the past thirteen years have continued to release and re-release various packages and compilations of Stones material.

DECCA STUDIOS
London recording studio where the Stones, along with Oldham as producer, recorded three songs: "Poison Ivy," "Fortune Teller," and "It Should Be You."

DECEMBER'S CHILDREN (AND EVERYBODY'S)
Artist: The Rolling Stones
Producer: Andrew Loog Oldham
Release date: November 1965
Record label: London
Tracks: 12
"**She Said Yeah**" (Roderick/Christy/Jackson)
"**Talkin' 'Bout You**" (Berry)
"**You Better Move On**" (Alexander)
"**Look What You've Done**" (Morganfield)
"**The Singer Not the Song**"
"**Route 66**" (Troup)
"**Get Off of My Cloud**"
"**I'm Free**"
"**As Tears Go By**" (Jagger/Richards/Oldham)
"**Gotta Get Away**"
"**Blue Turns to Grey**"
"**I'm Moving On**" (Snow)
• 5th U.S. LP.

• Jack Nitzsche—piano, organ, percussion.
• Ian Stewart—piano, organ, marimbas, percussion.
• J. W. Alexander—percussion.
• Studios—RCA, Hollywood; Chess, Chicago; Olympic, London.
• Engineers—Dave Hassinger, Ron Malo, Glyn Johns.
• Arranged by the Rolling Stones.
• Cover photo—Gered Mankowitz.
• Liner notes are by ALO, who, in poetry form, states that there is no political message here.
• No "s."

"DEED I DO"/"IT'S IN MY MIND"
1967 single by Moon's Train, produced by Bill.

DEGAULLE, GENERAL
Brian's nickname.

DEGAULLE'S PARTY, GENERAL
Alias under which Brian and entourage would book restaurant/hotel/club reservations.

DEGREE OF MURDER, A — (MORD UND TOTSCHLAG)
1966 film in which Anita starred and for which Brian composed and produced the soundtrack, with a score performed by Jimmy Page on lead guitar, Nicky Hopkins on piano, and Brian playing sitar, organ, dulcimer, clarinet, and harmonica. Glyn Johns engineered the recording session. The film was Germany's entry at the Cannes Film Festival.

DELENA, EDDIE
Assistant engineer of 1 2 3 4.

"DELIA"
Written by: Trad
Recorded by: Ron Wood
Release date: May 1979
Record label: CBS
Album: GIMME SOME NECK

DELON, NATHALIE
Witness at Mick and Bianca's wedding.

DENTWEILER, CRAIG
Horn player on STONE ALONE.

DESHUFFLIN, INC.
Company that controls publishing rights to Bill's compositions.

"DEVIL IS MY NAME, THE"
Original title of "Sympathy for the Devil."

DEVON
English county where Keith and Mick went on holiday in 1961 with Keith's parents. The Glimmer Twins made their first public appearance together in a local pub here.

DIAMOND
Mick's favorite jewel, which he wears imbedded in his front tooth. The diamond replaced Mick's first choice, a ruby, which looked too much like blood, and then an emerald, which resembled lettuce.

DIARY OF A BAND VOL. 1
1968 album by John Mayall and the Blues Breakers featuring Mick Taylor.

DIARY OF A BAND VOL. 2
1968 album by John Mayall and the Blues Breakers, again featuring Mick Taylor.

DICKERMAN, ANDY
Photographer for the *Providence Journal and Bulletin* who accused Keith and Stanley Moore of assault at the Warwick Airport in Rhode Island in 1972.

DICKINSON, J.
Plays piano on STICKY FINGERS.

DICKSON, DEBRA
Girlfriend of Donald Cammell. She was arrested along with Keith, Anita, and Tom Keylock while they were driving through Spain. (See Arrests—Barcelona.)

"DID EVERYONE PAY THEIR DUES?"
Recorded during the BEGGARS BANQUET sessions in 1968, this song was never released, but it evolved into "Street Fighting Man."

DIDDLEY, BO
The man who invented "the beat" and an all-time American rock and Stones hero, Bo Diddley headlined along with the Everly Brothers on the Stones first U.K. tour. Keith, Mick, and Brian presented him with gold cufflinks when he came to London, and Brian, Bill,

and Charlie served as his backup band on a *Saturday Club* broadcast.

"DIDDLEY DADDY"
Song that the Stones recorded at their first recording session with Glyn Johns in early 1963 but never released.

DIGITAL DREAMS
Film by Bill and Astrid Wyman, starring James Coburn, shown at the Cannes Film Festival, 1983. This full-length feature includes fantasy and animated sequences, and tells of the life and times of Bill, with soundtrack by Bill. Footage shows Bill, Astrid, and the Stones.

DIJON, ROCKY
Plays congas on STICKY FINGERS and percussion on LET IT BLEED.

DINELEY, CHIEF INSPECTOR
Headed the raid on Keith's Redlands house the night of the infamous bust.

DISNEY WORLD
While in Orlando, Florida, on their 1981 U.S. tour, the Stones celebrated Bill's forty-fifth birthday on a rented boat here.

DIXON, P. C.
The Stones do a takeoff on this popular British TV personality on the last cut of BETWEEN THE BUTTONS.

"DO YOU THINK I CARE?"
Song recorded in Paris in 1977 but never released.

DOE, JOHN
Never-identified member of the audience at Altamont who fell into an irrigation canal and drowned.

DOMINO, FATS
American rock 'n' roll legend and the inspiration behind Mick's vocal style. Mick followed Fats' "you should never sing the lyrics out very clearly" theory.

"DONCHA BOTHER ME"
Written by: Jagger/Richards
Recorded by: The Rolling Stones
Release date: April 1966
Record label: Decca/London
Albums: AFTERMATH (U.K.)
　　　　　AFTERMATH (U.S.)

"DON'T LIE TO ME"
Written by: Chuck Berry
Recorded by: The Rolling Stones
Release date: June 1975
Record label: Decca/ABKCO
Album: METAMORPHOSIS

"DON'T WORRY"
Written by: Ron Wood
Recorded by: Ron Wood
Release date: May 1979
Record label: CBS
Album: GIMME SOME NECK
• Charlie Watts—drums.
• "Pops" Popwell—bass.
• Bobby Keys—tenor sax.

"DOO DOO DOO DOO DOO (HEARTBREAKER)"
Written by: Jagger/Richards
Recorded by: The Rolling Stones
Release date: August 1973
Record label: Rolling Stones Records
Albums: GOATS HEAD SOUP
　　　　　MADE IN THE SHADE
Single: B/w "Dancing with Mr. D"
　　　　(U.S. 12/73)
• Billy Preston—piano.
• Jim Price—horns, horn arrangements.

DORCHESTER HOTEL
London hotel where the party to celebrate the premiere of the Beatles' film *A Hard Day's Night* was held in July 1964. Keith, Bill, and Brian crashed the party as uninvited guests.

DOUGLASS, JIMMY
Engineer on LOVE YOU LIVE.

DOWD, STEVE
Assistant engineer on BLACK AND BLUE.

DOWD, TOM
Tape mixer on STONE ALONE.

"DOWN AND OUT"/"STOP RUNNING ROUND"
1964 Cheynes single produced by Bill, who also wrote the flip side.

"DOWN HOME GIRL"
Written by: Lieber/Butler
Recorded by: The Rolling Stones
Release date: January 1965
Record label: Decca/London
Albums: THE ROLLING STONES NO. 2
　　　　　THE ROLLING STONES, NOW!
• Jack Nitzsche—piano.

"DOWN IN THE HOLE"
Written by: Jagger/Richards
Recorded by: The Rolling Stones
Release date: June 1980
Record label: Rolling Stones Records
Album: EMOTIONAL RESCUE
Single: Flip of "Emotional Rescue"
　　　　(6/80)

"DOWN THE ROAD APIECE"
Written by: Raye
Recorded by: The Rolling Stones
Release date: January 1965
Record label: Decca/London
Albums: THE ROLLING STONES NO. 2
　　　　　THE ROLLING STONES, NOW!
　　　　　ROCK 'N' ROLLING STONES
• An early version of this song was chosen by Bill for THE BLACK BOX compilation.

"DOWN TO THE GROUND"
Written by: Ron Wood
Recorded by: Ron Wood
Release date: August 1981
Record label: Columbia
Album: 1 2 3 4
• Ian Wallace—drums.
• Jimmy Haslip—bass.
• Nicky Hopkins—piano.
• Ian McLagan—organ.

"DOWNTOWN SUZIE"
Written by: Bill Wyman
Recorded by: The Rolling Stones
Release date: June 1975
Record label: Decca/ABKCO
Album: METAMORPHOSIS
• This was originally an outtake jam from BEGGARS BANQUET.

DOWNWIND
1979 Gong LP which features Mick Taylor.

DRIBERG, TOM
Member of Parliament, who in September 1966 asked the House of Commons to "deplore" the action of a magistrate who called the Stones "complete morons" who wore "filthy clothes."

DRINKIN' TNT 'N' SMOKIN' DYNAMITE
LP recorded live at the Montreux Jazz Festival, June 1974, and released on Bill's Ripple Records in 1982. The album consists of a set played by Buddy Guy and Junior Wells, with Bill, Pinetop Perkin, Terry Taylor, and Dallas Taylor.

DROVE, MARTIN
Horn player on "Jump Up."

DUKE ELLINGTON AND HIS ORCHESTRA
Perform "Take the A Train," the twenty-seven-second pre-recorded intro to STILL LIFE.

DUKE, GEORGE
Performer who opened for the Stones in St. Louis during their 1981 U.S. tour.

DUNBAR, JOHN
Art gallery owner and Marianne Faithfull's first husband. They were married in May 1965 and had a son, Nicholas. Through Dunbar's friendship with Paul McCartney, Marianne first met Mick. In September 1970 Dunbar cited Mick when he sued Marianne for divorce. The divorce was granted him six weeks later, and Mick had to pay £200 in court costs.

DUNN, ALAN
First became associated with the Stones when he was asked to keep an eye on Brian. In 1968 he became Mick's personal assistant, but when the band went on the road he served as road manager for all the Stones. When the Stones and entourage left Keith in Toronto after his drug bust, Dunn stayed on to help. He is currently employed as "logistics man" at Rolling Stones Records, U.K., and at the Rolling Stones Mobile Unit.

DUNN, ARNOLD
Head of "trucking" at the Rolling Stones Mobile Unit.

DUPONT FAMILY MANSION
Home for Charlie, Shirley, and Serafina, and the Stones' West Coast headquarters during their Los Angeles stay in 1969.

DUPREE, THEODORE AUGUSTUS
Keith's grandfather Gus, who was a saxophone player leading a dance band before World War II and a country band afterward. Keith felt a kinship with his grandfather and was much closer to him while he was growing up than to his own father.

DYLAN, BOB
American singer/songwriter and sixties legend. Brian felt particularly close to him and claims that Dylan asked him to join his backup band in 1965. Another 1965 rumor was that Dylan would be the best man at Anita and Brian's wedding. At a Carnegie Hall concert, also in 1965, Dylan said that his song, "Like a Rolling Stone" was written for Brian. Brian also felt that Dylan's "Ballad of a Thin Man" was about him and was devastated by the put-down of a "Mr. Jones." The Stones frequently attended Dylan's concerts. All of them plus friends saw him at the Royal Albert Hall in May 1966, and Keith, Bill, and Charlie saw his Isle of Wight concert in August 1969. Mick visited Dylan in the studio while he was recording BLOOD ON THE TRACKS but denies the rumors that he can be heard on the album. In early 1983 Charlie and Mick Taylor joined Dylan in the studio where he's working on his latest album.

DYNAMIC SOUND STUDIOS
Kingston, Jamaica, recording studio where the Stones recorded GOATS HEAD SOUP.

DZIDZORNU, ROCKI
Percussionist on "Wine & Wimmen."

Rolling Stones Tour Of Europe '76

EMI RECORDS
In 1978 the Rolling Stones signed with this company to distribute Rolling Stones Records worldwide except in America.

"EACH AND EVERYDAY OF THE YEAR"
Written by: Jagger/Richards
Recorded by: The Rolling Stones
Release date: June 1975
Record label: Decca/ABKCO
Album: METAMORPHOSIS
• Quincy Jones and Sarah Vaughn recorded this song before the Stones version was released.

EALES, STUART
Assistant engineer on BILL WYMAN.

EALING ART COLLEGE
Ron studied commercial art here for two years. He then worked as a signwriter for four months until he decided to pursue a musical career full-time.

EALING CLUB, THE
Alexis Korner and Cyril Davies helped found this R&B club in London in 1962. Brian attended the opening night show on St. Patrick's Day, watching Korner drummer Charlie Watts. Alexis Korner's Blues Incorporated was the resident band on Saturday nights at Ealing, and it was at one of their gigs

that Keith and Mick (of Little Boy Blue and the Blues Boys) met Brian (going under the name of Elmo Lewis). Often various future-Stones would play on stage, with Brian performing on slide guitar and harmonica, Keith singing the blues, and Mick playing harmonica and singing. The early Stones later played at the Ealing Club on Saturday nights also.

"EAMMON ANDREWS SHOW, THE"
In February 1967 Mick was a guest on this popular British TV show after *News of the World* published an article stating that he took LSD. On TV Mick accused the paper of lying.

EASTON, ERIC
Fifty-year-old talent agent, boss of Andrew Oldham, who first saw the Stones in April 1963 at the Crawdaddy Club and who, with Oldham, signed the Stones to an exclusive management contract the following day. Easton didn't like Mick's voice, and he and Brian agreed that they should get rid of Mick; Ian Stewart talked them out of that move, later himself to be thrown out by Oldham. Easton handled the financial matters, and because Brian convinced him that he was the leader of the band, Easton gave him five pounds extra per week until the rest of the band found out. Easton and Oldham coproduced the first Stones records. After Allen Klein entered the picture in August 1965, Easton officially parted with Oldham and the Stones. In August 1971, Mick, Keith, Bill, Charlie,

and Brian's father filed a High Court suit against Easton and Oldham (also no longer with the Stones) claiming that the two made a side deal with Decca Records in 1963, cheating the band of royalty monies. The suit claimed that Oldham convinced Brian to accept six percent of wholesale record prices for the band, while Decca was actually paying Oldham and Easton fourteen percent.
In May 1972, the Stones issued a press release stating that they had assigned their claims against Easton to ABKCO Industries and would cooperate with ABKCO in that action. (In the same press release, the Stones stated that they, ABKCO, and Klein had "settled all outstanding differences to the satisfaction of all parties," making it clear however that ABKCO would no longer act as business manager for the Stones. As Mick succinctly put it, "The settlement means that Allen Klein never has anything else to do with us.") Not to stand idly by, in October 1972 Easton sued Oldham, Nanker Phelge Music, Decca Records, London Records, and Allen Klein—and hasn't been heard from since.

"ED SULLIVAN SHOW, THE"
American Sunday night TV institution. After the Stones' first appearance on the show in October 1964, non-fan Sullivan said, "I promise you they'll never be back on our show," because of the hundreds of complaint letters he received. But because of the Stones'

popularity, they appeared on the show many more times, with the most famous appearance of all in January 1967 when the Stones were forced to change the lyrics of "Let's Spend the Night Together." Legend has it that Mick sang, "Let's spend some time together," although he claims to have mumbled, "Let's spend some m-m-m-m-m together." (See song for more details.) After that, whenever the Stones were on the show, Mick's microphone was turned down if the sound engineers thought his lyrics might be questionable.

EDDY, KEVIN
Assistant engineer on 1 2 3 4.

EDITH GROVE
No. 102. Chelsea flat where Keith, Mick, and Brian all lived for a time in 1962. Charlie also occasionally stayed here. Bill says that he would sometimes bring them food.

EDMUNDS, DAVE
British guitar virtuoso, true rockabilly believer, and then-member of Rockpile (with Nick Lowe). Keith attended his show at New York's Bottom Line rock club twenty-four hours after he received a suspended sentence at his Toronto bust trial. Keith wore the same T-shirt ("Robbie Rocker") at the show as he did in court. The audience cheered Keith, and he was given free champagne and a bodyguard. He later jammed with Rockpile during their set, performing "Let It Rock" and "Down, Down, Down."

ELECTRIC LADYLAND
New York recording studio where the Stones mixed EMOTIONAL RESCUE and recorded parts of EMOTIONAL RESCUE and TATTOO YOU.

ELEKTRA STUDIO
Los Angeles recording studio where the Stones recorded the album version of "Country Honk," "Live with Me," and overdubbed "Gimmie Shelter" in 1969.

ELLIS, BOB
Ron Wood's former manager.

ELTINGVILLE LUTHERAN CHURCH
Staten Island, New York, church where rumor had it that Keith and Patti Han-

sen were to marry in late 1982/early '83. Due to Patti's father's death in January 1983, the wedding was postponed, and sadly Alfred Hansen's funeral was held here instead. Keith served as a pallbearer at the military funeral.

ELY, JOE
Performer who opened some of the shows during the Stones 1981 U.S. tour.

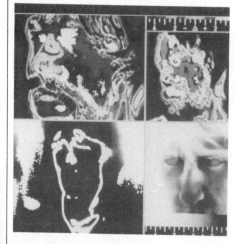

EMOTIONAL RESCUE
Artist: The Rolling Stones
Producer: The Glimmer Twins
Release date: June 1980
Record label: Rolling Stones Records
Tracks: 10
"Dance" (Jagger/Richards/Wood)
"Summer Romance"
"Send It to Me"
"Let Me Go"
"Indian Girl"
"Where the Boys Go"
"Down in the Hole"
"Emotional Rescue"
"She's So Cold"
"All about You"
• 28th U.K. LP.
• 27th U.S. LP.
• Ian Stewart—piano.
• Bobby Keys—sax.
• Nicky Hopkins—piano.
• Sugar Blue—harmonica.
• Michael Shrieve—percussion.
• Max Romeo—backup vocals.
• Studio—Pathé-Marconi Studios, Paris, France; Compass Point Studio, Nassau, Bahamas; Rolling Stones Mobile Unit.
• Associate producer—Chris Kimsey.
• Engineer—Chris Kimsey.
• Assistant engineers—Sean Fullen, Brad Samuelsohn, "Snake" Reynolds, Jon Smith.
• Arranged by Jack Nitzsche.
• The Stones had approximately forty songs in the works for EMOTIONAL RESCUE. They finished twenty-five of the forty, but had to narrow down to ten for the LP.
• During the recording sessions, Keith

broke his own record, staying up for nine consecutive days without sleep.

"EMOTIONAL RESCUE"
Written by: Jagger/Richards
Recorded by: The Rolling Stones
Release date: June 1980
Record label: Rolling Stones Records
Album: EMOTIONAL RESCUE
Single: B/w "Down in the Hole" (U.S./U.K. 6/80)

"EMPTY HEART"
Written by: Nanker Phelge
Recorded by: The Rolling Stones
Release date: October 1964
Record label: Decca/London
Album: 12 X 5
EP: FIVE BY FIVE (U.K. 8/64)

EMPTY ROOMS
1970 John Mayall album featuring Mick Taylor.

END, THE
Group on the Stones' seventh tour of Britain in September/October 1965. The mid-sixties Philips recording artists were managed by Bill. They eventually evolved into Tucky Buzzard, a band Bill also produced.

ENGLAND'S NEWEST HIT MAKERS —THE ROLLING STONES
Artist: The Rolling Stones
Producer: Andrew Loog Oldham and Eric Easton for Impact Sound
Release date: May 1964
Record label: London
Tracks: 12
"Not Fade Away" (Petty/Hardin)
"Route 66" (Troup)
"I Just Want to Make Love to You" (Dixon)
"Honest I Do" (Hurron/Calvert)
"Now I've Got a Witness" (Nanker Phelge)
"Little by Little" (Phelge/Spector)
"I'm a King Bee" (Moore)
"Carol" (Berry)
"Tell Me"
"Can I Get a Witness" (E. & B. Holland/Dozier)
"You Can Make It if You Try" (Jarrett)

"Walking the Dog" (Thomas)
• 1st U.S. album.
• Gene Pitney—piano.
• Phil Spector—maracas.
• Ian Stewart—piano and organ.
• Studio—Regent Sound, London.
• Arranged by the Rolling Stones.
• Cover photo—Nicholas Wright.
• In his liner notes Andrew Loog Oldham declared: "The Rolling Stones are more than just a group—they are a way of life." (Same liner notes as first UK LP.)
• No "s."

"ENGLISH SUMMER"
Two versions of this song were recorded by the Stones during the BE-TWEEN THE BUTTONS sessions, neither of which was ever released.

EPPS, STUART
Co-engineer, with Chris Kimsey, of BILL WYMAN, for which he mixed "Come Back Suzanne," in addition to singing backup vocals.

ERRICO, GREG
Drummer on "No More Foolin'."

ERTEGUN, AHMET
President of Atlantic Records. In April 1971 he threw a society party in New York to announce the signing of the Stones to Atlantic Records through a newly formed label, Rolling Stones Records. Mick guaranteed that the group would deliver six albums in four years, including STICKY FINGERS. The deal was off to a fitting start when Keith left the party early because he didn't like the company.

ETHERINGTON, ALLEN
Original member of Little Boy Blue and the Blue Boys, along with Dick Taylor, Mick, Bob Beckenwith, and eventually Keith.

EVERLY BROTHERS, THE
American singing duo who headlined, along with Bo Diddley, the first tour of Britain the Stones did, in the autumn of 1963.

"EVERY BEAT OF MY HEART"/ "TOMORROW"
1965 Bobbie Miller single produced by Bill.

EVERY PICTURE TELLS A STORY
1971 Rod Stewart LP featuring Ron.

"EVERY SIXTY SECONDS"
Written by: Bill Wyman
Recorded by: Bill Wyman
Release date: February 1976
Record label: Rolling Stones Records
Album: STONE ALONE
• Joe Walsh—slide guitar.
• Joe Vitale—piano.
• Jim Kelter—drums.
• Van Morrison—harmonica.
• Ruth and Bonnie Pointer—backup vocals.

"EVERYBODY NEEDS SOMEBODY TO LOVE"
Written by: Russell/Burke/Wexler
Recorded by: The Rolling Stones
Release date: January 1965
Record label: Decca/London
Albums: THE ROLLING STONES NO. 2
THE ROLLING STONES, NOW!
PROMOTIONAL ALBUM
ROCK 'N' ROLLING STONES
EP: GOT LIVE IF YOU WANT IT (U.K.) (live version)
Single: B/w "Street Fighting Man" and "Surprise Surprise" on a maxi single (U.K. 1972)
• Ian Stewart—piano.
• The version on THE ROLLING STONES, NOW! album was a studio run-through that was released by mistake.

"EVERLASTING IS MY LOVE"
Song recorded during the SOME GIRLS sessions, but never released.

"EVERYTHING IS TURNING TO GOLD"
Written by: Jagger/Richards/Wood
Recorded by: The Rolling Stones
Release date: June 1978
Record label: Rolling Stones Records
Album: SUCKING IN THE SEVENTIES
Single: Flip of "Shattered" (U.S./U.K. 6/78)
• Previously unavailable on an LP.

EVERYTHING STOPS FOR TEA
1972 John Baldry album for which Ron did the cover painting.

"EVERYWHERE I GO"/"STU-BALL"
1966 single produced by Bill. The A side is by Bobbie Miller. The B side is by Ian Stewart and the Railroaders, co-written by Bill and Ian, and features Keith, Bill, and Ian, with Tony Meehan on drums.

EXILE ON MAIN ST.

Artist: The Rolling Stones
Producer: Jimmy Miller
Release date: May 1972
Record label: Rolling Stones Records
Tracks: 18

"Rocks Off"
"Rip This Joint"
"Shake Your Hips" (Moore, aka Slim Harpo)
"Casino Boogie"
"Tumbling Dice"
"Sweet Virginia"
"Torn and Frayed"
"Sweet Black Angel"
"Loving Cup"
"Happy"
"Turd on the Run"
"Ventilator Blues" (Jagger/Richards/Taylor)
"I Just Want to See His Face"
"Let It Loose"
"All Down the Line"
"Stop Breaking Down" (Traditional —arranged by Jagger/Richards/Wyman/Taylor/Watts)
"Shine a Light"
"Soul Survivor"

• 18th U.S. album.
• 15th U.K. album.
• Bobby Keys (sax), Jim Price (trumpet and trombones), and Nicky Hopkins (piano) appear on all tracks. They were joined by fifteen assorted backup musicians and vocalists (see individual tracks for credit).
• Studio—Rolling Stones Mobile Unit, recorded at Nellcote, Villefranche, France.
• Engineers—Glyn and Andy Johns, Joe Zaganno, and Jeremy Gee.
• Mixed at Sunset Sound, Hollywood.
• Cover photography and concept —Robert Frank.
• Layout and design—John Von Hamersveld, Norman Seeff.
• Included with the album is a chain of twelve picture postcards—scenes one through twelve of "the fall from exile on Main St."—which tell and illustrate the story of the arrival of Mick's "Auntie," shows the band's fall, and ends with Mick Taylor suggesting "early retirement."
• Postcards photographed and directed —Norman Seeff.
• Postcard design—John Von Hamersveld.
• Postcard story dialogue—Kendrew Lascelles.
• This was the Stones' first double-LP, which in retrospect Keith feels could have been a single LP.
• It was re-released by EMI in the U.K. in March 1980.
• "Shake Your Hips" is referred to as "Hip Shake" on the album cover; "I Just Want to See His Face" is "I Just *Wanna…*"; and "Sweet Black Angel" isn't sweet.
• EAT IT and TROPICAL DISEASES were among the tentative titles for the album.
• The album cover has an "s"; no "s" on the disc itself.

EXPRESSO 2

1978 Gong LP featuring Mick Taylor.

"F.U.C. HER"
Written by: Ron Wood
Recorded by: Ron Wood
Release date: May 1979
Record label: CBS
Album: GIMME SOME NECK
• "Pops" Popwell—bass.
• Dave Mason—guitar.

FABULOUS THUNDERBIRDS
Band who opened for the Stones in
Texas during their 1981 tour.

FACES, THE
Originally the Small Faces, who recorded for Andrew Oldham's Immediate Records, this band contained Steve
Marriott, Ronnie Lane, Ian McLagan,
and Kenney Jones. Marriott left in
1969 to form Humble Pie, and Rod
Stewart replaced him, followed shortly
thereafter by Ron, both of whom were
tired of waiting for their former band
leader, Jeff Beck, to decide his next
move. Since Rod and Ron were not as
short as the band's original members,
and a new image was sought anyway,
the word "small" was dropped from
the band's name, leaving just the Faces,
who were to become the ultimate good-
time fun band of Britain (and the world)
in the early seventies.
Rod, with a solo contract to another
label, was becoming more and more
popular as an individual, to the point
that, in 1974, Ron decided "I've Got
My Own Album to Do." He did
—with help from his friends Keith
Richards, Mick Jagger, and Mick Taylor,
who in one configuration or another
appear on all but one of the album's
eleven tracks.
Ron was the Stones' guitarist of choice
for Mick Taylor's replacement in 1975.
(He had even been rumored to be
joining the Stones in 1973 for touring
only—of all things, to *replace* Keith,
who, because of tax and drug and
other rock 'n' roll problems, almost
found himself trapped in Jamaica
[Switzerland was the only other country that would have him] unable to
enter other countries and hence to
travel and tour.) Ron, however, remained a member of the Faces while
accompanying the Stones on tour in
1975. When Rod officially left the band
in pursuit of a solo career in late 1975,
Ron felt he was finally free to join the
Stones.
As for the rest of the Faces, Ronnie
Lane composed and played on the
original motion picture soundtrack for
Mahoney's Last Stand with Ron in
1976, performed with Paul McCartney's

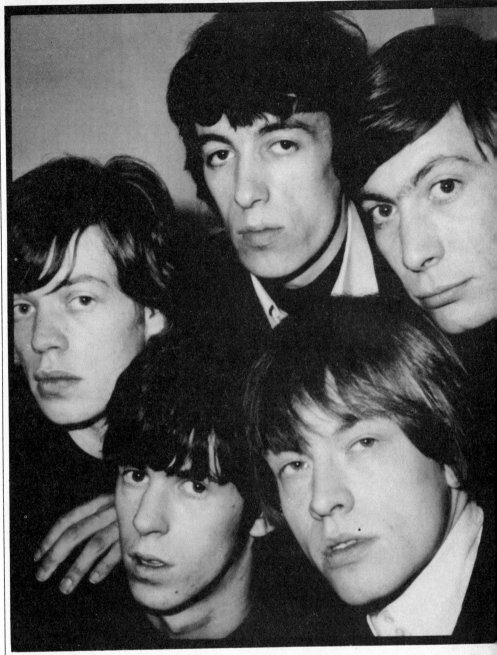

Rockestra in 1979, and is now, sadly,
terminally ill. The Stones helped pay
some of Lane's hospital bills when he
underwent special treatments in Florida.
Kenney Jones replaced Keith Moon in
the Who, and Ian McLagan somewhat
replaced Keith Moon in real life, marrying Keith's former wife, Kim, with the
blessings of the other Mrs. Moon
(Keith's mom). Ian also performs keyboard duties with the Stones, though
not as an official member of the band.

"FACTORY GIRL"
Written by: Jagger/Richards
Recorded by: The Rolling Stones
Release date: November 1968
Record label: London/Decca
Album: BEGGARS BANQUET

"FAERIE TALE THEATRE"
1983 cable TV Showtime series in which

Mick plays the part of the Chinese
Emperor in Hans Christian Andersen's
The Nightingale.

FAITHFULL, MARIANNE
Marianne was *the* mod sixties girl. She
was blond, beautiful, and dating Mick
Jagger. Marianne's background gave
her an upper-class sophistication that
Mick's then current girlfriend, Chrissie
Shrimpton, lacked. Marianne's mother
was an Austrian baroness (it didn't
matter that she was penniless) and her
father was a professor and/or a secret
agent. Marianne first met Mick at a
party in 1964. He was so attracted to
her that he threw champagne down
her dress to get her attention, but she
was in love with soon-to-be husband,
John Dunbar, and ignored Mick. She
preferred to get to know Oldham, who

Mick and Marianne attend a performance of the Royal Ballet at Covent Garden Opera House, London, 1967.

Mick and Marianne arrive in Sydney, Australia for the filming of NED KELLY, July 8, 1969.

offered to manage her without even hearing her sing. He knew he could sell her on looks alone. And he was probably right, but her association with the Stones didn't hurt.

She had her first hit with "As Tears Go By," a song written especially for her by Mick, Keith, and Andrew, and she toured with the Stones in 1965. She had married John Dunbar and had his son, Nicolas, but she wanted excitement and glamour. Despite her innocent looks she knew exactly how to get what she wanted. She had affairs with Brian and Keith before "...deciding the lead singer was the best bet."

In 1966 Mick and Chrissie broke up and Marianne left her husband to move in with Mick. Marianne starred in *Hamlet* and *The Three Sisters* on stage and in the movie *Girl on a Motorcycle*. In real life she was the infamous "Miss X. in a fur rug" at the Redlands bust trial, saved from arrest by Mick who gallantly claimed the illegal pills in *her* jacket pocket were his.

Mick and Marianne appeared to be the perfect couple—so hip that the fact she was married to another man only added to her appeal. But behind the cool facade Marianne couldn't cope with her role as Mick's leading lady. It was painful for her to watch Mick turn her sorrow into hit songs, but it seemed to be all that she could give him once she had gotten hooked on drugs. In October 1968 Marianne announced she was pregnant with Mick's child, but a month later she lost the baby. In many ways Marianne felt a kinship with Brian; they were both dependent on drugs and on Mick—and Brian's death shattered Marianne, causing her attempted suicide in Sydney, Australia. While in a coma, she claims that Brian spoke to her and convinced her to go on with her life.

She was happy to see Mick when she recovered, but the suicide attempt had driven Mick further from her, thus causing her heroin addiction. By May 1970, when Mick told Marianne he was moving to France for tax purposes,

she decided to stay in Britain. Ironically, Marianne's divorce from John Dunbar came through just as she and Mick broke up, but Mick paid the legal fees. On the day of Mick's wedding to Bianca, Marianne was arrested for drunk and disorderly conduct.

In 1979 Marianne married Ben Brierely (former bassist of the Vibrators) and in the late seventies embarked on a musical comeback. She and Brierely were recently divorced.

FAMILY
British band who opened for the Stones at their free concert at Hyde Park, July 5, 1969.

"FAMILY"
Written by: Jagger/Richards
Recorded by: The Rolling Stones
Release date: June 1975
Record label: Decca/ABKCO
Album: METAMORPHOSIS

"FANFARE FOR THE COMMON MAN"
An excerpt from this Aaron Copland piece serves as the introduction to the

live double album, LOVE YOU LIVE. During the Stones 1975 Tour of the Americas, the band appeared as this played from the loudspeakers.

"FANNY MAE"
Song recorded by the Stones in 1965 but never released. It was chosen by Bill for THE BLACK BOX compilation.

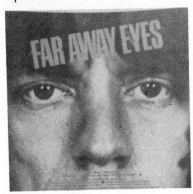

"FAR AWAY EYES"
Written by: Jagger/Richards
Recorded by: The Rolling Stones
Release date: May 1978
Record label: Rolling Stones Records
Album: SOME GIRLS
Single: Flip of "Miss You" (U.S./U.K. 5/78)

FARLOWE, CHRIS
British rhythm and blues singer backed by the Thunderbirds (no relation to Ron Wood), whose lineup boasted drummer Carl Palmer. He had a few top-thirty hits in the mid-sixties, and though he received a lot of help from his friends Keith and Mick as producers and songwriters along the way, he never really made it big. In the late sixties/early seventies, he was briefly in Colosseum and Atomic Rooster.

FARLOWE IN THE MIDNIGHT HOUR
Chris Farlowe EP, produced by Keith, Mick, and Andrew Oldham in 1966. It contains Farlowe's version of "(I Can't Get No) Satisfaction."

FARREN, MICK
Co-compiler (with David Dalton) of *The Rolling Stones in Their Own Words.*

FAT ALBERT PRODUCTIONS
Company formed by Howard and Ron Albert, who performed engineering, mixing, and production chores on MONKEY GRIP and STONE ALONE.

FAULK, KEN
Member of Boneroo Horn Section on MONKEY GRIP.

FAYE, KARROT
Assistant engineer on 1 2 3 4.

FEEL YOUR GROOVE
1971 Ben Sidran LP featuring Charlie.

"FEET"
Written by: Kortchmar
Recorded by: Bill Wyman
Release date: February 1976
Record label: Rolling Stones Records
Album: STONE ALONE
• Ronnie Wood—guitar.
• Danny Kortchmar—guitar.
• Dallas Taylor—percussion.
• Joe Vitale—drums.
• Joe Walsh—guitar.
• Al Kooper—piano.
• Guille Garcia—percussion.
• Ruth and Bonnie Pointer—backup vocals.

FEIGER, MARK
Man killed, along with his friend Richard Savlov, at Altamont when a car plowed into their campsite hours after the concert was over.

FEINSTEIN, BARRY
Photographer of the original graffitied-toilet-wall cover of BEGGARS BANQUET, which Decca and London both refused to distribute. Mick, Keith, and Anita found this real-life toilet and brought Feinstein in to take the photo.

FEITLER, BEA
Layout artist of the BLACK AND BLUE LP cover.

FENDER JAZZ
Make and model of Ron's first bass.

FERSON, RICKY
Cyril Davies' sideman who sat in on bass with the Stones at one of their early Crawdaddy Club dates.

FIELDS, VANETTA
Backup vocalist on EXILE ON MAIN ST. and STONE ALONE.

FIFTH AVENUE HOTEL
Greenwich Village, New York, building where the Stones held a "press conference" on May 1, 1975, to announce their forthcoming Tour of the Americas. The band appeared on a flatbed truck which stopped in front of the building, where the press was awaiting them. The Stones performed a ten-minute version of "Brown Sugar," and then prepared statements were thrown to the press from the truck as it continued down Fifth Avenue. Charlie's brainchild, the event attracted thousands of passers-by and made the front pages of New York's newspapers, the perfect start to a Stones tour.

"FIJI GIN"
Unreleased Stones song recorded in Paris, 1977.

FINE OLD TOWN
1975 Tom Newman album featuring Mick Taylor.

"FINGERPRINT FILE"
Written by: Jagger/Richards
Recorded by: The Rolling Stones
Release date: October 1974
Record label: Rolling Stones Records
Albums: IT'S ONLY ROCK 'N' ROLL
           LOVE YOU LIVE (live in Paris)
• On the studio version, Billy Preston plays piano and clavinet; Nicky Hopkins is on piano, and Charlie Jolly plays tabla.

FINLEY, CHUCK
Trumpet player on GOATS HEAD SOUP.

FIREARMS
What Keith gets arrested for the possession of when there are no drugs around; also sometimes when there *are* drugs around.

FIRST STEP
1970 Faces album featuring Ron.

FITTER, ALAN
Decca Records employee who co-compiled ROLLED GOLD with Roy Carr.

FITZCARRALDO
1982 film by German director Werner Herzog, which originally starred Jason Robards and Mick. The filming, which began in 1980 in the Peruvian Amazon, took so long that Mick was forced to drop out in order to rehearse for the Stones 1981 U.S. tour. Herzog felt he could not replace Mick and wrote the role out of the film. Mick's work, however, can be seen in the film *Burden of Dreams*, a documentary on the making of *Fitzcarraldo*.

FIVE BY FIVE (EP)
Artist: The Rolling Stones
Producer: Andrew Loog Oldham for Impact Sound
Release date: August 1964
Record label: Decca
Tracks: 5
"If You Need Me" (Pickett/Bateman/Sanders)
"Empty Heart" (Nanker Phelge)
"2120 South Michigan Avenue" (Nanker Phelge)
"Confessin' the Blues" (Brown/McShann)
"Around and Around" (Berry)
• Studio—Chess, Chicago.
• Engineer—Ron Malo.

FIXX, THE
MCA recording artists who are totally unrelated to Keith.

FLAMINGO CLUB
London club where the Rolling Stones performed on Monday nights in early 1963. The Cyril Davies memorial concert was held here.

FLEETWOOD, MICK
Fleetwood Mac drummer, who plays on "Seven Days."

FLICK, AMANDA
Assistant to Jimmy Wachtel on the album design and artwork for MONKEY GRIP.

"FLIGHT 505"
Written by: Jagger/Richards
Recorded by: The Rolling Stones
Release date: April 1966
Record label: Decca/London
Albums: AFTERMATH (U.K.)
          AFTERMATH (U.S.)

FLOWERS

Artist: The Rolling Stones
Producer: Andrew Loog Oldham
Release date: June 1967
Record label: London
Tracks: 12
"Ruby Tuesday"
"Have You Seen Your Mother, Baby,
Standing in the Shadow?"
"Let's Spend the Night Together"
"Lady Jane"
"Out of Time"
"My Girl" (Robinson/White)
"Back Street Girl"
"Please Go Home"
"Mother's Little Helper"
"Take It or Leave It"
"Ride On, Baby"
"Sittin' on a Fence"
• 10th U.S. LP.
• Arranged by the Rolling Stones.
• Photography—Guy Webster.
• Graphics—Tom Wilkes.
• Design execution—The Corporate Head.
• Title concept by "Lou-in Adler."
• On the cover of FLOWERS, each Stone's face appears in an oval on a stem of a flower. Brian has the only stem without leaves. Were they trying to tell him something?

FLY

1973 Yoko Ono album featuring Mick.

FLYING BURRITO BROTHERS

Country-rock band who performed at Altamont and recorded "Wild Horses" before the Stones version was released. (See Parsons, Gram.)

FLYNN, ERROL

Late swashbuckling actor who was one of Keith's idols and whose yacht was docked in Villefranche. Keith was determined to buy the yacht from the estate that owned it, but his offer was turned down due to legal technicalities. Keith thought up an elaborate scheme to sink the boat and then buy it from the salvage crew that would find it. The only hitch in the plan was that Keith couldn't find anyone to sink the boat!

"FOOL TO CRY"

Written by: Jagger/Richards
Recorded by: The Rolling Stones
Release date: April 1976
Record label: Rolling Stones Records
Albums: BLACK AND BLUE
    TIME WAITS FOR NO ONE
    SUCKING IN THE SEVENTIES
Singles: B/w "Hot Stuff" (U.S. 4/76)
    B/w "Crazy Mama" (U.S./U.K. 4/76)
• Wayne Perkins—guitar.
• Nicky Hopkins—piano, string synthesizer.
• Keith fell asleep on stage playing this song in concert.

FORD, GERALD

Former U.S. president, who admitted on TV in February 1974 that he had never heard of Mick Jagger. His comment: "Mick Jagger? Isn't he the motorcycle rider?"

FORD, JACK

Son of U.S. President Gerald Ford who certainly heard of Bianca Jagger and invited her to the White House while his family was living there. She and Jack happily posed for press pictures on the White House lawn and went out together in New York while Bianca was still married to Mick.

FOREIGNER

Top-selling Anglo-American band who opened for the Stones on some of their shows during the 1978 U.S. tour.

"FORTUNE TELLER"

Written by: Neville
Recorded by: The Rolling Stones
Release date: January 1964
Record label: Decca/London
Albums: SATURDAY CLUB
    GOT LIVE IF YOU WANT
    IT! (LIVE)
    GIMME SHELTER
    MORE HOT ROCKS
• There were *two* original versions of this song, one produced by Andrew Oldham and the second produced by Eric Easton.
• It's rumored that the SATURDAY CLUB version appears on GOT LIVE IF YOU WANT IT!, with the screams overdubbed to make it sound like it was recorded live at Royal Albert Hall.

"FOUNTAIN OF LOVE"

Written by: R. Wood/J. Ford
Recorded by: Ron Wood
Release date: August 1981

James Fox and Mick in PERFORMANCE.

Record label: Columbia
Album: 1 2 3 4
• Ian Wallace—drums.
• Bobby Womack—bass, twelve-string guitar.
• Ian McLagan—electric piano.
• Clydie King and Shirley Matthews —backup vocals.

FOURTEEN
Decca Records compilation album released in May 1964 and featuring the Stones along with Dave Berry, the late Billy Fury, Tom Jones, Them (with Van Morrison) and others. The Stones contributed "Surprise, Surprise" to this LP, the entire profits of which, together with artist royalties, were donated to The Lords Taverners National Playing Fields Association.

FOX, JAMES
British actor who starred in *Performance*, playing the part of Chas Devlin. Taking *Performance*'s theme of good vs. evil very much to heart, Fox became a devout Christian, and spent the seventies involved in Christian missionary work. He is now making a comeback, acting in several BBC productions, working on a feature film, and has just published a book entitled *Comeback: An Actor's Direction*.

FOXX, CHARLIE AND INEZ
Soul duo who opened for the Stones on their fifth British tour, September/October 1964.

FRAMPTON, PETER
Britain's "Face of 1968" and the world's "Face of 1977," this extraordinarily talented guitarist cum pretty boy would have missed his chance at his second title had he been chosen for Stoneship in the "Great Guitarists Hunt" of February 1975. As it was, after the auditions Frampton continued the solo career he had begun after leaving Humble Pie, recording the largest-selling live double album in history, conquering the musical world in 1977, and sadly, accepting the kamikaze mission of acting the lead role of Billy Shears in the film version of *Sgt. Pepper's Lonely Hearts Club Band*. With the exception of an unacclaimed album every so often, he's been virtually unheard of since.

FRANCIS SERVICE STATION
Stratford, West Ham, England, gas station where Bill, Brian, and Mick were arrested in March 1965.

FRANK, ROBERT
Director who followed the Stones 1972 tour and filmed *Cocksucker Blues*. During the tour, he was arrested along with Mick and Keith for assaulting a photographer. (See Warwick Airport.) He is also responsible for the cover photography and concept of EXILE ON MAIN ST.

FRASER, ROBERT
Hip London art gallery owner who was a close personal friend of the Stones after meeting them in Paris in 1965. He was busted at Redlands in February 1967 for possession of heroin, and was sentenced to six months in jail and a £200 fine. Although Mick and Keith beat their rap after a day in jail, Fraser stayed in for the full six months. When he got out of jail, Keith and Anita moved into his London flat, while Keith was recording LET IT BLEED.

FROM THE INSIDE
1978 Alice Cooper album featuring Keith and Ron.

FULLEN, SEAN
Assistant engineer on EMOTIONAL RESCUE.

FULLER, DETECTIVE-CONSTABLE EVELYN
Testified at Redlands bust trial that "Miss X." was clad only in a fur rug when the police raided the house.

G & M RECORDS
British record company formed in 1973. They were the first rock-related outfit to throw a party at London's exclusive Ritz Hotel. Mick and Bianca attended, of course—to celebrate one of the label's first signings, Chris Jagger.

GALLAGHER, RORY
Plaid-shirted Irish wonder guitarist who in February 1975 was spied rehearsing with the Stones in Rotterdam, during the post-Taylor "Great Guitarists Hunt." Keith cast the no vote.

GALUTEN, ALBHY
Synthesizer player on STONE ALONE.

"GANGSTER'S MAUL"
EMOTIONAL RESCUE outtake.

GARCIA, GUILLE
Percussionist on STONE ALONE.

GARDNER, ERIC
Bill's personal manager, who was stopped at the Munich Airport in 1980 when guard dogs there lunged for his suitcase. Guard people grabbed Gardner and pointed submachine guns at him while his suitcase was searched.

The contraband, to be delivered to Bill, was two boxes of Milk Bones dog biscuits, an imported treat for Bill's pet.

GARRICK CLUB
Exclusive London's men club which Judge Block was thrown out of after sentencing Mick and Keith during the Redlands bust trial.

GASOLINE ALLEY
1970 Rod Stewart LP featuring Ron.

GATHER MOSS
12-minute British newsreel featuring the Stones released in 1964.

GATHER NO MOSS
British name of the *T.A.M.I. Show* film.

GEE, JEREMY
Assistant engineer on BLACK AND BLUE and engineer on EXILE ON MAIN ST.

GERMAN, BILL
Charming young publisher of *Beggars Banquet*.

GEORGE, LOWELL
Late Little Feat guitarist who performed on "Monkey Grip Glue."

GEORGE COOPER ORGANIZATION
Promoters who gave the Stones their first headlining British tour in January 1964.

"GET BACK TO THE ONE YOU LOVE"
Song recorded by the Stones in 1965 but never released.

GEORGE THOROGOOD AND THE DESTROYERS
American band who opened many of the shows on the Stones 1981 U.S. tour, including the first show at JFK Stadium, and some shows in Europe 1982.

"GET IT ON"
Written by: Bill Wyman
Recorded by: Bill Wyman
Release date: February 1976
Record label: Rolling Stones Records
Album: STONE ALONE
• Dallas Taylor—drums.
• Hubie Heard—organ.
• Danny Kortchmar—guitar.
• Terry Taylor—slide guitar.
• Nicky Hopkins—piano.
• Albhy Galuten—synthesizer.

"GET OFF OF MY CLOUD"
Written by: Jagger/Richards
Recorded by: The Rolling Stones
Release date: September 1965
Record label: London/Decca
Albums: DECEMBER'S CHILDREN
      BIG HITS (U.S.)
      BIG HITS (U.K.)
      GOT LIVE IF YOU WANT IT! (live)
      HOT ROCKS
      MILESTONES

ROLLED GOLD
LOVE YOU LIVE (live in Paris)
TIME WAITS FOR NO ONE
Singles: B/w "I'm Free" (U.S. 9/65)
B/w "The Singer Not the Song"
(U.K. 10/65)
• This was the first time the Stones had a number-one hit in the U.S. and U.K. simultaneously.
• Keith thinks that this was one of Andrew Oldham's worst productions.

GET OFF OF MY CLOUD
1975 Alexis Korner LP featuring Keith as guitarist and lead singer (for a few lines) of the title track.

'GET YER YA-YA'S OUT'
The Rolling Stones in concert

GET YER YA-YA'S OUT (THE ROLL-ING STONES IN CONCERT)
Artist: The Rolling Stones
Producer: The Rolling Stones and Glyn Johns
Release date: September 1970
Record label: Decca/London
Tracks: 10
"Jumpin' Jack Flash"
"Carol" (Berry)
"Stray Cat Blues"
"Love in Vain" (Payne)
"Midnight Rambler"
"Sympathy for the Devil"
"Live with Me"
"Little Queenie" (Berry)
"Honky Tonk Women"
"Street Fighting Man"
• 15th U.S. LP.
• 11th U.K. LP.
• Ian Stewart—piano at both recorded concerts.
• Recording by Wally Heider Mobile.
• Recording and mixing engineer —Glyn Johns.
• Front cover photo—David Bailey.
• Liner photos—Ethan Russell.
• Design—John Kosh and Steve Thomas Associates.
• Originally intended to be a double album with the other disc featuring B.B. King and the Ike and Tina Turner Revue, but Decca wasn't interested.
• This album was released in the hope of keeping people from buying the bootleg LIVE R THAN YOU'LL EVER BE.

• Recorded at the 1969 Madison Square Garden shows.
• The title of the album is an African voodoo phrase.
• No "s."

GIBBS, CHRISTOPHER
An old friend of Brian, Mick, and Keith (though not Barry, Maurice, and Robin) who suggested the name for the BEGGARS BANQUET album. He was also the antique dealer who decorated Mick's Cheyne Walk home.

GILLETTE, MICK
Horn player and arranger on STONE ALONE.

"GIMME A LITTLE DRINK"
LET IT BLEED outtake.

"GIMME JUST ONE CHANCE"
Written by: Bill Wyman
Recorded by: Bill Wyman
Release date: February 1976
Record label: Rolling Stones Records
Album: STONE ALONE
• Dallas Taylor—drums.
• Bob Welch—acoustic guitars.
• Dr. John—organ, marimbas.
• Clydie King and Vanetta Fields —backup vocals.

"GIMME MICK"
Song performed by "Candy Slice," aka Gilda Radner doing her Patti Smith parody, on "Saturday Night Live" and in the Broadway revue *Gilda Live* and in the film of the stage show. Song was written by Radner and Paul Shaffer.

GIMME SELTZER
New York City club soda delivery service.

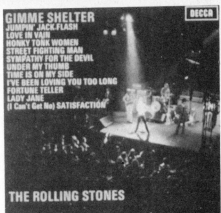

GIMME SHELTER
JUMPIN' JACK FLASH
LOVE IN VAIN
HONKY TONK WOMEN
STREET FIGHTING MAN
SYMPATHY FOR THE DEVIL
UNDER MY THUMB
TIME IS ON MY SIDE
I'VE BEEN LOVING YOU TOO LONG
FORTUNE TELLER
LADY JANE
(I Can't Get No) SATISFACTION

THE ROLLING STONES

GIMME SHELTER
Artist: The Rolling Stones
Producer: Compilation album
Release date: August 1972
Record label: Decca/London
Tracks: 12
"Jumpin' Jack Flash"
"Love in Vain" (Payne)
"Honky Tonk Women"
"Street Fighting Man"
"Sympathy for the Devil"
"Gimmie Shelter"
"Under My Thumb"
"Time Is on My Side" (Meade/ Norman)
"I've Been Loving You Too Long" (Redding/Butler)
"Fortune Teller" (Neville)
"Lady Jane"
"(I Can't Get No) Satisfaction"
• Not a soundtrack!
• Side two of this album (starting from "Under My Thumb") is from GOT LIVE IF YOU WANT IT!

In a scene from GIMME SHELTER, Keith and Mick view a film of the murder of Meredith Hunter at Altamont.

GIMME SHELTER

1970 documentary film produced by Ronald Schneider, directed by the Maysles Brothers—David and Albert—and Charlotte Zwerin, about the Stones' infamous Altamont concert. It includes appearances by Ike and Tina Turner and the Jefferson Airplane and shows the killing of Meredith Hunter. The ninety-minute film, released by Cinema V, also features their performance at Madison Square Garden, New York, earlier in 1969. The Stones wanted to give away the money they made from the film, but the distribution company wouldn't give away any of their profits. The Jefferson Airplane would only allow their segment to be included in the film if the money went to charity—as long as it wasn't the "Allen Klein Retirement Fund." Other suggested film titles by Stones and Co. included: "Old Glory," "Too Many Crooks," "Love in Vain," "Naughty Ladies," "Naughty Ladies '70," "Everybody's Got to Go," and "Perry Mason Strikes Again."

GIMME SOME NECK

Artist: Ron Wood
Producer: Roy Thomas Baker
Year first released: May 1979
Record label: CBS
Tracks: 11
"Worry No More" (Williams)
"Breakin' My Heart"
"Delia" (Trad)
"Buried Alive"
"Come to Realize"

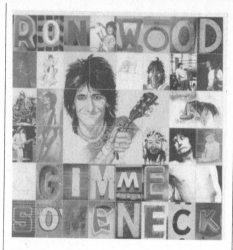

"Infekshun"
"Seven Days" (Dylan)
"We All Get Old"
"F.U.C. Her"
"Lost and Lonely"
"Don't Worry"
• Several musicians including Mick and Keith surround the core of Charlie on drums, "Pops" Popwell on bass, and Ian McLagan on organ. (See individual songs for credits.)
• Studio—Cherokee Studios, Paris.
• Engineer—Geoff Workman.
• The self-portrait on the cover was painted by Ron while looking in the mirror. When he decided to use it on the LP, he added makeup and jewelry.

"GIMMIE SHELTER"

Written by: Jagger/Richards
Recorded by: The Rolling Stones
Release date: November 1969
Record label: Decca/London
Albums: LET IT BLEED
HOT ROCKS
GIMME SHELTER
ROLLED GOLD
• Nicky Hopkins—piano.
• Jimmy Miller—percussion.
• Merry Clayton—backup vocals.

GIRL ON A MOTORCYCLE

Film Marianne Faithfull starred in while pregnant with Mick's child in 1968. After filming, she was ordered to bed for a week by her doctors.

"GIRLS"

Written by: Bill Wyman
Recorded by: Bill Wyman
Release date: 1981
Record label: A & M Records
Album: BILL WYMAN
Single: Flip of "A New Fashion" (U.K. 1981)

GITLIS, IVRY

Violinist who performed Paganini's First Violin Concerto on the violin and played country fiddle while Yoko Ono wailed during "The Rolling Stones' Rock and Roll Circus."

GITOMER, PHIL

Assistant engineer on STILL LIFE.

"GLASS EYE"

EMOTIONAL RESCUE outtake.

GLEASON, RALPH

Rolling Stone columnist who criticized prices of tickets on the Stones 1969 U.S. tour. In response to his condemnation, Mick said that Gleason would have to pay fifty dollars to attend the

"free" concert at Altamont.

GLENROWAN GANG
Australian gang who threatened to kidnap Mick and cut off all his hair upon his arrival in Sydney, Australia, to begin the filming of *Ned Kelly*.

GLIMMER TWINS, THE
Mick and Keith.

G'NAOUA
Musicians Brian recorded with Glyn Johns in Marrakesh in the spring of 1968.

GO GOS, THE
Eighties girl group who opened for the Stones during their 1981 U.S. tour in Illinois.

"GO ON HOME"
Song recorded by the Stones in 1965 but never released.

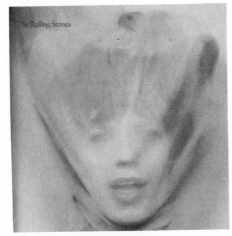

GOATS HEAD SOUP
Artist: The Rolling Stones
Producer: Jimmy Miller
Release date: August 1973
Record label: Rolling Stones Records

Tracks: 10
"Dancing with Mr. D"
"100 Years Ago"
"Coming Down Again"
"Doo Doo Doo Doo Doo (Heartbreaker)"
"Angie"
"Silver Train"
"Hide Your Love"
"Winter"
"Can You Hear the Music"
"Star Star"
• 20th U.S. album.
• 18th U.K. album.
• The album features Nicky Hopkins on piano, Billy Preston on piano and clavinet, Ian Stewart on piano and "jangle," plus others. (See individual songs for credits.) Bobby Keys plays tenor and baritone sax throughout; Jim Horn plays flute and alto sax throughout; Chuck Finley is on trumpet throughout, and percussion is played throughout by Pascal, Rebop, and Jimmy Miller.
• Studio—Dynamic Sound Studios, Kingston, Jamaica.
• Engineer and mixer—Andy Johns.
• Assistant engineers—Carlton Lee, Howard Kilgour, and Doug Bennett.
• Photography and album design —David Bailey, who took photos at a session which Keith didn't show up for.
• Album designer—Ray Lawrence.
• Goats Head Soup—John Pasche.
• The song "Star Star" was remixed for the U.S. LP. Therefore the U.S. and the U.K. albums differ.
• Goats head soup is a Jamaican delicacy.
• The album was reissued by EMI in the U.K. in March 1980.
• On the inner sleeve of GOATS HEAD SOUP appears the warning: "Since 1969, The Rolling Stones only on Rolling Stones Records. This is a new record—beware of re-packaging." This is the only reference to the year 1969 as relates to Rolling Stones Records, a company formed in 1971!
• No "s."

GODARD, JEAN-LUC
World-renowned director who worked with the Stones on ONE PLUS ONE.

GODDARD, PETER
Writer of the text for *The Rolling Stones: The Last Tour*.

GODS, THE
The band Mick Taylor was in before joining John Mayall's Blues Breakers. Greg Lake was in this mid-sixties band, along with members who were later to become Uriah Heep.

"GODZI"
Song chosen by Bill for THE BLACK BOX compilation.

"GOIN' HOME"
Written by: Jagger/Richards
Recorded by: The Rolling Stones
Release date: April 1966
Record label: Decca/London
Albums: AFTERMATH (U.K.)
              AFTERMATH (U.S.)
• At eleven minutes and thirty-five seconds, this was the longest rock song ever on an LP at that time.

"GOING TO A GO GO"
Written by: Robinson/Tarplin/Moore/Rogers
Recorded by: The Rolling Stones
Release date: June 1982
Record label: Rolling Stones Records
Album: STILL LIFE
Single: B/w "Beast of Burden" (live) (U.S./U.K. 82)

"GOLD PAINTED NAILS"
Unreleased 1966 recording, which Bill chose for THE BLACK BOX compilation.

GOLDIE AND THE GINGERBREADS
Group who opened for the Stones on their sixth British tour, in March 1965. Goldie, later known as Genya Raven, went on to Ten Wheel Drive.

GOLDSBORO, BOBBY
American teeny-bop hero who opened for the Stones on their first U.S. tour, 1964.

GOMELSKY, GIORGIO
London-based Russian film producer who promoted the National Blues Festival, bringing Chicago blues artists to the U.K. for the first time in the early sixties. He operated the Crawdaddy Club at the Station Hotel in Richmond, giving the Stones their first major booking, a Sunday afternoon residency, and acting as their sort-of manager until Oldham stepped into the picture. He filmed a short documen-

tary of the Stones in April 1963.

"GOMPER"
Written by: Jagger/Richards
Recorded by: The Rolling Stones
Release date: November 1967
Record label: London/Decca
Album: THEIR SATANIC MAJESTIES
   REQUEST

"GOOD DAYS"/"MIDNIGHT MORNING"
1973 single by John Walker produced by Bill.

"GOOD TIME WOMEN"
Original title of the music that became "Tumbling Dice," with different lyrics.

"GOOD TIMES"
Written by: Sam Cooke
Recorded by: The Rolling Stones
Release date: July 1965
Record label: London/Decca
Albums: OUT OF OUR HEADS (U.S.)
   OUT OF OUR HEADS (U.K.)

"GOOD TIMES, BAD TIMES"
Written by: Jagger/Richards
Recorded by: The Rolling Stones
Release date: June 1964
Record label: Decca/London
Albums: 12 x 5
   BIG HITS (U.S).
   MORE HOT ROCKS
Single: Flip of "It's All Over Now"
   (U.K. 6/64) (U.S. 7/64)

GOODMAN, PETER
Author of *Our Own Story by the Rolling Stones*.

GOODMAN, SHIRLEY
Backup vocalist on "Let It Loose."

GORE HOTEL
Hotel in Kensington, London, which was the site of the actual beggars banquet held in celebration of the release of BEGGARS BANQUET. The bash cost over £1,000 and ended with the Stones throwing custard pies in the faces of Decca Record executives, who had caused the LP's late release, and their other guests.

GOT LIVE IF YOU WANT IT! (BRITISH EP)
Artist: The Rolling Stones
Producer: Andrew Loog Oldham for

Impact Sound
Release date: June 1965
Record label: Decca
Tracks: 6
"We Want the Stones" (Nanker Phelge)
"Everybody Needs Somebody to Love"
(Russell/Burke/Wexler)
"Pain in My Heart" (Neville)
"Route 66" (Troup)
"I'm Moving On" (Snow)
"I'm Alright" (Nanker Phelge)
• Recorded on the Rolling Stones'
March 1965 tour of Great Britain in
Liverpool, Manchester, Edmonton,
Greenford.
• Engineer—Glyn Johns.
• This was the only live recording the
Stones did that wasn't overdubbed or
"fixed" in a studio.
• This is entirely different from the
U.S. album of the same name.

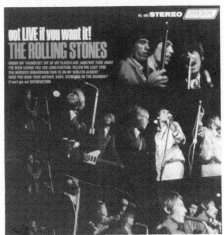

GOT LIVE IF YOU WANT IT!

Artist: The Rolling Stones
Producer: Andrew Loog Oldham
Release date: November 1966
Record label: London
Tracks: 12
"Under My Thumb"
"Get Off of My Cloud"
"Lady Jane"
"Not Fade Away" (Petty/Hardin)
"I've Been Loving You Too Long"
(Redding/Butler)
"Fortune Teller" (Neville)
"The Last Time"

"19th Nervous Breakdown"
"Time Is on My Side" (Meade/Norman)
"I'm Alright" (Nanker Phelge)
**"Have You Seen Your Mother, Baby,
Standing in the Shadow?"**
"(I Can't Get No) Satisfaction"
• 8th U.S. album.
• Recorded live at Royal Albert Hall,
September 1966.
• Recorded by—Glyn Johns.
• Photography—Gered Mankowitz.
• Cover design—Stephen Inglis.
• "I've Been Loving You Too Long"
and "Fortune Teller" are possibly
outtakes. "I've Been Loving You Too
Long" could also possibly be from the
SATURDAY CLUB compilation
album. Either way, both songs, if not
really live, feature overdubbed audi-
ence screams.
• Totally different from the U.K. EP of
the same name.
• Six tracks resurfaced on Decca's
GIMME SHELTER LP six years later.
• "s."

"GOTTA GET AWAY"
Written by: Jagger/Richards
Recorded by: The Rolling Stones
Release date: September 1965
Record label: Decca/London
Albums: OUT OF OUR HEADS (U.K.)
          DECEMBER'S CHILDREN
Single: Flip of "As Tears Go By"
          (U.S. 12/65)

GRABURN, JUDGE LLOYD
Handed down Keith's Toronto trial
sentence.

GRAHAM, BILL
Owner of the Fillmores, East and West.
He was tour director of the Stones'
1978 U.S. tour, the 1981 U.S. tour, and

the 1982 European tour. (See Rainbow
Productions.)

GRANADA CINEMA
Harrow, England theater where the
Stones played their first headlining gig
on January 6, 1964.

GRATEFUL DEAD
America's favorites, they helped the
Stones arrange Altamont but didn't
get to play.

GRAVES, PETER
Co-arranged horns, with Bill, on MON-
KEY GRIP, and performed on the
same album as part of the Boneroo
Horn Section.

GREAT FATSBY, THE
1975 Leslie West album on which Mick
(yes, Jagger) plays (yes) guitar.

"GREAT GUITARISTS HUNT, THE"
In February/March 1975, a few months after Mick Taylor's departure from the Stones, the band was in Rotterdam, Holland, recording tracks for BLACK AND BLUE. With an eye toward picking a replacement Stone, they invited practically every guitarist known to the instrument to jam with them—including Jeff Beck; Peter Frampton; Wayne Perkins; Robert A. Johnson; Harvey Mandel; Leslie West; Rory Gallagher; the eventual winner, Ron Wood; and a score of others. (Individual contenders are listed throughout this book.) Reports circulated daily among guitar fans as to who was last seen carrying a Fender case through the Rotterdam airport, and an indecisive time was had by all. (See BLACK AND BLUE for some recorded contributions during this period.)

GREAT SOUTHEAST STONED-OUT WRESTLING CHAMPIONS, THE
Name under which tickets for the Stones performance at a Florida club in 1978 were sold.

GREEN, JOE
Backup vocalist on "Let It Loose" and "Shine a Light."

GREEN ICE
1981 British adventure film, starring Ryan O'Neal and Omar Sharif for which Bill scored the music.

GREENFIELD, ROBERT
Author of the book *STP.*

GREENIDGE, ROBERT
Steel drum player on "Soul Satisfying."

GREG KIHN BAND
Band which opened in Seattle for the Stones during their 1981 U.S. tour.

GREHAN, ELLEN
British TV personality who interviewed Mick on "Ready Steady Go" in late 1964. Her mother, who was backstage, got to know Brian, and they became pen pals.

GRETSCH
Drum manufacturer which features Charlie in its ads.

GROSS, MICHAEL
Designed jacket for HOT ROCKS 1964-1971.

GROUNDHOGS, THE
John Lee's Groundhogs, in one of their attempts to "save the world," opened for the Stones during their ninth British tour in March of 1971.

"GROWN UP WRONG"
Written by: Jagger/Richards
Recorded by: The Rolling Stones
Release date: October 1964
Record label: Decca/London
Albums: THE ROLLING STONES NO. 2
12 x 5

GRUBER, MICHAEL
The Stones' road manager in 1965.

GUINNESS BOOK OF WORLD RECORDS
Listed the Stones as "loudest rock band in the world" in 1976.

GULF MOTEL
Clearwater, Florida, inn where the Stones stayed in May 1965 and Keith played "Satisfaction" for Mick for the first time. Ten years later, the cover photos for BLACK AND BLUE were shot here.

GUYMAN, LINDA
Did graphics for METAMORPHOSIS LP jacket.

GYSIN, BRION
Stones' eccentric associate who befriended Brian after Anita ran off with Keith in Morocco in 1967. He took Brian to Joujouka, where Brian recorded the Maalimin Musicians, and later wrote about his adventures with the Stones in a piece titled: "Moroccan Mishaps with the Strolling Ruins."

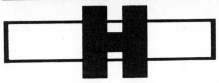

HAFFKINE, RON
Producer of MICK JAGGER AS NED KELLY.

HAHN, LEW
Assistant engineer on LOVE YOU LIVE; engineer on BLACK AND BLUE.

HALL, JERRY
Hailing from Texas, this top fashion model has lived with Mick since December 1977, when their affair became public two years prior to Mick and Bianca's divorce. Jerry and Mick own adjoining ranches in Texas, where she breeds horses; furthering her cowgirl image, she's slated to appear in the upcoming film version of the book *Even Cowgirls Get the Blues*. Jerry's boyfriend before Mick was Brian Ferry, the suave leader/singer of Roxy Music. "Life is wonderful. It always is when you've got the right girl," Mick said in December 1982 as he and Jerry were off on a vacation trip to Mustique. In the fall of 1983, it was rumored that Jerry was pregnant with Mick's baby. A week later it was denied. Wedding plans for the couple are always up in the air.

HALSBAND, MICHAEL
Photographer of STILL LIFE sleeve photos.

"HAMBURGER TO GO"
BEGGARS BANQUET outtake.

HAMPTON, VIRGINIA
Site of the last two shows of the 1981 U.S. tour. A closed-circuit cable TV hookup connected to seventeen cities enabled 800,000 people to see the show.

"HAND OF FATE"
Written by: Jagger/Richards
Recorded by: The Rolling Stones
Release date: April 1976
Record label: Rolling Stones Records
Albums: BLACK AND BLUE
       TIME WAITS FOR NO ONE
• Wayne Perkins—guitar.

• Billy Preston—piano.
• Ollie E. Brown—percussion.

HANESS, ABIGAIL
Backup vocalist on "Mighty Fine Time."

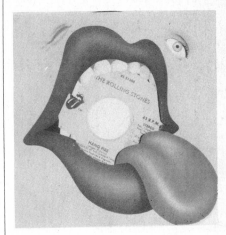

"HANG FIRE"
Written by: Jagger/Richards
Recorded by: The Rolling Stones
Release date: October 1981
Record label: Rolling Stones Records
Album: TATTOO YOU
Single: B/w "Neighbors" (U.S./U.K. 1981)
• This song is about the economic problems in England. As Keith put it: "They're going through their little traumas over there. It serves them right for kickin' us out."

HANSEN, JERRY
Assistant engineer on LET IT BLEED.

HANSEN, PATTI
Staten Island, New York-born model/actress whose career began when a total stranger approached her as she was leaving a 1975 Rolling Stones concert (!) and told her she had what it took to be a model. Five years later, her modeling career was at its height (Calvin Klein, Revlon) and her boyfriend was a Rolling Stone. At first Patti was seen about town in the company of Keith and Anita, but soon it was Anita who was relegated to third wheel. Yearly rumors abound as to a wedding date for Keith and Patti, but so far (as of this writing, 8/83), the Stones have not gathered to play for free at *anyone's* wedding, though rumors say within the next six months . . . .

"HAPPY"
Written by: Jagger/Richards
Recorded by: The Rolling Stones
Lead singer: Keith
Release date: May 1972
Record label: Rolling Stones Records
Albums: EXILE ON MAIN ST.
      MADE IN THE SHADE
      LOVE YOU LIVE (live in Paris)
Single: B/w "All Down the Line"
    (U.S. 6/72)
• Jimmy Miller—drums.
• Bobby Keys—percussion.

"HAPPY BIRTHDAY TO YOU"
Song sung by audience and accompanied on drums by Charlie at Madison Square Garden, New York City, for Mick's twenty-ninth birthday (July 26, 1972). The Stones threw pies at one another and Bianca came on stage to give her husband a stuffed panda bear and a kiss.

HARBOUR CASTLE HILTON
Hotel in Toronto, Canada, where all the Stones plus entourage stayed in February/March 1977. Keith and family had various suites on the thirty-second floor, where he was busted by the Royal Canadian Mounted Police when they found almost an ounce of heroin and cocaine in the room where he was ironically registered under the name of Redlands. All the Stones except Keith soon left Canada; Keith was detained for his trial.

HARD TO HOLD
Soon-to-be released Universal film starring Rick Springfield and Patti Hansen, in which a glimpse of Keith is rumored.

HARD-UP HEROES
1974 U.K. compilation album which features one track by Ron's Birds, plus Mick singing with the Andrew Loog Oldham Orchestra and Chorus.

"HARDER THEY COME, THE"
Written by: Jimmy Cliff
Recorded by: Keith
Lead singer: Keith
Release date: December 1978
Record label: Rolling Stones Records
Single: Flip side of "Run Rudolph
    Run" (U.S./U.K. 12/78)
• Reissued November 1979.
• Keith is backed by Ron, Charlie, and Ian McLagan.

HARRIS, JET
Former member of the Shadows, who opened for the Stones on their third tour of Britain in February/March 1964.

HARRIS, PAUL
Organist on "Soul Satisfying."

HARRIS, STEVE
Replacement drummer for Tony Chapman.

HARRISON, GEORGE
Ex-Beatle and first celebrity to see the Stones play at the Crawdaddy Club, in March 1963. His visit motivated the *Richmond and Twickenham Times* to report on the Stones and to get Andrew Oldham to see them.

HARRISON, NICKY
String arranger on "Angie" and "Winter."

HARRISON, PAULA
Backup vocalist on "Feet."

HARROW ART COLLEGE
School Charlie attended, majoring in drawing to enable him to pursue a career as a graphic artist or a fashion designer. He graduated from here.

HARWOOD, KEITH
Engineer on IT'S ONLY ROCK 'N' ROLL (where he mixed all the tracks but "Fingerprint File"), BLACK AND BLUE, and LOVE YOU LIVE, which is dedicated to his memory. He died in a car crash in 1977.

HASLIP, JIMMY
Bassist on "Down to the Ground" and "She Never Told Me."

HASSINGER, DAVE
Engineer who worked with Jack Nitzsche at RCA Studios in Hollywood when the Stones came there to record. He worked with the Stones on most of THE ROLLING STONES NO. 2, 12 X 5, and THE ROLLING STONES, NOW!, in addition to other tracks.

HASON, RANDY
Assistant engineer on LOVE YOU LIVE.

HATTRELL, DICK
Friend of Brian's who shared a flat with him in Cheltenham and went with him to London, eventually becoming one of the Stones' early road managers.

HAUSMAN, NEIL
Assistant engineer on STONE ALONE.

"HAVE YOU SEEN YOUR MOTHER, BABY, STANDING IN THE SHADOW?"
Written by: Jagger/Richards
Recorded by: The Rolling Stones
Release date: September 1966
Record label: Decca/London
Albums: BIG HITS (U.K.)
      GOT LIVE IF YOU WANT IT! (live)
      FLOWERS
      THROUGH THE PAST, DARKLY U.S.
      MORE HOT ROCKS
      ROLLED GOLD
Single: B/w "Who's Driving Your Plane?" (U.S./U.K. 9/66)
• Keith feels that the incorrectly mixed version was released as a single.
• The cover of the U.S. single shows the Stones in drag, with Bill sitting in a wheelchair.

HAVE YOU SEEN YOUR MOTHER, LIVE
Original title for the GOT LIVE IF YOU WANT IT! album.

HAVERS, MICHAEL
Mick and Keith's lawyer at their Redlands bust trial.

HAWKINS, SCREAMIN' JAY
Opened for the Stones in New York during their 1981 tour.

HEARD, HUBIE
Keyboardist on MONKEY GRIP and STONE ALONE.

HEART
Wilson sisters' band who opened for the Stones during parts of their 1981 U.S. tour.

"HEART OF STONE"
Written by: Jagger/Richards
Recorded by: The Rolling Stones
Release date: December 1964
Record label: Decca/London/ABKCO
Albums: THE ROLLING STONES, NOW!
      OUT OF OUR HEADS (U.K.)
      BIG HITS (U.S.)
      BIG HITS (U.K.)
      METAMORPHOSIS
      HOT ROCKS
      SLOW ROLLERS
Single: B/w "What a Shame" (U.S.12/64)
• The version which appears on META-MORPHOSIS is a demo featuring Jimmy Page and John McLaughlin.

"HEAVEN"
Written by: Jagger/Richards
Recorded by: The Rolling Stones
Release date: October 1981
Record label: Rolling Stones Records
Album: TATTOO YOU

HEID, TOM
Assistant engineer on LOVE YOU LIVE.

HELL'S ANGELS
International motorcycle gang whose London branch peacefully policed the Stones' free Hyde Park Concert in July 1969. America's West Coast division was called in to perform the same function at Altamont. They did the job for $500 worth of beer, but generated tons of bad publicity. During the concert one of the Angels allegedly stabbed a member of the audience who aimed a gun at Mick. The Angel was acquitted and sued the Stones for £2,000, claiming invasion of privacy when the incident was shown in the film *Gimme Shelter.* In early 1983 it was revealed in a Senate hearing by an ex-Hell's Angel that the Angels had put a contract out on Mick in retaliation for what happened at Altamont. Angel leaders deny the story.

HENDRIX, JIMI
Late, all-time guitar superhero who performs the forty-four-second prerecorded "Star-Spangled Banner" outro on STILL LIFE and who once unsuccessfully attempted to steal Marianne Faithfull away from Mick at least for a night.

HENNING, JOHN
Assistant engineer on STONE ALONE.

HENRY, DR. LEONARD
One of Brian's many psychiatrists who testified on his behalf during his appeal after his first drug trial (Courtfield bust). He felt that Brian couldn't handle being in prison and should be hospitalized.

HENRY PAUL BAND
Band who opened for the Stones in Orlando, Florida, during the 1981 U.S. tour.

HER SATANIC MAJESTY REQUESTS AND REQUIRES
Second selected title (after COSMIC CHRISTMAS) for the album which became THEIR SATANIC MAJESTIES REQUEST. Decca did not accept this title because it parodied too closely the words printed on a British passport.

HEROIN
Drug which Keith claimed is the cure for the common cold. Mick claims that the sound of the Velvet Underground's "Heroin" influenced "Stray Cat Blues."

HEWITT, DAVID
Recording engineer on STILL LIFE.

"HEY, GOOD LOOKIN' "
Bo Diddley song which Bill called his fave song of 1965.

"HEY, NEGRITA"
Written by: Jagger/Richards
Recorded by: The Rolling Stones
Release date: April 1976
Record label: Rolling Stones Records
Album: BLACK AND BLUE
• Pre-Stone Ron Wood—guitar.
• Billy Preston—piano, organ, backup vocals.
• Ollie E. Brown—percussion.
• Inspiration by Ron Wood.

HICKS, TONY
Member of the Hollies who appears on selected demos/outtakes on METAMORPHOSIS.

"HIDE YOUR LOVE"
Written by: Jagger/Richards
Recorded by: The Rolling Stones
Release date: September 1973
Record label: Rolling Stones Records
Album: GOATS HEAD SOUP

"HIGH AND DRY"
Written by: Jagger/Richards
Recorded by: The Rolling Stones
Release date: April 1966
Record label: Decca/London
Albums: AFTERMATH (U.K.)
AFTERMATH (U.S.)

"HIGH-HEELED SNEAKERS"
Song recorded by the Stones but never released.

HILLINGDON, BRITAIN
Middlesex town where Ron was born.

HIRO
Photographer of BLACK AND BLUE cover.

HIT FACTORY, THE
New York recording studio where EMOTIONAL RESCUE and the 1983 album were mixed.

"HITCH HIKE"
Written by: Gaye/Stevenson/Paul
Recorded by: The Rolling Stones
Release date: July 1965
Record label: London/Decca
Albums: OUT OF OUR HEADS (U.S.)
OUT OF OUR HEADS (U.K.)

"HOLD ON I'M COMING"
Song recorded by the Stones in 1968-69 but never released.

HOLLIES, THE
British quintet extremely popular on both sides of the Atlantic. They appeared as "guest artists" on some of the shows during the Stones' third tour of Britain (February/March 1964), and they opened the Stones' sixth British tour in March 1965.

HOLLY, BUDDY
Bespectacled American musical legend who cowrote "Not Fade Away" and whose voice and music the Stones heard when they tried to play one of their own gold records in 1966.

"HOLLYWOOD PALACE"
Dean Martin hosted the show when the Stones made their first American TV appearance in June 1964. They performed three numbers, but not all of their segment was aired. Martin made fun of the Stones when they were on, but when the show was rerun, a voice-over was dubbed in announcing, "And now the fabulous Rolling Stones," and screams and cheers were added during their performance.

"HONEST I DO"
Written by: Hurron/Calvert
Recorded by: The Rolling Stones
Release date: April 1964
Record label: Decca/London
Albums: THE ROLLING STONES
ENGLAND'S NEWEST HIT MAKERS

"HONEST" RON WOOD
Ron's nickname.

"HONEY, WHAT'S WRONG?"
Stones recorded this song at their first recording session with Glyn Johns in early 1963; it was never released.

"HONKY TONK WOMEN"
Written by: Jagger/Richards
Recorded by: The Rolling Stones
Release date: July 1969
Record label: Decca/London/Rolling Stones Records
Albums: THROUGH THE PAST, DARKLY
(U.K.)
THROUGH THE PAST, DARKLY
(U.S.)
GET YER YA-YA'S OUT (live)
GIMME SHELTER
ROLLED GOLD
LOVE YOU LIVE (live in Paris)
Single: B/w "You Can't Always Get What You Want" (U.S. 7/69)

B/w "Sympathy for the Devil"
(U.K. 4/76)
• The single version is the first song that Mick Taylor recorded with the Stones.
• Brian's father claims that Brian played him a tape of this song, with his arrangements, but for the released version the Stones re-recorded it without Brian.
• Ry Cooder (and probably his father) claimed to have written the opening chords to this song. Keith and his entire family disagree.
• Four hundred copies of the single were given away to people who cleaned up Hyde Park after the free concert the Stones gave there in July 1969.
• When this song was performed during one of the shows on the 1981 U.S. tour, a parade of "honky tonk women" came out, including Shirley Watts, Jerry Hall, Patti Hansen, and Jo Howard. This was captured in the film *Let's Spend the Night Together*.

HOPKINS, CANNON HUGH EVAN
Church official who read Brian's self-penned epitaph, "Please don't judge me too harshly," at Brian's funeral.

Jerry Hall, Charlie and Jim Callaghan at the premiere of LET'S SPEND THE NIGHT TOGETHER.

HOPKINS, NICKY

The most famous session keyboardist of all time, Nicky joined the Stones on piano for the recording of THEIR SATANIC MAJESTIES REQUEST and has since appeared on all their studio albums with the exception of SOME GIRLS and TATTOO YOU. He can be seen in the film *One Plus One*, and heard playing on STONE ALONE and 1 2 3 4. He also accompanied the Stones on several tours, performing in the jam session at Mick and Bianca's wedding, and is an avid on-the-road photographer.

HOPKINS-JONES, BARBARA

Brian's sister. She was born in 1946 and studied piano and the violin as a child. She is now a physical education teacher. She and Brian were never close.

HOPKINS-JONES, LEWIS

Brian's father. Employed as an aeronautical engineer at Dowty's Aircraft Works, Lewis did not get along with his son while Brian was growing up, but he started an investigation to look fully into Brian's death and cooperat-

ed with the Stones in lawsuits against Eric Easton and Andrew Oldham.

HOPKINS-JONES, LEWIS BRIAN

Brian's real name.

HOPKINS-JONES, LOUISA

Brian's mother, a piano teacher. "Of course I am very glad that he has done so well. But as a typical mother, I think it would have been nice if he had become a dentist."

HORN, JIM

Flute and alto sax player on GOATS HEAD SOUP; horn player on 1 2 3 4.

HOT

Another one of the nonexistent film projects Mick planned to star in. He worked on the idea for three years, from 1977 until 1980, but it never came to be.

HOT ROCKS 1964-1971

Artist: The Rolling Stones
Producer: Andrew Loog Oldham/ Jimmy Miller/The Rolling Stones/ Glyn Johns
Release date: January 1972

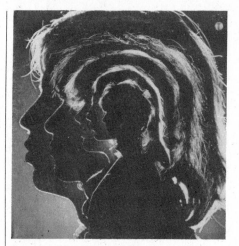

Record label: London
Tracks: 20
"Time Is on My Side" (Meade/Norman)
"Heart of Stone"
"Play with Fire" (Nanker Phelge)
"(I Can't Get No) Satisfaction"
"As Tears Go By" (Jagger/Richards/ Oldham)
"Get Off of My Cloud"
"Mother's Little Helper"

"19th Nervous Breakdown"
"Paint It, Black"
"Under My Thumb"
"Ruby Tuesday"
"Let's Spend the Night Together"
"Jumpin' Jack Flash"
"Street Fighting Man"
"Sympathy for the Devil"
"Gimmie Shelter"
"Midnight Rambler" (live version)
"You Can't Always Get What
You Want"
"Brown Sugar"
"Wild Horses"
• 17th U.S. album.
• Cover photo—Ron Raffaelli.
• Design—Michael Gross.
• London Records released this album after they had lost their recording contract with the Stones.
• No "s."

"HOT STUFF"
Written by: Jagger/Richards
Recorded by: The Rolling Stones
Release date: April 1976
Record label: Rolling Stones Records
Albums: BLACK AND BLUE
       LOVE YOU LIVE (live in Paris)
       SUCKING IN THE SEVENTIES
Single: Flip side of "Fool to Cry"
    (U.S. 4/76)
• Harvy Mandel—guitar.
•• Billy Preston—piano, backup vocals.
• Ian Stewart—percussion.
• This was to be the original title of BLACK AND BLUE.

HOTEL ASTOR
New York hotel where the Stones held their first American press conference, in 1964.

HOWARD, JO
A model who is the mother of Ron's children. She and Ron once lived in Esther Williams' Hollywood mansion but sold it when they decided they'd rather live in New York. They recently purchased a town house on New York's Upper West Side.

HULKO, LEE
Mastered tapes for BLACK AND BLUE.

HUNT, MARSHA
A singer/actress who appeared in the British version of the hit musical *Hair*, she gave birth to Mick's daughter Karis while he was still involved with Marianne Faithfull. The child's birth was kept quiet until Marsha sued Mick for child support payments in 1978. She wanted the payments raised from $17 a week to over $2,000 a month. Pending the outcome of the court case, the money Mick earned from his California concerts was held. Mick felt the matter could have been handled privately and was annoyed that Marsha went public with the news because his mother didn't know about her grandchild. The case was eventually settled privately for the sake of the child.

HUNTER, MEREDITH
Man in the audience who pointed a gun at Mick while he was singing at Altamont. Hunter was stabbed to death by one of the Hells' Angels hired to guard the Stones. The event was captured on film in *Gimme Shelter*.

HUSH PUPPIES
At a December 1965 concert in Sacramento, California, Keith was knocked unconscious from an electrical shock on stage. Bill unplugged him, but doctors claim that it was his Hush Puppies shoes that cushioned the electrical jolt, thereby saving his life.

HYDE PARK CONCERT

On June 13, 1969, the Stones held a "photo call" at the bandstand in this London park to introduce Brian's replacement, guitarist Mick Taylor, to the press, and to announce that they would be giving a free show at the park. On July 5, 1969, two days after Brian's death, the Stones gave their first live concert performance in three years. "Brian would have wanted it to go on. We will now do the concert for Brian. I hope people will understand that it is because of our love for him that we are doing it," Mick announced from the stage at the start of the Stones' segment of the free concert. It was Mick Taylor's first live public performance with the Stones. Also on the bill were Alexis Korner's New Church, Third Ear Band, King Crimson, Screw, Family, and Battered Ornaments. In memory of Brian, Mick read part of a poem by Shelley and let off hundreds of white butterflies, many of them dead.

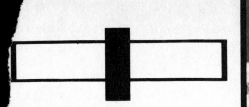

IBC STUDIOS
London recording studio where the Stones, with Ian Stewart, first recorded a demo with Glyn Johns in late January/early February 1963. The six songs recorded were: "Diddley Daddy," "Road Runner," "Bright Lights, Big City," "I Want to Be Loved," "Honey, What's Wrong?" and "Crackin' Up." The record companies found this work to be too rough, and eventually Oldham bought the demo back from the studio for ninety-eight pounds. They subsequently recorded more songs at IBC Studios which were released.

ICI
Major British chemical company which Ian Stewart worked for in the early sixties. As the only employed Stone, he used his paycheck to feed his bandmates. In true cosmic world balance, the Stones have supported both Ian Stewart and the chemical industry ever since.

"I AM WAITING"
Written by: Jagger/Richards
Recorded by: The Rolling Stones
Release date: April 1966
Record label: Decca/London
Albums: AFTERMATH (U.K.)
   AFTERMATH (U.S.)

"I AM YOURS AND SHE'S MINE"
LET IT BLEED outtake.

"I CAN FEEL THE FIRE"/"BREATHE ON ME"
1974 Ron Wood solo single. The A side is from I'VE GOT MY OWN ALBUM TO DO; the flip from NOW LOOK.

I CAN TELL
1968 John Hammond LP featuring Bill.

"I CAN'T BE SATISFIED"
Written by: Muddy Waters
Recorded by: The Rolling Stones
Release date: January 1965
Record label: Decca/London
Albums: THE ROLLING STONES NO. 2
   MORE HOT ROCKS

"(I CAN'T GET NO) SATISFACTION"
Written by: Jagger/Richards
Recorded by: The Rolling Stones
Release date: May 1965
Record label: London/Decca
Albums: OUT OF OUR HEADS (U.S.)
   BIG HITS (U.S.)
   BIG HITS (U.K.)
   GOT LIVE IF YOU WANT IT! (live)
   MILESTONES
   GIMME SHELTER
   HOT ROCKS
   ROLLED GOLD

  STILL LIFE (live)
Singles: B/w "The Under Assistant West Coast Promotion Man" (U.S. 5/65)
   B/w "The Spider and the Fly" (U.K. 8/65)
• Studio—Chess, Chicago; RCA, Hollywood.
• Engineer—Ron Malo, Dave Hassinger.
• "Satisfaction" was originally taped at Chess on May 19, 1965, but recut two days later in Hollywood during the Stones' third U.S. tour.
• The single was released in the U.S. in May 1965 but not released in the U.K.

until August, when it was already number one in America.
• Keith wrote all the music and the chorus to this song. It's ironic that the rock anthem of all time was originally conceived as a folk song by Keith, who never believed it would be a hit. Mick disagreed.
• This was the Stones' first major hit in the U.S., and it glued a generation's ears to their radio and record player (we didn't have *stereos* then) speakers hunting for the word "pregnant" after Mick's phrase "try to make some girl," as the Stones intentionally blurred the suggestive vocals by burying them in the music.

"I CAN'T HELP IT"
SOME GIRLS outtake.

"I DON'T KNOW WHY"
Written by: Wonder/Riser/Hunter/Hardaway
Recorded by: The Rolling Stones
Release date: May 1975
Record label: Decca/ABKCO
Album: METAMORPHOSIS
Single: B/w "Try a Little Harder" (U.S./U.K. 5/75)
• The first 1,000 pressings of the single credit Jagger/Richards as the writers.
• The U.S. METAMORPHOSIS al-

Record label: Decca/London
Albums: READY, STEADY, GO!
 MILESTONES
 ROLLED GOLD
Singles: B/w "Stoned" (U.K. 11/63)
 Flip of "Not Fade Away"
 (U.S. 3/64)
• Studio—Kingsway Studios, England.
• Producer—Impact Sound.
• Engineer—Eric Easton.
• The U.K. single was released three days before the end of the Stones' first headlining British tour, where the group performed sixty concerts in thirty days.
• London Records released and then immediately withdrew "I Wanna Be Your Man" in the U.S., making "Not Fade Away" the A side instead.
• Lennon and McCartney wrote this song especially for the Stones when they learned the Stones wanted a song of theirs to record.

"I WANNA GET ME A GUN"
Written by: Bill Wyman
Recorded by: Bill Wyman
Release date: May 1974
Record label: Rolling Stones Records
Album: MONKEY GRIP
• Danny Kootch—guitars.
• Joe Lala—percussion.
• Mac Rebennack—piano.
• Dallas Taylor—drums.
• Betty Wright, George McCrae, Gwen McCrae—backup vocals.
• Boneroo Horn Section—Peter Graves, Mark Colby, Ken Faulk, Neal Bonsanti.

"I WANT TO BE LOVED"
Written by: Dixon
Recorded by: The Rolling Stones
Release date: June 1963
Record label: Decca
Album: None
Single: Flip side of "Come On"
 (U.K. 6/63)
• First U.K. single.

"I'D MUCH RATHER BE WITH THE BOYS"
Written by: Oldham/Richards
Recorded by: The Rolling Stones
Release date: June 1975
Record label: Decca/ABKCO
Album: METAMORPHOSIS
• One of the two songs chosen by

bum credits Jagger/Richards/Taylor as writers.
• The Stones were recording this song when they learned Brian had died.

"I GOT THE BLUES"
Written by: Jagger/Richards
Recorded by: The Rolling Stones
Release date: April 1971
Record label: Rolling Stones Records
Album: STICKY FINGERS
• Bobby Keys—sax.
• Billy Preston—organ.
• Jim Price—trumpet.

"I GOT YOU BABE"
Sonny and Cher hit which Mick and Andrew Oldham parodied on the British TV show "Ready Steady Go," September 1965.

"I JUST WANT TO MAKE LOVE TO YOU"
Written by: Dixon
Recorded by: The Rolling Stones
Release date: April 1964
Record label: Decca/London
Albums:THE ROLLING STONES
 ENGLAND'S NEWEST HIT MAKERS
 MILESTONES
 ROCK 'N' ROLLING STONES
Single: Flip side of "Tell Me" (U.S. 6/64)

"I JUST WANT TO SEE HIS FACE"
Written by: Jagger/Richards
Recorded by: The Rolling Stones
Release date: May 1972
Record label: Rolling Stones Records
Album: EXILE ON MAIN ST.
• Bill Plummer—bass.
• Jimmy Miller—percussion.
• Clydie King, Vanetta Fields, J. Kirkland—backup vocals.
• Album sleeve says: "I Just Wanna See His Face."

"I NEED YOU BABY (MONA)"
Written by: McDaniels (pronounced Bo Diddley!)
Recorded by: The Rolling Stones
Release date: April 1964
Record label: Decca/London
Albums: THE ROLLING STONES
 THE ROLLING STONES, NOW!
• The song appears with its better known backward title, "Mona (I Need You Baby)" on THE ROLLING STONES, NOW!

"I WANNA BE YOUR MAN"
Written by: Lennon/McCartney
Recorded by: The Rolling Stones
Release date: November 1963

Bill for THE BLACK BOX compilation, which actually appeared on METAMORPHOSIS.

"IF I WAS A DANCER (DANCE PT. 2)"
Written by: Jagger/Richards/Wood
Recorded by: The Rolling Stones
Release date: May 1981
Album: SUCKING IN THE SEVENTIES
• This song was previously unavailable on an LP.

"IF YOU CAN'T ROCK ME"
Written by: Jagger/Richards
Recorded by: The Rolling Stones
Release date: October 1974
Record label: Rolling Stones Records
Albums: IT'S ONLY ROCK 'N' ROLL
      LOVE YOU LIVE (live in Paris)
      TIME WAITS FOR NO ONE
• Billy Preston—piano, clavinet.

"IF YOU DON'T WANT MY LOVE"/"I'VE GOT A FEELING"
1975 Ron solo single.

"IF YOU LET ME"
Written by: Jagger/Richards
Recorded by: The Rolling Stones
Release date: June 1975
Record label: Decca/ABKCO
Album: METAMORPHOSIS
• One of the two songs chosen by Bill for THE BLACK BOX compilation, which appeared on METAMORPHOSIS.

"(IF YOU THINK YOU'RE) GROOVY"/ "THOUGH IT HURTS"
1968 P. P. Arnold single, the flip side of which was produced by Mick.

"IF YOU NEED ME"
Written by: Bateman/Pickett
Recorded by: The Rolling Stones
Release date: August 1964
Record label: Decca/London
Albums: 12 x 5
      STONE AGE
EP: FIVE BY FIVE (U.K. 8/64)
• Ian Stewart—organ.

"IF YOU REALLY WANT TO BE MY FRIEND"
Written by: Jagger/Richards
Recorded by: The Rolling Stones
Release date: October 1974
Record label: Rolling Stones Records
Album: IT'S ONLY ROCK 'N' ROLL
• Nicky Hopkins—piano.
• Blue Magic—backup vocals.

"IF YOU WANNA BE HAPPY"
Written by: Guida/Guida/Royster
Recorded by: Bill Wyman
Release date: February 1976
Record label: Rolling Stones Records
Album: STONE ALONE
• Dallas Taylor—drums.
• Hubie Heard—organ.
• Danny Kortchmar—guitar.
• Albhy Galuten—synthesizer.
• Mark Colby—sax.
• Clydie King, Vanetta Fields—backup vocals.

IKE AND TINA TURNER REVUE
Husband and wife act which the Stones first saw when Ike and Tina were recording "River Deep Mountain High" with Phil Spector in 1966. Mick asked them to open for the Stones' eighth British tour in the fall of 1966, and Tina feels that Mick based his "stage dancing" on her moves. Ike and Tina

also accompanied the Stones on their 1969 U.S. tour, including Altamont. Tina opened for the Stones in New Jersey during the 1981 U.S. tour. Currently, Tina as a solo performer is waiting on a friend, either Mick or Keith, to produce an LP for her.

"I'LL PULL YOU THRO'"
Written by: Bill Wyman
Recorded by: Bill Wyman
Release date: May 1974
Record label: Rolling Stones Records
Album: MONKEY GRIP
• Jackie Clark—guitar.
• Hubie Heard—organ.
• Danny Kootch—twelve-string guitar.
• Joe Lala—percussion.
• Dallas Taylor—drums.
• George Terry—guitar.
• Betty Wright, George McCrae, Gwen McCrae—backup vocals.
• Boneroo Horn Section—Peter Graves, Mark Colby, Ken Faulk, Neal Bonsanti.

"IMAGINATION"
See "Just My Imagination . . .".

IMMEDIATE RECORDS
Record company started by Andrew Loog Oldham in 1966. The Small Faces, P. P. Arnold, the Nice, and others were signed to the label. In 1969 Immediate Records went bankrupt, and in 1976 NEMS bought up the old Immediate catalogue, reissuing some of the records. When Oldham became the American director, the label was relaunched.

IMPACT SOUND
Andrew Oldham's and Eric Easton's 1963 management deal with the Stones included the formation of this company to supervise the Stones' recording sessions.

IMPERIAL HOTEL
London hotel where Brian was living when he was busted in the spring of 1968. (For details see Arrests: London [Imperial Hotel Bust].)

"I'M A COUNTRY BOY"
EXILE ON MAIN ST. outtake.

"I'M A KING BEE"
Written by: Moore (Slim Harpo)
Recorded by: The Rolling Stones
Release date: April 1964
Record label: Decca/London
Albums: THE ROLLING STONES
ENGLAND'S NEWEST HIT MAKERS

"I'M ALL RIGHT"
Written by: Nanker Phelge
Recorded by: The Rolling Stones
Release date: July 1965
Record label: London/Decca
Albums: OUT OF OUR HEADS (U.S.) (live)

GOT LIVE IF YOU WANT IT! (live)
EP: GOT LIVE IF YOU WANT IT!
(U.K. 6/65) (live)
• The lyrics are "It's all right" throughout the song. "I'm all right" is never sung.

"I'M FREE"
Written by: Jagger/Richards
Recorded by: The Rolling Stones
Release date: September 1965
Record label: Decca/London
Albums: OUT OF OUR HEADS (U.K.)
DECEMBER'S CHILDREN
PROMOTIONAL ALBUM
MORE HOT ROCKS
Single: Flip of "Get Off of My Cloud"
(U.S. 9/65)

"I'M GOING DOWN"
Written by: Jagger/Richards
Recorded by: The Rolling Stones
Release date: June 1975
Record label: Decca/ABKCO
Album: METAMORPHOSIS

"I'M MOVING ON"
Written by: Snow
Recorded by: The Rolling Stones
Release date: June 1965
Record label: Decca/London
Albums: DECEMBER'S CHILDREN
NO STONE UNTURNED
EP: GOT LIVE IF YOU WANT IT!
(U.K. 6/65) (live)

"I'M NOT THE MARRYING KIND"/"MY LOVE BELONGS TO YOU"
1967 single by Hamilton and the Movement produced by Bill, who also co-wrote the A side.

"IN ANOTHER LAND"
Written by: Bill Wyman
Recorded by: The Rolling Stones
Lead singer: Bill
Release date: November 1967
Record label: London/Decca
Album: THEIR SATANIC MAJESTIES REQUEST
• Original track features only Bill, Charlie, Nicky Hopkins, and Steve Marriott. Legend has it that Bill got his big break because he and Charlie were the only Stones to show up at Olympic Studios the night of the recording session. The rest of the Stones added backup vocals later.

"IN CROWD, THE"
As performed by the Ramsey Lewis Trio, this was Charlie's favorite song of 1965.

"IN THE MIDNIGHT HOUR"
Wilson Pickett song that was Mick's pick hit of 1965.

"INDIAN GIRL"
Written by: Jagger/Richards
Recorded by: The Rolling Stones
Release date: June 1980
Record label: Rolling Stones Records
Album: EMOTIONAL RESCUE

"INFEKSHUN"
Written by: Ron Wood
Recorded by: Ron Wood
Release date: May 1979
Record label: CBS
Album: GIMME SOME NECK
• "Pops" Popwell—bass.
• H. Phillips—piano.

INGLIS, STEPHEN
Cover designer of AFTERMATH (U.S.) and GOT LIVE IF YOU WANT IT!

INNER COURT SESSIONS
Courthouse where Brian's trial was held when he was busted at his Kings Road flat.

"INTERNATIONAL TV FESTIVAL"
Montreux, Switzerland television taping, which took place in April 1964 and was the Stones' first trek out of the U.K.

INTERVIEW WITH MICK JAGGER BY TOM DONAHUE, APRIL 1971, AN
1971 Rolling Stones Records promo album given to disc jockeys.

INTROSPECTION
1969 album by the End produced by Bill, featuring Charlie on tabla on one track.

INVOCATION OF MY DEMON BROTHER
Twelve-minute Kenneth Anger film made in 1969 containing several shots of the Rolling Stones in concert at Hyde Park and an original synthesizer score by Mick.

ISHTAR
Film about the Assyrian and Babylonian goddess of love and war which Mick is planning to co-star in and/or produce.

ISLEY BROTHERS
American soul act the Stones wanted at their "Rock and Roll Circus." The Isleys couldn't make it.

IT AIN'T EASY
1971 Long John Baldry album featuring Ron.

"IT'S A LIE"
EMOTIONAL RESCUE outtake.

"IT SHOULD BE YOU"
First-ever Jagger/Richards composition, recorded by George Bean on Decca. The Stones' version of this song was never released.

"IT WAS A NORMAL DAY FOR BRIAN, A MAN WHO DIED EVERY DAY"
Unreleased Pete Townshend song, written when he heard that Brian had died.

"IT'S A WONDER"
Written by: Bill Wyman
Recorded by: Bill Wyman
Release date: May 1974

Record label: Rolling Stones Records
Album: MONKEY GRIP
• Hubie Heard—piano, organ.
• Danny Kootch—guitars.
• Joe Lala—percussion.
• Dallas Taylor—drums.
• Betty Wright, George McCrae, Gwen McCrae—backup vocals.

"IT'S ALL OVER NOW"
Written by: B. & S. Womack
Recorded by: The Rolling Stones
Release date: June 1964
Record label: Decca/London
Albums: 12 x 5
   BIG HITS (U.S.)
   BIG HITS (U.K.)
   STONE AGE
   MORE HOT ROCKS
   ROLLED GOLD
Single: B/w "Good Times, Bad Times"
   (U.K. 6/64) (U.S. 7/64)

- "It's All Over Now" was the Stones' first number one in the U.K.
- The single version was reprocessed for albums.
- Famous American DJ and "fifth Beatle," Murray the K, first played this song for the Stones—as recorded by the Valentinos featuring Bobby Womack on lead vocals. The Stones decided then and there to record it.

"IT'S ALRIGHT, BABE"
Unreleased Stones song, recorded in 1963.

"IT'S NOT EASY"
Written by: Jagger/Richards
Recorded by: The Rolling Stones
Release date: April 1966
Record label: Decca/London
Albums: AFTERMATH (U.K.)
       AFTERMATH (U.S.)

IT'S ONLY ROCK 'N' ROLL
Artist: The Rolling Stones
Producer: The Glimmer Twins
Release date: October 1974
Record label: Rolling Stones Records
Tracks: 10
"If You Can't Rock Me"
"Ain't Too Proud to Beg" (Whitfield/Holland)
"It's Only Rock 'n' Roll (But I Like It)"
"Till the Next Goodbye"
"Time Waits for No One"
"Luxury"
"Dance Little Sister"
"If You Really Want to Be My Friend"
"Short and Curlies"
"Fingerprint File"
- 21st U.S. album.
- 20th U.K. album.
- Special guests include Billy Preston, Nicky Hopkins, Ian Stewart, and more (see individual songs for credits).
- Ray Cooper plays percussion throughout.
- Studio—Musicland, Munich, West Germany.
- Engineers—Andy Johns, Keith Harwood.
- Assistant engineers—Tapani

Tapanainen, Rod Thear, Howard Kilgour, Mac "Munich."
- Overdub engineer—George Chkiantz.
- The first Mick and Keith production.
- Mixing—Keith Harwood, except for "Fingerprint File," mixed by Glyn Johns.
- Album designed and painted by Guy Peellaert.
- Reissued by EMI in March 1980 in the U.K.
- "s."

"IT'S ONLY ROCK 'N' ROLL (BUT I LIKE IT)"
Written by: Jagger/Richards
Recorded by: The Rolling Stones
Release date: July 1974
Record label: Rolling Stones Records
Albums: IT'S ONLY ROCK 'N' ROLL
      MADE IN THE SHADE
      LOVE YOU LIVE (live in Paris)
      BY INVITATION ONLY
Single: B/w "Through the Lonely Nights" (U.S./U.K. 7/74)
- Ian Stewart—piano.
- David Bowie—backup vocals.
- Kenney Jones plays drums and Willy Weeks bass on the original backing track, which still remains under layers

of overdubbing.
- The song was begun at Ron's home studio in London, during the recording of I'VE GOT MY OWN ALBUM TO DO.
- Inspiration by Ron Wood.

"I'VE BEEN LOVING YOU TOO LONG"
Written by: Redding/Butler
Recorded by: The Rolling Stones
Release date: November 1966
Record label: London/Decca
Albums: GOT LIVE IF YOU WANT IT! (live)
      GIMME SHELTER (live)
- Legend has it that this was not actually recorded live at Royal Albert Hall but was an outtake from the May 1965 RCA Hollywood session which produced "Satisfaction" and that the audience screams were overdubbed.

I'VE GOT MY OWN ALBUM TO DO
Solo album by Face/pre-Stone Ron Wood, released in September of 1974, featuring Keith (who contributed two songs) on guitar and vocals, with the Micks Jagger and Taylor also appearing on some tracks. Possibly in deference to his future bandmate, Ron's last name on the album cover is spelt "Woods," with the "s" boldly crossed out.

J. GEILS BAND
"The bad boys from Boston" and America's all-time party rockers, who opened for the Stones on some dates of their 1981 U.S. tour and on their 1982 European tour.

JFK INTERNATIONAL AIRPORT
On June 1, 1964, the Stones landed at this New York airport to start their first U.S. tour.

JACK DANIELS
"If alcohol is a crutch, Jack Daniels is a wheelchair."

—Robin Williams

Keith and Ron's beverage of choice.

JACKSON, J.J.
MTV "video jockey" who served as master of ceremonies at the Learning Annex's "Evening with Ron Wood."

JAGGER, BIANCA
Bianca Rose Perez-Mora, aka Bianca Perez Moreno de Macias, aka the ex-Mrs. Mick, was born on May 2, 1945, in Nicaragua, the daughter of shop-keepers, though Bianca claimed her father was a wealthy plantation owner and a diplomat. With eyes glued to the top, Bianca met Mick in Paris in September 1970 at a party. After Mick and Bianca's first night together, the Stones went on to Vienna and Bianca flew to Rome and followed the rest of the tour. The band could tell that the situation was serious when Mick turned gentleman and booked Bianca a sepa-rate room at the hotel.

Many people have noted the striking physical similarity between Mick and Bianca, and Bianca summed up the situation when she said, " . . . Actually he [Mick] wanted to achieve the ulti-mate by making love to himself."
Bianca was pregnant when she wed Mick in St. Tropez on May 12, 1971, but the wedding almost didn't take place due to the fight the bride-to-be and her groom had minutes before. Bianca wanted Mick to sign a joint ownership agreement, but he refused, demanding that she sign *his* prenuptial agreement. She agreed to his demands when he threatened to call off the wedding. Their next eight years togeth-er were equally as rocky and they spent much of their married time liv-ing in separate homes and countries, though Bianca did introduce Mick to the jet-set life-style and people. Bianca's the definition of the word jet-setter, though her pet cause has always been the people of her mother

country, Nicaragua.
"I think she's had a bigger negative influence on Mick than anyone would have thought possible."

—Keith

Bianca's presence and influence isolat-ed Mick from the band and created much friction in his private life and in his life as a Rolling Stone.
"Mick marrying Bianca stopped certain possibilities of us writing together. . . . "

—Keith

Mick and Bianca's 1979 divorce came as no surprise to anyone, but the settle-ment battle continued for over a year. Bianca wanted the case to be decided in Los Angeles, where her chances for joint ownership were better due to liberal community property laws; Mick opted for London. Bianca claimed that she was entitled to half of the money

Mick earned while they were married. It amounted to $25 million. A secret settlement was agreed upon in Novem-ber 1980, and Bianca received custody of their only child, Jade.
Mick's comment: *"She has been so difficult and devious that I'll never be friends with her again."*

Bianca was to star in *Trick or Treat* (the follow-up to the rock film *Stardust*), but she caused such trouble on the set that the film was shelved in mid-production. Her next role was in *Flesh Color*, followed by *The American Suc-cess Company*, a two-year-old film which has finally been released with the new title, *Success*.

JAGGER, CHRIS
Mick's younger brother, who is also a pop singer, but spent most of the six-

An unmarried man. Mick leaves court after his divorce from Bianca.

ties winning Mick Jagger look-alike contests. In October 1967, he protested in front of the court house when Brian was sentenced to nine months in jail. Chris was arrested at the demonstration and charged with "abusive behavior" and "obstructing police." He was let out on twenty-five pounds bail.

JAGGER, EVA

Mick's mother. Mick borrowed twenty pounds from her to make a down payment on an amplifier and a microphone. The question is: Did he pay her back?

Mick, daughter Jade, and Jane Rose backstage at a 1982 Who concert.

JAGGER, JADE

Daughter of Mick and Bianca, born on October 21, 1971, in Paris. "She's the one thing about it that I don't regret." —Mick.

JAGGER, JESSE JAMES

What Mick and Bianca would have named Jade had she been a boy.

JAGGER, MICK

Born: July 26, 1943

The following is reprinted from a fact sheet sent to American fans in spring 1964:

MICK JAGGER

REAL NAME Michael Philip Jagger.
BIRTH PLACE Dartford, Kent.
BIRTH DATE 26.7.44. [Authors' note: Missed by a year!]
HEIGHT 5'10".
WEIGHT 10st. 6lbs.
COLOUR OF EYES Blue.
COLOUR OF HAIR Mousy.
PARENTS' NAMES Joe and Eva.
BROTHERS AND SISTERS Christopher.
PRESENT HOME Hampstead.
INSTRUMENTS PLAYED Harmonica.
WHERE EDUCATED Dartford Grammar School, London School of Economics.
MUSICAL EDUCATION None.
ENTERED SHOW BUSINESS AT: 18.
FIRST PUBLIC APPEARANCE Marquee Club.
BIGGEST BREAK IN CAREER Meeting the rest of the Stones.
TV DEBUT "Thank Your Lucky Stars".
RADIO DEBUT "Saturday Club".
DISC LABEL Decca.
HOBBIES Boats, records.
FAVOURITE SINGERS Chuck Berry, Jimmy Reed.
FAVOURITE ACTORS/ACTRESSES Sophia Loren, Steve McQueen.
FAVOURITE COLOUR Blue, pink.
FAVOURITE FOOD Continental.
FAVOURITE DRINK Milk.
FAVOURITE CLOTHES Casual.
FAVOURITE COMPOSERS Lieber/Stoller.
MISC. LIKES Driving at night by myself, girls.
MISC. DISLIKES Motorway cafes, intolerant people.
TASTES IN MUSIC R & B, pop.
PROFESSIONAL AMBITION To make a million seller.
PERSONAL AMBITION To enjoy myself.

Michael Philip Jagger, a child who worked as an ice cream man for extra money and hoped to grow up to be a lawyer or politician, became lead singer in a rock 'n' roll band called the Rolling Stones and changed the world through different channels.

"I must say I don't really like singing very much. I'm not really a good enough singer to really enjoy it. . . . I enjoy playing the guitar more than I enjoy singing, and I can't play the guitar either. But I know that if I keep on playing the guitar, I can get better, whereas I can't improve much as a singer."

—Mick Jagger, 1969

"It's a true friendship when you can bash somebody over the head and not be told, 'You're not my friend anymore.' That's a true friendship. You put up with each other's bitching. . . . He's my wife. And he'll say the same thing about me."

—Keith Richards, 1981

"It's very hard to be Mick's friend despite how much you want *to be 'cause he* never *opens up. He just doesn't."*

—Keith Richards

"Mick is very hard to work for if you're at all sensitive."

—Charlie Watts

"Mick is always flitting about; never happy or always happy."

—Charlie Watts

"It is a tremendous hassle to keep Mick in reality. . . ."

—Keith Richards

"Nobody believes me that I came into music just because I wanted the bread. It's true."

—Mick Jagger, 1974

"I might have kids and I might get married, but I'll never settle down. I'm not the type."

—Mick Jagger, 1970

"Let's go watch Mick put on his makeup, that's always good for a laugh."
—Ron Wood, 1975

"When I'm thirty-three, I quit."

—Mick Jagger, 1972

"If you can't take a joke, it's too fuckin' bad."

—Mick Jagger

JAGGER, JOE
Mick's father. He was a physical education teacher, who didn't want Mick to get into music.

JAGGER, MICHAEL PHILIP
Born on July 26, 1943, this is Mick's legal name. Until he got famous everyone called him Mike.

JAGGER/RICHARDS
Well-known songwriting team who were encouraged in this endeavor by Andrew Oldham, who dangled Lennon/McCartney in front of the future Glimmer Twins as the perfect examples of "self-sufficiency." Oldham believed that someday the Stones would run out of old blues tunes to cover, and the team heeded his advice, with over two hundred compositions to their credit so far.
"Mick writes the words."

—Keith
"When I'm writing I feel terrible. It's the time I feel the worst."

—Mick
". . . The best songs are the ones we've written together."

—Mick

"JAH IS NOT DEAD"
EMOTIONAL RESCUE outtake.

"JAMAICA"
GOATS HEAD SOUP outtake.

JAMES, ETTA
Singer who opened for the Stones during their 1978 U.S. tour and in Ohio during the 1981 U.S. tour. In April of 1982 Keith played on stage with her at the Other End, a New York club. They did "Rock Me Baby."

JAMMING WITH EDWARD
(Also called: NICKY HOPKINS, RY COODER, MICK JAGGER, BILL WYMAN, CHARLIE WATTS—JAMMING WITH EDWARD)
1972 "budget" release on Rolling Stones Records of a jam session produced by Glyn Johns at Olympic Studios, London, with all of the above musicians. Keith didn't show up one night during the 1969 LET IT BLEED sessions, rumored to be due to his feud with Ry Cooder, but three-fifths of the band played on without him. The album came complete with a letter of apology from Mick making reference

to this "piece of bullshit," cut in London while "waiting for our guitar player to get out of bed," and noting that Glyn Johns and Marshall Chess unearthed the soon-forgotten tapes and felt that Stones fans might want to hear this "historic" jam session.

JAN AND DEAN
American duo who appeared on the *T.A.M.I. Show* with the Stones in 1964.

JAPANESE EMBASSY
In 1973 they denied Mick a visa to perform in Japan because of his 1969 cannabis bust, causing the Stones to cancel the Pacific segment of their tour.

"JAPANESE THING, THE"
Working title of "Moonlight Mile."

"JAZZ CLUB"
BBC radio program whose July 12, 1962 show was a milestone in the Stones' career. Alexis Korner's Blues Incorporated appeared on the show, but because of strict union fees, only six musicians were budgeted and Mick was dropped from the lineup. Because the broadcast was on a Thursday, coinciding with Blues Incorporated's residency at the Marquee Club, a replacement band was needed. The Stones were available and played their first gig that night.

JAZZ NEWS
British paper where Brian placed an ad for musicians to join his rhythm and blues band. Ian Stewart was among those who answered the ad.

JEFFERSON AIRPLANE
Sixties version of the Jefferson Starship. They performed at Altamont with the Stones, and member Marty Balin was hurt onstage, a prelude to the violence to come.

JEFFREYS, GARLAND
American singer who opened for the Stones in Connecticut during their 1981 U.S. tour.

JENKINS, BOB
Photographer of MONKEY GRIP LP cover.

JENSEN, TED
Mastered tapes for SOME GIRLS and BILL WYMAN.

JETHRO TULL
Group who played on "The Rolling Stones' Rock and Roll Circus." In February 1972 they broke the Stones' box office records all across Europe.

"JIG-SAW PUZZLE"
Written by: Jagger/Richards
Recorded by: The Rolling Stones
Release date: November 1968
Record label: London/Decca
Album: BEGGARS BANQUET

JIMI HENDRIX
1973 documentary film in which Mick can be seen briefly.

"JIVING SISTER FANNY"
Written by: Jagger/Richards
Recorded by: The Rolling Stones
Release date: June 1975
Record label: Decca/ABKCO
Album: METAMORPHOSIS

JOHN, DR. (MAC REBENNACK)
The Louisiana-based "night tripper," who was asked to perform at "The Rolling Stones' Rock and Roll Circus," sings backup on "Let It Loose," and performs various keyboard chores on MONKEY GRIP and STONE ALONE.

JOHN F. KENNEDY STADIUM
Philadelphia outdoor arena where the Stones opened their 1981 U.S. tour. On September 25, 1981, 90,000 fans watched the show, portions of which can be seen in the film *Let's Spend the Night Together*. George Thorogood and Journey opened the show.

JOHN HAMMOND
1967 John Hammond album featuring Bill on three tracks.

JOHN KEEN'S TRAD BAND
A band Brian was in in Cheltenham.

JOHNNY KIDD AND THE PIRATES
Guest artists during parts of the Stones second British tour, January 1964.

JOHNS, ANDY
Glyn Johns' younger brother, who was a tape operator at Olympic Studios in London. He first worked on a Stones project while they were recording THEIR SATANIC MAJESTIES REQUEST. By spring 1970, he had advanced to engineer, performing that chore on STICKY FINGERS (for which he mixed some of the tracks with Jimmy Miller). He also engineered EXILE ON MAIN ST., mixed and engineered GOATS HEAD SOUP, and engineered IT'S ONLY ROCK 'N' ROLL. Johns also co-produced (with Ron) and engineered (except for "Wind Howlin' Through") 1 2 3 4.

JOHNS, GLYN
Engineer who first recorded the Stones in January/February 1963 at IBC Studios in London. He had seen them at his club, the Red Lion, and brought them to the studio to cut a demo tape. Many people felt that in the early days, when Oldham called himself the producer, it was actually Glyn Johns who was producing the records. Johns engineered portions of OUT OF OUR HEADS, DECEMBER'S CHILDREN, GOT LIVE IF YOU WANT IT!, THEIR SATANIC MAJESTIES REQUEST, LET IT BLEED, STICKY FINGERS, EXILE ON MAIN ST., BLACK AND BLUE, and mixed "Fingerprint File" on IT'S ONLY ROCK 'N' ROLL. With the Rolling Stones, he coproduced GET YER YA-YA'S OUT and is credited as the recording and mixing engineer of that album. Johns also engineered Brian's A DEGREE OF MURDER soundtrack and went with Brian to Marrakesh in the spring of 1968 to record the G'naoua musicians. Johns' association with the Stones came to an end in the mid-seventies because he couldn't handle their extreme and chronic tardiness at the studio, feeling it was a waste of valuable time.

JOHNSON, JIMMY
Assistant engineer on STICKY FINGERS.

JOHNSON, ROBERT A.
Guitarist who cut two tracks with Keith and Jeff Beck when he auditioned for the Stones as a possible replacement for Mick Taylor during the "Great Guitarists Hunt" of 1975.

JOHNSON, WILKO
U.K.'s rockin' Dr. Feelgood guitarist who auditioned for the Stones during the "Great Guitarists Hunt" of 1975. He was not asked "Back in the Night."

JOLLY, CHARLIE
Tabla player on "Fingerprint File."

JONES, BRIAN

Born: February 28, 1942
Died: July 3, 1969

The following is reprinted from a fact sheet sent to American fans in spring 1964:

BRIAN JONES

REAL NAME Brian Jones.
BIRTHPLACE Cheltenham.
BIRTH DATE 28.2.44. [Authors' note: Two years off!]
HEIGHT 5'8".
WEIGHT 10st. 1lb.
COLOUR OF EYES Greeny-blue.
COLOUR OF HAIR Blonde.
PARENTS' NAMES Lewis and Louisa.
BROTHERS AND SISTERS Barbara (17).
PRESENT HOME London.
INSTRUMENTS PLAYED Guitar, Harmonica.
WHERE EDUCATED Cheltenham Grammar School.
MUSICAL EDUCATION Self-taught.
ENTERED SHOW BUSINESS AT: 18.
FIRST PUBLIC APPEARANCE Marquee, Oxford Street.
BIGGEST BREAK IN CAREER Meeting the other "Stones".
TV DEBUT "Thank Your Lucky Stars".
RADIO DEBUT "Saturday Club".
DISC LABEL Decca.
HOBBIES Women. [Authors' note: He was honest!]
FAVOURITE SINGERS, ARTISTS Johnny Cash, Bo Diddley, Jimmy Reed.
FAVOURITE ACTRESSES, ACTORS Tony Perkins.
FAVOURITE COLOUR Black/White/Grey.
FAVOURITE FOOD Steaks.
FAVOURITE BAND Muddy Waters.
FAVOURITE DRINK Milk/Whiskey.
FAVOURITE CLOTHES "Gear", "Anello Boots".
FAVOURITE COMPOSERS Willy Dixon, Bach, Beatles.
MISC. LIKES Having a shower.
MISC. DISLIKES Public Transport.
TASTES IN MUSIC Very Catholic, but I hate Brass Bands.
ORIGIN OF STAGE NAME Title of an old Muddy Waters Blues.
PERSONAL AMBITION To stop smoking 60 fags a day.
PROFESSIONAL AMBITION To tour the States. To get a no. 1.

The beautiful Brian Jones (born Lewis Brian Hopkins-Jones) began studying clarinet as a child, also singing in his church choir. He taught himself guitar on a Spanish instrument bought for three pounds, and though music seemed to be his main interest, he did well in chemistry and physics in school, planning to become a dentist. His rebellious attitude, however, got him expelled from school several times, starting at the age of 10! When he finally left school in his teens, Brian hitchhiked through Europe, basically Scandinavia, accepting a myriad of odd jobs and playing clarinet and alto sax in jazz bands once back in his hometown of Cheltenham.

The "undisputed leader" of the early Rolling Stones and the band's original manager, Brian's interest in all musical instruments drove him to learn the harmonica, sitar, dulcimer, organ, piano, harpsichord, marimbas, and all percussive instruments, in addition to clarinet, sax, and guitar. He experimented with some of these—a rarity for rock 'n' roll—on the Rolling Stones' records.

With his fabulous face, brilliant hair, "mod" stance, and flamboyant clothing, Brian personified the "Swinging London" of the mid-sixties. But behind that beautiful dream facade lay a nightmare. Brian was a brutal womanizer, fathering at least six known illegitimate children. He kept a "box score" of women, once calculating that he slept with sixty-four in one month. He carried dog chains to beat his girlfriends with.

Brian overdosed for the first time in 1964; he was a closet alcoholic, taking pills to combat his drinking. By 1967 he had been hospitalized twice with nervous breakdowns. All this, in addition to his asthma condition, prevented Brian from functioning as a performer and prevented the Stones from touring in 1968. In addition, Brian always suffered from a paranoia that he made it on his looks and was totally talentless. He also felt that Keith, Mick, and Andrew Oldham were in alliance against him.

On June 8, 1969, Brian left the Rolling Stones, after a meeting with Mick, Keith, and—for good faith—Charlie. His official statement was: "I want to play my kind of music, which is no longer the Stones music." Brian was to be paid $240,000 a year for as long as the Stones stayed together as a band. He began talking with Alexis Korner and other musicians and hoped to continue in his musical endeavors.

On July 3, l969, Brian died in the swimming pool of his home at Cotchford Farm. The coroner's report concluded: "Death by misadventure . . . death due to immersion in fresh water . . . under the influence of drugs and alcohol." His funeral was held on July 9, at the same church where he had once served as choirboy. It was attended by his family, some former lovers, Brian's and Linda Lawrence's son, Julian, and Charlie, Bill, and Ian Stewart. When Brian's estate was settled a year later, he was found to be $360,000 in debt. His was the first self-inflicted rock 'n' roll death, and to this day remains the most poignant. Brian's gravestone bears his self-composed epitaph: "Please don't judge me too harshly."

"Brian was the first person in England to play bottleneck guitar and nobody knew what it was."

—Bill Wyman

"When it comes to life-styles, Brian wrote the definition of an English popstar."
—Al Aronowitz

"He was six years old all the time."

—Jo Bergman

"He was one of those people who are so beautiful in one way, and such an asshole in another."

—Keith Richards

"We felt like we had a wooden leg."

—Mick Jagger

"I'm wordless and sad and shocked. We were like a pack, we Stones. Like a family. I just say my prayers for him. I hope he is, at last, finding peace. . . . I wasn't ever really close to him."

—Mick Jagger

"If he gave nothing else to the world, Brian Jones was the first heterosexual male to start wearing costume jewelry from Saks Fifth Avenue."
—Al Aronowitz

"With his death, a chapter of rock is concluded. Who can forget his clothes, his angelic/demonic smile, his poses on album covers?"

—Fusion magazine

"There are some people who you know aren't going to get old. . . . Brian and I agreed that he, Brian, wouldn't live very long. . . . I remember saying, 'You'll never make thirty, man,' and he said, 'I know.'"

—Keith Richards

(For Brian's relatives, see the surname Hopkins-Jones.)

Brian on his way to sentencing at Inner Court Sessions, October 1967.

JONES, BUSTA CHERRY
Bass player rumored to be set to re-place Bill in August 1981.

JONES, ELMORE
One of Brian's stage names; "Elmore" taken from his idol Elmore James.

JONES, JOHN PAUL
Bass player/keyboardist of Led Zep, who worked as a studio musician in the sixties. He played on many of the Rolling Stones demos, which later surfaced on METAMORPHOSIS. He also plays strings on "She's a Rainbow."

JONES, JULIAN BRIAN LAWRENCE
Son born to Brian and Linda Lawrence in July 1964 and later adopted by Donovan when he married Linda. At eighteen, Julian traveled on tour with the Stones.

JONES, JULIAN MARK ANDREWS
Son born to Brian and Pat Andrews in 1963. He was named after Julian "Cannonball" Adderly, another one of Brian's idols.

JONES, KENNEY
Drummer on the original backing track of "It's Only Rock 'n' Roll (But I Like It)" which remains under layers of overdubbing. He also performed, along with Bill, on Bill's "A New Fashion" when they performed it on European TV. (See Faces, The.)

JONES, PAUL
Lead singer of Manfred Mann and star of the cult classic film *Privilege,* which many people believe to be based on Brian's life story. Under the name of P. P. Pond, he performed blues numbers with Elmo Lewis (Brian). He also sang as a guest in Blues Incorporated when the Stones were first starting out. Brian wanted Jones to be the lead singer in the Stones instead of Mick. Paul and at least part of the Stones met again when his latest band, the Blues Band, opened for Jim Carroll at New York's Trax Club the night Keith jammed with Carroll in 1980.

JONES, PETER, AND JOPLING, NORMAN
Jones was a free-lance writer for Britain's *Record Mirror* who was invited by Giorgio Gomelsky to see the Stones at the Crawdaddy Club. Jones in turn invited R & B writer Norman Jopling, who penned the Stones' first national review, "The Rolling Stones —Genuine R & B," for *Record Mirror.* Jones took the event one step further by informing Andrew Loog Oldham that Jopling was about to file this ecstatic report, and Oldham wasted no time in getting to the Crawdaddy Club himself.

JORDAN, DAVE
Remix engineer on LOVE YOU LIVE, who also engineered and mixed "Before

They Make Me Run'' on SOME GIRLS.

JOSEPH, MICHAEL
Photographer of BEGGARS BAN-QUET inside LP cover.

JOURNEY
Opening act at the first three shows of the Stones 1981 U.S. tour.

JOVAN
Perfume company which reportedly spent between $2 and $4 million on the Stones' 1981 U.S. tour in exchange for the appearance of the name of their men's cologne on the concert tickets and radio promotion spots. Keith's response to this corporate merger: "We've never done any of this crap before, but we can use the money constructively to pay for small gigs that otherwise we wouldn't have been able to do." The three-month tour of fifty-one concerts grossed the band over $50 million.

"JUKE BOX JURY"
BBC TV show on which the Stones appeared as panelists in July 1964. When their appearance was announced, 8,000 people clamored for passes—the biggest demand ever for studio tickets.

"JUMP UP"
Written by: Bill Wyman
Recorded by: Bill Wyman/C. Kimsey
Release date: 1981
Record label: A & M
Album: BILL WYMAN
• Mel Collins, Martin Drove, Annie Whitehead—horns.

"JUMPIN' JACK FLASH"
Written by: Jagger/Richards
Recorded by: The Rolling Stones
Release date: May 1968
Record label: Decca/London

Albums: THROUGH THE PAST, DARKLY U.K.
THROUGH THE PAST, DARKLY U.S.
GET YER YA-YA'S OUT (live)
HOT ROCKS
GIMME SHELTER
ROLLED GOLD
LOVE YOU LIVE (live in Paris)
Single: B/w "Child of the Moon" (U.S./U.K. 5/68)
• Studio—Olympic Studios, London.
• Producer—Jimmy Miller.
• This song was originally slated to appear on BEGGARS BANQUET, but the Stones wanted it released sooner.
• The promo film clip (directed by Michael Lindsay-Hogg) was so successful that it inspired the Stones to do the "Rock and Roll Circus," with Lindsay-Hogg also directing. Mick also claims that it was this live performance film clip which made the song a number-one hit in the U.S. and U.K.
• Bill claims that he wrote the song's original riff.
• This song was performed by the Stones at the "Rock and Roll Circus."

• When performed in concert, Mick often throws either buckets of water or flower petals at the audience, the latter of which makes sense if Keith is being truthful when he said the song was written about his gardener.

JUST A STORY FROM AMERICA
1977 Elliot Murphy album featuring Mick Taylor.

"JUST MY IMAGINATION (RUNNING AWAY WITH ME)"
Written by: Whitfield/Strong
Recorded by: The Rolling Stones
Release date: June 1978
Record label: Rolling Stones Records
Albums: SOME GIRLS
STILL LIFE (live)
• Ian "Mac" McLagan—organ.

KDAY
Los Angeles radio station, which started playing an "exclusive" copy of "All Down the Line"/"Stop Breaking Down" in February 1972. Program director Bob Wilson claimed that this pre-release playing was with Mick's blessings, but it turned out that the Stones had never authorized it, and the acetate pressing of the single had been stolen from Marshall Chess' Los Angeles home.

KAHN, VICTOR
Designer of album sleeve and poster for LET IT BLEED.

KALKI
Gore Vidal novel for which Mick bought the movie rights in 1981.

KAMIN, PHILIP
Photographer who co-created *The Rolling Stones: The Last Tour.*

KARSLAKE, JO
Maiden name of Jo Howard.

KATCHEN, JULIAN
Classical pianist who performed in "The Rolling Stones' Rock and Roll Circus."

KAUFMAN, MURRAY (THE K)
Leading New York disc jockey in the sixties, known as "the fifth Beatle." Murray was probably the first person to play the Stones on U.S. radio during a show taped with John Lennon from London. During the Stones' first American tour in the summer of 1964, Murray played the song "It's All Over Now" for the group, who loved it and decided to record it. Murray also promoted the Stones June 1964 Carnegie Hall concert.

KEEF
Nickname for Keith.

KEELEY, CHARLES
Gas station attendant at Francis Service Station the night Bill, Mick, and Brian were arrested there in 1965.

KEITH, LINDA
British model who was Keith's girlfriend in 1965. They broke up when he fell in love with Anita, but Linda kept trying to get him back. When Keith and Anita moved in together, *Brian* moved in with Linda. In March 1968, while Brian was recording, Linda attempted suicide, causing such a commotion in the apartment that Brian was immediately evicted.

KEITH RICHARDS
Book by Barbara Charone published by Futura in the U.K., 1979; Doubleday in the U.S., 1982.

KELTNER, JIM
Session percussionist who has played with *everyone* at one time or another, and can be heard on GIMME SOME NECK and 1 2 3 4.

KENNEDY, TED
Massachusetts senator who in his bid for the Democratic candidacy for U.S. president received support from Mick, who showed up at a New York fund raiser.

KERSHAW, DOUG
Country/western artist who Bill saw performing in New Orleans and invit-

ed to open some of the Stones shows during their 1978 U.S. tour, which he did. In 1979, Doug was in the band that Bill arranged to perform at the Jerry Lewis Muscular Dystrophy Labor Day Telethon. It is rumored that he plays fiddle in the never seen "Rolling Stones' Rock and Rock Circus."

"KEY TO THE HIGHWAY"
Song which the Stones recorded in 1965 but never released.

KEYLOCK, MRS. TOM
Tom's wife broke the news of Brian's death to Mick over the phone.

KEYLOCK, TOM
Brian's chauffeur, who in early 1967, drove with Keith, Brian, and Anita to Morocco. Brian overdosed in Toulon, France and was left behind in a hospital. On the way south, Tom and Keith were arrested with other friends in Barcelona, Spain and detained briefly. When Brian finally rejoined everyone in Morocco, he proved to be so difficult to get along with that Tom helped Keith and Anita "escape" from him. After the "Moroccan Incident," Tom became Keith's chauffeur.

KEYS, BOBBY
Saxophone player who Mick and Keith saw performing with Delaney and Bonnie in California in 1969. The Glimmer Twins had Jimmy Miller contact Keys, and he came to the studio while they were mixing LET IT BLEED, adding horns to "Live with Me." He and Keith became close friends due to the fact that they were born on the same day and year (December 18, 1943). Keys played sax on STICKY FINGERS, sax and percussion on EXILE ON MAIN ST., tenor and baritone sax on GOATS HEAD SOUP, and sax on EMOTIONAL RESCUE. He also played tenor sax on the song "Don't Worry" on Ron's GIMME SOME NECK, and he performs on several songs on 1 2 3 4. Keys was on the Stones 1972 STP tour, their 1973 European tour, and in the New Barbarians in 1979. In 1971, he played at the jam session at Mick and Bianca's wedding reception. In actuality, Bobby had first been in the company of the Stones when in 1964 at the San Antone Teen Fair in Texas, Bobby was in the backup band of the Stones' opening artist, Bobby Vee. Keith, though not recalling this precisely, is so

impressed with his ultracosmic connections with Keys, that he has no fear of drugs, accidents, or anything that would take him even further off the planet. "Mr. Unhealth" claims that his safety is insured because, "I'm not gonna die till Bobby Keys dies." And apparently, Keys is in no danger.

KIDS ARE ALRIGHT, THE
1979 "rockumentary" film on the Who featuring the band doing "A Quick One," as filmed for "The Rolling Stones' Rock and Roll Circus" (intro by Keith). This is the first and only authorized public airing of any segment of the "Circus."

KILBURN STATE AUDITORIUM
London concert hall where Keith joined pre-Stone Ron on stage along with Ian McLagan, Andy Newmark, and Willie Weeks for two nights in July 1974 during Ron's "If You Gave Him Half a Chance" tour.

KILGOUR, HOWARD
Assistant engineer on IT'S ONLY ROCK 'N' ROLL and GOATS HEAD SOUP.

KIMSEY, CHRIS
Assistant engineer on STICKY FINGERS, who also engineered and mixed all of SOME GIRLS, except for "Before They Make Me Run." He also served as associate producer and engineer on EMOTIONAL RESCUE and associate producer and engineer on TATTOO YOU. He coproduced, coengineered, mixed, and mastered tapes for BILL WYMAN and is currently working with Bill on his forthcoming solo LP. Chris and the Cookham Cookies sing backup vocals on BILL WYMAN.

KING, B.B.
Blues favorite who opened for the Stones on their 1969 U.S. tour.

KING, BEN
Assistant engineer on SOME GIRLS.

KING, BILL
Photographer of STONE ALONE LP sleeve.

KING, CLYDIE
Very in-demand backup singer, who can be heard on EXILE ON MAIN ST., STONE ALONE, and 1 2 3 4.

KING, DENNIS
Mastered tapes for STONE ALONE.

KING, REG
Andrew Oldham's chauffeur, who must've listened and learned from the dealings in the backseat, becoming the manager of Decca recording artists, Thee, in the mid-sixties.

KING CRIMSON
Robert Fripp's electric/techno band which played at the Stones' free Hyde Park Concert on July 5, 1969.

KINGSWAY RECORDING STUDIOS
London studio where the Stones recorded with Eric Easton as producer. In September/October 1963, they recorded their hit, "I Wanna Be Your Man," plus "You'd Better Move On," "Money,"

"Bye Bye Johnny," and "Stoned." In November of 1963 they re-recorded "Poison Ivy," "Fortune Teller," and "You'd Better Move On," again with Eric Easton.

KIRKLAND, J.
Backup vocalist on EXILE ON MAIN ST.

KJELLGREN, GARY
Engineer and production assistant on STONE ALONE; he also mixed the album.

KLEIN, ALLEN
New York accountant who was appointed co-manager with Andrew Loog Oldham of the Stones in August 1965. The basic agreement was that Oldham managed the Stones and Klein managed Oldham. The Stones were eager to sign with Klein because he promised them *big* money. His first major triumph was renegotiating their contract with Decca Records in 1965. Klein was able to get them a $1.4 million advance (unheard of until then) against their royalties, plus a five-movie film deal to be financed by Decca. Everyone was thrilled with this until the truth came out years later when it was discovered that the Stones never got the $1.4 million. The Stones thought the advance was to be deposited into their account, Nanker Phelge Music, *Ltd.* Allegedly Klein deposited all the money into Nanker Phelge Music, *Inc.* —Klein's own U.S. company. When the Stones learned the truth, Klein pointed out that there was a clause in the contract with the Stones which stated that he had up to twenty years to give them the $1.4 million, thus giving him the opportunity to use the money himself and just give the Stones the principal back after he had earned all the interest. The Stones claimed Klein, also using this company, Nanker Phelge Music, *Inc.*, got them to sign away unknowingly their publishing rights by telling them this was the company they owned, when in fact it was Klein's company! In the U.S. the Stones were under contract to Klein's company ABKCO, which in turn had a contract with London Records, making Klein the middleman for all Stones releases.
In July 1970 the Stones announced that "neither he [Klein] or ABKCO Industries, Inc., nor any other company have any authority to negotiate

recording contracts on their behalf." A year later, 1971, the Stones, plus Brian's father, filed a $29 million lawsuit against Klein (and ABKCO) for mishandling their funds and trying to "deceive and defraud" them. In May 1972, during final negotiations with Klein to sort out their business problems, Mick brought along a film crew, who filmed the entire twenty-four-hour session. The final settlement gave ABKCO the rights to some past Stones recordings and publishing, plus one more album for ABKCO Records to be released through Atlantic Records. The Stones got a million dollars and their freedom. Klein went on to wreak havoc within the Beatles, also managing other stars of the day. In July of 1980 Klein surrendered to authorities in New York to begin serving a two-month prison sentence for filing a false income tax return. He is currently producing a Broadway play.

KLEIN, MARCI
Daughter of fashion designer Calvin Klein, whose Sweet Sixteen party at Studio 54 was attended by the dateless Mick, who danced with all of Marci's friends and gave an in-public hello kiss to his ex, Bianca, who was escorted to the event by Watergate-crasher Carl Bernstein.

KLEIN'S REVENGE
Nickname of the METAMORPHOSIS LP, because litigations forced the release of this album.

KNIGHT, BRIAN
British blues singer who in the early sixties was the leader of the Blues by Six, a group Charlie was in. Twenty years later, in early 1980, Charlie played drums on Knight's album. Other notables on the LP are Ian Stewart and Geoff Bradford.

KOCH, EDWARD
Lovable mayor of "the greatest city in the world," and thus the only appropriate host when the "greatest rock 'n' roll band in the world" appeared on "Saturday Night Live" in 1978.

KOOPER, AL
Brooklyn-born musician and songwriter, member of the Blues Project and founder of Blood, Sweat, and Tears, who plays piano, french horn, and organ on LET IT BLEED, and piano on "Feet." He also plays piano on an unreleased live version of "Brown Sugar," which was recorded at a birthday party for Keith held at Olympic Studios, London.

KOOTCH, DANNY
Using this cuter name and various guitars, Danny Kortchmar headed the core of Los Angeles musicians who performed on MONKEY GRIP. He did STONE ALONE under his real name.

KORNER, ALEXIS

Born in Paris in 1928, Korner moved to England while a child and grew up listening to "trad" jazz. He fell in love with American blues music, a sound not often heard in Britain in the fifties, and through his dedication to that music found himself pioneering the cause of British blues. By 1961 he and harmonica player Cyril Davies were together in Alexis Korner's Blues Incorporated, searching for places for their band to play. They talked the Marquee Club into running a "Blues Evening" every Tuesday. They were also influential in the creation of the Ealing Club, which featured their band, with drummer Charlie Watts and vocalist Art Wood (Ron's brother), on its opening night in March 1962.

Blues enthusiasts like Paul Jones, Long John Baldry, and most importantly, Mick, Keith, and Brian, flocked to hear Blues Incorporated. Mick started singing with the band occasionally (the others sometimes jammed), and was offered a permanent spot, which he declined, preferring to work with Brian and Keith, who, being Keith, would not change his Chuck Berry–influenced style for Korner. Watts left Blues Incor-porated in spring 1962 because the band's work was becoming too regular and was conflicting with his steady ad-agency job. It was Alexis' wife who, a while later, talked him into joining the Rolling Stones. An invitation from BBC Radio's *Jazz Club* to perform on its July 12, 1962 show sent Alexis Korner's Blues Incorporated off to the studio, leaving the Marquee Club without its Thursday-night resident band, and giving the Stones the opportunity to play their first gig!

After Brian left the Stones, Mick and Keith, seeing the depression he was in, asked Alexis, one of Brian's most-beloved fellow musicians, to talk to him. Brian wanted to join Korner's then-forming band, New Church, but Korner recommended that he start his own.

Korner has continued crusading for the blues through the decades. A quite lucrative career doing voice-overs for TV commercials has allowed him to continue performing the music of his heart with integrity and no concessions to any forms of musical commercialism. Through the years, the cream of British musicians have passed through Korner's Blues Incorporated—including Ginger Baker, Jack Bruce, Dick Heckstall-Smith, and countless others. They all owe him.

KORTCHMAR, DANNY

Popular Los Angeles session guitarist, best known for his work with James Taylor and Carole King. He was part of the three-man nucleus of musicians on MONKEY GRIP and STONE ALONE, along with Bill and Dallas Taylor. Danny is willing to travel "anywhere at any time" to play with his all-time idol, Keith Richards.

KOSH, JOHN

Designer of GET YER YA-YA'S OUT LP cover.

KOSSOFF, PAUL

Guitarist in Free who Mick Taylor beat out for Stoneship after Brian left the band. Kossoff was later in the band Back Street Crawler, and Kossoff unfortunately died of a drug-induced heart attack in 1976.

KRAMER, EDDIE

Engineer on LOVE YOU LIVE.

KUPKA, STEVE (THE DOCTOR)

Horn player on STONE ALONE, who also did horn arrangements.

L

"LABOR DAY TELETHON"
Astrid Lundstrom was the promotion consultant for Jerry Lewis' 1979 muscular dystrophy telethon show, getting rock groups to donate promotional clips. Bill arranged a live band to perform, which included himself, Dave Mason, Todd Rundgren, Ringo Starr, and Doug Kershaw. Among the songs the band performed were "Money," "Twist and Shout," and "Jumpin' Jack Flash."

LADIES AND GENTLEMEN, THE ROLLING STONES
1974 film of the Stones in concert, filmed in Fort Worth, Texas, June 1972. Directed by Rollin Binzer and produced by Marshall Chess, Rollin Binzer, Bob Fries, and Steve Gebhardt, the color film is ninety minutes long and features Stones' guest musicians Nicky Hopkins, Bobby Keys, Jim Price, and Ian Stewart. It was released by Dragon Aire, Ltd., and premiered at New York's Ziegfeld Theater in April 1974, the first concert film to have a full quadraphonic soundtrack.

"LADIES AND GENTLEMEN, THE ROLLING STONES"
Not the movie, but a TV special filmed at the Marquee Club in March 1970. Directed by Bruce Gowers, the Stones sang eight numbers. Partly intended as a promo film for STICKY FINGERS, it was never shown on British TV, although it has been shown in Europe.

"LADY JANE"
Written by: Jagger/Richards
Recorded by: The Rolling Stones
Release date: April 1966
Record label: Decca/London
Albums: AFTERMATH (U.K.)
    AFTERMATH (U.S.)
    BIG HITS (U.K.)
    GOT LIVE IF YOU WANT IT! (live)
    FLOWERS
    GIMME SHELTER
    MORE HOT ROCKS
    ROLLED GOLD
    SLOW ROLLERS
Single: Flip of "Mother's Little Helper" (U.S. 6/66)
• Brian plays dulcimer on this song.

LALA, JOE
Percussionist on MONKEY GRIP, last seen on the Neil Young *Trans European* tour.

LANE, CHANCERY
One of Andrew Oldham's pseudonyms.

LANE, RONNIE
Former Small Face and Face (see Faces, The), who may or may not have sung backup vocals on "Wild Horses." By

mistake, he may have contributed even more to the Stones: When Mick called the Faces' office and asked to speak to Ron, wanting him to leave the Faces and join the Stones, his call was put through to Ronnie Lane instead of Ronnie Wood. Lane turned Mick down.

LANE, TONY
Designer of the LP jackets for GIMME SOME NECK and 1 2 3 4.

"LANTERN, THE"
Written by: Jagger/Richards
Recorded by: The Rolling Stones
Release date: November 1967
Record label: London/Decca
Album: THEIR SATANIC MAJESTIES REQUEST
Single: Flip of "In Another Land" (U.S. 12/67)

LAPPING TONGUE, THE
The name of the airplane the Stones used during their tour of the U.S. in 1972. "In" people called it simply, the Tongue.

LAROCHE, PIERRE
David Bowie makeup man who "did" Bill for the cover of STONE ALONE. He is also credited with cover concept and set design of the album.

LASCELLES, KENDREW
Dialogue writer for the chain of twelve postcards enclosed with EXILE ON MAIN ST.

LASFARQUE, JUDGE ANDRÉ
French official who questioned Mick, Charlie, Bill, and Mick Taylor concerning violation of drug laws while they were living in France.

LASLO, LARRY
Title calligrapher for STONE ALONE LP cover.

LASSO FROM EL PASSO
1976 Kinky Friedman LP featuring Ron.

"LAST TIME, THE"
Written by: Jagger/Richards
Recorded by: The Rolling Stones
Release date: February 1965
Record label: Decca/London
Albums: OUT OF OUR HEADS (U.S.)
      BIG HITS (U.S.)
      BIG HITS (U.K.)
      GOT LIVE IF YOU WANT IT! (live)
      STONE AGE
      MORE HOT ROCKS
      ROLLED GOLD
Single: B/w "Play with Fire" (U.K. 2/65) (U.S. 3/65)
• "The Last Time" was the first Jagger/Richards self-penned A side.

LAST WALTZ, THE
Martin Scorsese's 1978 film of the Band's 1976 Thanksgiving Day farewell concert featuring Ron on "I Shall Be Released." Ron also appears on the triple album of the same name.

"LAUGH IN"
American comedy TV show which was the last TV show Brian ever watched, July 3, 1969. Upon shutting off his television, he went out to the pool.

LAVENDER, ERIC
A customer at the Francis Service Station who testified against Bill, Mick, and Brian at their trial in 1965.

LAWRENCE, LINDA
Woman who met Brian at the Ricky Tick Club in Windsor, 1961. Brian encouraged her in her modeling career. Some claim that Linda was the only woman whom Brian ever really loved, and she was the only "girlfriend" allowed to accompany the Stones on their early tours. She gave birth to Brian's son, Julian, but did not sue for paternity because she didn't want to generate negative publicity for Brian. The couple broke up in 1965, and Linda moved to America with her son. Opting for a more acoustic life-style, she is now married to Donovan Leitch (the famed sixties folkie, Donovan).

LAWRENCE, RAY
Designer of the GOATS HEAD SOUP LP cover.

LAWSON, DAVE
Synthesizer player on BILL WYMAN.

LAWSON, JANET
Nurse who lived in the guest apartment at Cotchford and was with Brian the night he died. She pumped water out of him and massaged his chest for fifteen minutes in an attempt to save him.

LE'MESURIER, ROBIN
Guitarist on "Priceless."

LEACH, ED
Cowbell player on "Ain't Too Proud to Beg."

LEANDER, MIKE
Coarranger with Keith of "As Tears Go By."

LEARNING ANNEX, THE
New York City adult education "school," which sponsored "An Evening of Talk, Music, and Dance" with Professor Ron Wood at New York's Town Hall, January 1983. Ron was witty, charming, and above all, patient, as all around him fell apart—from incorrect videos to stolen guitars.

"LEATHER JACKET"
EXILE ON MAIN ST. outtake.

"LEAVE ME ALONE"
Song recorded by the Stones in 1965 but never released.

LEAVELL, CHUCK
Ex-Allman Brother member who opened for the Stones during their 1982 European tour and joined them in the studio in Paris when they recorded their new album.

LED ZEPPELIN
THE band of the seventies (and subjects of a stunning photo book, *Led Zeppelin: Portraits,* just released by our cover photographer Neal Preston). Mick commenting on the ballyhoo and fanfare surrounding the Stones' 1981 U.S. tour: "Well, Led Zeppelin's not touring; they have to go see *someone.*"

LEE, CARLTON
Assistant engineer on GOATS HEAD SOUP.

LEEDS UNIVERSITY
British school from which the Stones did a live broadcast for the BBC in April 1971.

LEIBOVITZ, ANNIE
Rolling Stone magazine photographer who was co-photographer of the book *The Rolling Stones on Tour.*

LENNEAR, CLAUDIA
Popular backup singer who "Brown Sugar" is rumored to be about.

LENNON, JOHN, AND ONO, YOKO
Participants in "The Rolling Stones' Rock and Roll Circus"—John as a member of A. N. Other, and Yoko on "wails."

LEONARD, BIG LEROY
Security chief for the Stones 1972 U.S. tour.

LET IT BLEED
Artist: The Rolling Stones
Producer: Jimmy Miller
Release date: November 1969
Record label: London/Decca
Tracks: 9
"Gimmie Shelter"
"Love in Vain" (Payne)
"Country Honk"
"Live with Me"
"Let It Bleed"
"Midnight Rambler"
"You Got the Silver"
"Monkey Man"
"You Can't Always Get What You Want"
• 14th U.S. LP.
• 10th U.K. LP.
• Guest musicians include Nicky Hopkins, Leon Russell, Al Kooper, and a dozen other musicians and back-up vocalists including the London Bach Choir. (See individual songs for credits.)
• Studio—Olympic Studios, London.
• Engineer—Glyn Johns.
• Assistant engineers—Bruce Botnick, Jerry Hansen, George Chiantz.
• Photo—Don McAllester.
• Cover and liner design—Robert Brownjohn.
• Sleeve and poster design—Victor Kahn.
• LET IT BLEED came packaged with a poster of the Stones.
• The LP was originally to be called STICKY FINGERS.
• The title is rumored to be a pun on the Beatles' LET IT BE.
• "s."

"LET IT BLEED"
Written by: Jagger/Richards
Recorded by: The Rolling Stones

Release date: November 1969
Record label: London/Decca
Albums: LET IT BLEED
          MORE HOT ROCKS
• Ian Stewart—piano.

"LET IT LOOSE"
Written by: Jagger/Richards
Recorded by: The Rolling Stones
Release date: May 1972
Record label: Rolling Stones Records
Album: EXILE ON MAIN ST.
• Clydie King, Vanetta Fields,
Tammi Lynn, Shirley Goodman, Mac
Rebennack, Joe Green—backup
vocals.

"LET IT ROCK"
Written by: Anderson
Recorded by: The Rolling Stones

Release date: April 1971
Record label: Rolling Stones Records
Album: None, except for the Spanish
pressings of STICKY FINGERS, which
used this song as a replacement for
"Sister Morphine"
Single: Flip of "Brown Sugar" along
        with "Bitch" (U.K. 4/71)
• Recorded by Glyn Johns live at Leeds.
• Reappeared as a single with "Blow
with Ry" from JAMMING WITH
EDWARD. This was sold in Germany
in 1972, with proceeds going to Release,
a drug rehabilitation program.

"LET ME GO"
Written by: Jagger/Richards
Recorded by: The Rolling Stones
Release date: June 1980

Record label: Rolling Stones Records
Albums: EMOTIONAL RESCUE
        STILL LIFE (live)

"LET'S SPEND SOME TIME TOGETHER"
Song the Stones sang on the Ed Sulli-
van show, January 1967, because Mr.
Sullivan objected to the lyrics of "Let's
Spend the Night Together."

"LET'S SPEND THE NIGHT TOGETHER"
Written by: Jagger/Richards
Recorded by: The Rolling Stones
Release date: January 1967
Record label: London/Decca
Albums: BETWEEN THE BUTTONS (U.S.)
        FLOWERS
        THROUGH THE PAST, DARKLY U.K.
        THROUGH THE PAST, DARKLY U.S.
        HOT ROCKS

ROLLED GOLD
STILL LIFE (live)
Single: B/w "Ruby Tuesday" (U.S./U.K. 1/67)
• Radio stations bleeped out the word "night."
• Those stations that banned the song completely played the flip side, "Ruby Tuesday," causing the single to essentially be a double A-sided disc.

LET'S SPEND THE NIGHT TOGETHER
Film of the Stones' 1981 U.S. tour released in 1983 by Embassy Pictures. Directed by Hal Ashby, with creative associate Pablo Ferro, the film shows the Stones performing twenty-five songs, filmed at three different shows, in addition to backstage footage. It is produced by Ronald L. Schwary. Ashby had wanted the ninety-four-minute film to be shown in large clubs where people could dance to the music, but it is being shown in standard movie theaters instead.

"LET'S TALK IT OVER"
Song chosen by Bill for THE BLACK BOX compilation.

LEWES PRISON
Mick was held here for one night pending sentencing after his Redlands bust trial.

LEWIS, ELMO
An early "blues" stage name used by Brian when he and P. P. Pond (Paul Jones, later of Manfred Mann) played together at the Ealing Club, performing Muddy Waters and Elmore James material.

LEWIS, JERRY LEE
For a Dick Clark TV special he taped, July 1983, "The Killer" requested Keith's participation in his hand-picked

band. Also included were Little Richard, Mick Fleetwood, singer Emmylou Harris, and the Celluloid Buddy Holly, Gary Busey. Everybody (including Mr. Richards!) got all dressed up for the event.

LEWIS, SIR EDWARD
Chairman of Decca Records when the Stones were with that label.

LEWISHAM
Bill's birthplace.

LEX HOTEL
Hotel at London's Heathrow Airport that opened in 1973 with ads in the *London Times* showing portraits of the Rolling Stones, Edward Heath (Britain's prime minister at the time), David Frost, Barbra Streisand, and Olympic swimming champ Mark Spitz. Heath was the only one to complain about the company.

LIBRARIAN
The job which Mick was scheduled to perform as an inmate at prison after the Redlands bust. However, due to not being sentenced, Mick was forced to continue in his previous occupation as singer of a rock 'n' roll band.

LICHFIELD, LORD
Gave the bride away at Mick and Bianca's church wedding ceremony.

LIEBERSON, SANFORD
Executive producer of the "The Rolling Stones' Rock and Roll Circus"; producer of *Performance*.

"LIES"
Written by: Jagger/Richards
Recorded by: The Rolling Stones
Release date: June 1978
Record label: Rolling Stones Records
Album: SOME GIRLS

"LIKE A ROLLING STONE"
Bob Dylan song that Keith listed as his favorite song of 1965. He didn't realize it wasn't about him.

"LIKE UNCLE PHIL AND UNCLE GENE"
British subtitle of "Now I've Got a Witness." Gene is Gene Pitney; Phil is Phil Spector.

LINCOLN SQUARE MOTOR INN
During New York City's famous blackout in November 1965, Dylan, Robbie Robertson, Bobby Neuwirth, and Brian were here, jamming in Brian's hotel room. They switched to acoustic guitars by candlelight when the power failed.

"LINDA LU"
EMOTIONAL RESCUE outtake.

LINDSAY-HOGG, MICHAEL
Director of the British rock TV show "Ready Steady Go," he directed the promo film for "Jumpin' Jack Flash," to which Mick credits the song's success, and "The Rolling Stones' Rock and Roll Circus." Most recently, he captured Keith staggering the New York streets toward his Glimmer Twin in the rock video classic "Waiting on a Friend."

"LITTLE T & A"
Written by: Jagger/Richards
Recorded by: The Rolling Stones
Release date: October 1981
Record label: Rolling Stones Records
Album: TATTOO YOU
Single: Flip of "Waiting on a Friend" (U.S./U.K. 81)
• This song was originally an EMOTIONAL RESCUE outtake called "Bulldog."

LITTLE, CARLO

Drummer for Cyril Davies, who played with the Stones on their third date at the Crawdaddy Club. Brian preferred him to Charlie but was outvoted.

LITTLE BOY BLUE AND THE BLUES BOYS

1960 rhythm and blues band originally composed of Mick, Dick Taylor, Bob Beckwith, and Allen Etherington. Keith joined shortly thereafter. After a jam session at the Ealing Club with Cyril Davies and his drummer Charlie Watts, Mick got up the nerve to send the band's demo tape of "La Bamba," "Around and Around," "Reelin' and Rockin'," and "Bright Lights, Big City" to Alexis Korner.

"LITTLE BY LITTLE"

Written by: Phelge/Spector
Recorded by: The Rolling Stones
Release date: February 1964
Record label: Decca/London
Albums: THE ROLLING STONES
      ENGLAND'S NEWEST HIT MAKERS
Single: Flip of "Not Fade Away"
    (U.K. 2/64)
• Gene Pitney—piano.
• Phil Spector—maracas.

"LITTLE QUEENIE"

Written by: Chuck Berry
Recorded by: The Rolling Stones
Release date: September 1970
Record label: Decca/London
Albums: GET YER YA-YA'S OUT (live)
    ROCK 'N' ROLLING STONES

"LITTLE RED ROOSTER"

Written by: Dixon
Recorded by: The Rolling Stones
Release date: November 1964
Record label: Decca/London
Albums: THE ROLLING STONES, NOW!
    BIG HITS (U.K.)
    ROLLED GOLD
    LOVE YOU LIVE (live in Toronto)
Single: B/w "Off the Hook"
    (U.K. 11/64)
• The Stones' second number-one single in the U.K., this song features Brian on slide guitar and was Brian's favorite Stones track.
• An early live version of the song was chosen by Bill for THE BLACK BOX compilation.

LITTLE RICHARD

Mick's original idol, Little Richard was flown in to help floundering ticket sales on the Stones' first U.K. tour in 1963. Richard is currently writing an autobiography, which Mick is contributing to, and is featured along with Keith on the Jerry Lee Lewis TV special.

LITTLEJOHN, DAVID

Author of *The Man Who Killed Mick Jagger.*

"LIVE WITH ME"

Written by: Jagger/Richards
Recorded by: The Rolling Stones
Release date: November 1969
Record label: Decca/London
Albums: LET IT BLEED
    GET YER YA-YA'S OUT (live)
• Nicky Hopkins—piano.
• Leon Russell—piano, also horn arrangement.
• Bobby Keys—tenor sax.

LIVE R THAN YOU'LL EVER BE

Live concert bootleg of the Stones 1969 U.S. tour. Its underground success caused Decca and London Records to release GET YER YA-YA'S OUT. Created out of love for the dollar or love for the band, Rolling Stones bootlegs have flooded the market since LIVE R. There are probably more than 300 bootleg records, not to mention tapes and cassettes—and now videos—currently in circulation, though all are hard to find due to their illegal status. Among many other things, bootlegs

• commemorate Stones tours in almost every city (GARDEN STATE—the Stones at the Capitol Theatre, Passaic, New Jersey, 1978; WE NEVER REALLY GOT IT ON TILL DETROIT, from 1969 recordings) and foreign country (PARIS 1964; LONDON ROUNDHOUSE 1971);

Mick accepting honorary Liberty Bell in Philadelphia at the start of the 1981 U.S. tour.

• cover radio and TV broadcasts (the highly touted COPS AND ROBBERS EP of 1964 and 1965 British radio performances; SUMMER RERUNS, the Stones on American TV shows, including "The Ed Sullivan Show," "Hollywood Palace," "Shindig," "Hullaballoo");
• release studio outtakes (GRAVE-STONES includes the jam of "Brown Sugar" recorded on Keith's birthday, plus various Stones rehearsals in the early seventies);
• celebrate events (HYDE PARK 1969; FIRST NIGHT STAND, a recording of Ron's first concert performance with the Stones in 1975);
• show prejudices toward particular band members (CHARLIE WATTS AND HIS FABULOUS ROLLING STONES 1975 TOUR OF THE AMERICAS);
• and at the height of fandom, reflect the personal likes and dislikes of the Stones themselves (JACK DANIELS ON TOUR from 1972; and OUT ON BAIL, New Jersey and Philadelphia recordings from 1978).

LIVINGSTONE HOSPITAL
Dartford, England hospital where Keith was born a living Stone.

LOEWENSTEIN, PRINCE RUPERT
Mick's business adviser who convinced the band to become tax exiles and move to France in 1971. He eventually became the Stones' business adviser.

LOFGREN, NILS
Songwriter, singer, pianist, and of course, guitarist extraordinaire, Neil Young protégé and sideman, and the *ultimate* fan. The Washington Bullets basketball team was ecstatic over his fight song for them, "Bullets Fever," but no such sentiments from our man Keith, who didn't want to know from Nils after Lofgren's heartfelt "Keith Don't Go (Ode to the Glimmer Twin)," a 1975 plea to his hero not to do himself in on drugs. Although the choice of quite a few American rock

critics during the "Great Guitarists Hunt" of 1975 (as Ben Edmonds wrote, "You couldn't assemble a better Rolling Stone if they came in do-it-yourself kits"), Lofgren wasn't even granted an audition. In 1977 Nils released a cover version of "Happy," repeating the words he misheard on EXILE and coming out with a version much more suggestive than the original. In March of the same year he amended his own lyrics, singing "to the town called Toronto" in "Keith Don't Go," thereby immortalizing Keith's Canadian drug bust in concert and on his live album NIGHT AFTER NIGHT.

LONDON BACH CHOIR
Performed vocals on "You Can't Always Get What You Want," with choral arrangement by Jack Nitzsche.

LONDON HOWLIN' WOLF SESSIONS, THE
1971 LP recorded by Glyn Johns in Olympic Studios, London, and released on Chess Records in the U.S. and Rolling Stones Records in the U.K. It features Bill on bass guitar, shakers, and cowbell, and Charlie on drums, conga, and assorted percussion instruments.

LONDON RECORDS
American record label which released the Rolling Stones' records in the U.S. from the beginning of their recorded career through July 31, 1970, when the Stones' contract with them expired. London launched its biggest promotional campaign ever for the Stones in 1964, but since the end of their contract they have been much more noble than Decca about flooding the marketplace with old Rolling Stones material in various compilations.

LONDON REVISITED
1974 Howlin' Wolf album featuring Charlie and Bill.

LONDON ROCK AND ROLL SHOW, THE
Film of a 1973 rock 'n' roll revival concert at Wembley Stadium with Chuck Berry, Little Richard, Bo Diddley, and more, interspersed with comments by Mick.

LONDON SCHOOL OF ECONOMICS, THE
College Mick entered at age sixteen or seventeen, his good grades at Dartford Grammar School winning him a grant. Aiming to be a lawyer, journalist, or politician (and not a "Street Fighting Man"), Mick studied economics and

political science and did not leave school until after the Stones signed their contract with Decca Records. In 1962, during phys ed class here, Mick accidentally bit off the tip of his tongue and was unable to speak for days. 21 years later, it has still not been determined whether it has affected his singing.

LONDON TIMES, THE
Newspaper which printed the editorial "Who Breaks a Butterfly on a Wheel" after Mick's incarceration in prison for possession of pills in 1967 (see Arrests: Redlands Bust). A copy of the editorial was thrown through the window at Lewes Prison the night Mick spent in jail so that he could read it.

LONDON UNDERGROUND
1974 Herbie Mann album featuring Mick Taylor.

"LONG LONG WHILE"
Written by: Jagger/Richards
Recorded by: The Rolling Stones
Release date: May 1966
Record label: London/Decca
Albums: MORE HOT ROCKS
        NO STONE UNTURNED
Single: Flip of "Paint It, Black"
    (U.K. 5/66)

LONG PLAYER
1971 Faces album featuring Ron.

LONG VIEW FARM
Studio and estate located in Massachusetts, where the Stones rehearsed for their 1981 U.S. tour. Long View comes equipped with two twenty-four-track studios, in addition to the rehearsal rooms, pool room, lodgings, and security. A 100-foot-wide sound stage was built specifically for the Stones at a cost of $40,000.

"LOOK WHAT YOU'VE DONE"
Written by: Morganfield
Recorded by: The Rolling Stones
Release date: November 1965
Record label: London/Decca
Albums: DECEMBER'S CHILDREN
      STONE AGE

LOOKING BACK
1970 John Mayall album featuring Mick Taylor.

"LOOKING TIRED"
Unreleased 1965 Stones recording.

LORD OF THE MANOR OF GEDDING AND THORNSWOODS
Bill. The title came with his house, Gedding Hall, a mansion in Suffolk, England, which was built during the reign of Henry VIII.

LORD TAVERNERS NATIONAL PLAYING FIELDS ASSOCIATION, THE
Organization which received the entire profits (including royalties) from the FOURTEEN compilation LP which featured the Stones doing "Surprise, Surprise."

LOS ANGELES FORUM
The Stones performed a concert here for the aid of Nicaraguan earthquake victims in January 1973. Cheech and Chong and Santana opened the bill, which helped the Stones raise the funds that they donated to the Pan American Development Foundation.

"LOST AND LONELY"
Written by: Ron Wood
Recorded by: Ron Wood
Release date: May 1979
Record label: CBS
Album: GIMME SOME NECK
• Charlie Watts—drums.
• "Pops" Popwell—bass.
• Jim Keltner—percussion.
• Ian McLagan—organ.

LOUISIANA STATE UNIVERSITY ASSEMBLY CENTER
Arena located in Baton Rouge, Louisiana, where on June 1, 1975 (Ron's birthday), he played in concert with the Stones for the first time.

LOUISIANA SUPERDOME
New Orleans stadium where the Stones broke records during their 1981 U.S. tour for the largest crowd gathered for an indoor rock concert. 87,000 fans saw the Stones perform there.

LOVE, JOHN A.
Governor of Colorado, who declared "Rolling Stones Day" when the band played there in November 1965.

"LOVE IN VAIN"
Written by: Payne
Recorded by: The Rolling Stones
Release date: October 1969
Record label: London/Decca
Albums: PROMOTIONAL ALBUM
      LET IT BLEED
      GET YER YA-YA'S OUT (live)
      GIMME SHELTER
• Ry Cooder—mandolin.
• Nicky Hopkins—piano.
• The mixes on LET IT BLEED and the PROMOTIONAL ALBUM differ.
• *Love in Vain* was the original film title of *Gimme Shelter*.

"LOVE POTION NO. 9"
Song which the Stones recorded in May 1963 at their first session with Oldham and Easton. It was never released.

LOVE STORY
Film whose theme music was played at Mick and Bianca's wedding. Her choice, of course.

LOVE YOU LIVE

Artist: The Rolling Stones
Producer: The Glimmer Twins
Release date: September 1977
Record label: Rolling Stones Records
Tracks: 19
(Introduction) Excerpt from "Fanfare for the Common Man" (Copland)
"Honky Tonk Women"
"If You Can't Rock Me"
"Get Off of My Cloud"
"Happy"
"Hot Stuff"
"Star Star"
"Tumbling Dice"
"Fingerprint File"
"You Gotta Move" (McDowell/Davis)
"You Can't Always Get What You Want"
"Mannish Boy" (London/McDaniel/Morganfield)
"Crackin' Up" (McDaniel)
"Little Red Rooster" (Dixon)
"Around and Around" (Berry)
"It's Only Rock 'n' Roll"
"Brown Sugar"
"Jumping Jack Flash"
"Sympathy for the Devil"
• 25th U.S. LP.
• 25th U.K. LP.
• Billy Preston—keyboards, backup vocals.
• Ian Stewart—piano.
• Ollie E. Brown—percussion.
• Recorded live in Paris, 1976-77. Side three ("Mannish Boy" through "Around and Around") recorded live at El Mocambo, Toronto, March 4 and 5, 1977.
• Engineers—Keith Harwood, Eddie Kramer, Ron Nevison.
• Remix engineers—Dave Jordan, Jimmy Douglass.
• Assistant engineers—Mick McKenna, Tom Heid, Randy Hason, Bobby Warner, Lew Hahn, Tapani Tapanainen.
• Tape mastering—Lee Hulko/Sterling Sound.
• Artwork—Andy Warhol.
• Lettering—Francis Pessin.
• LOVE YOU LIVE is a double album.
• "Jumpin'" (as in "Jack Flash") ap-

pears as "Jumping" (with a "g") on the cover and label.
• LOVE YOU LIVE is dedicated to the memory of engineer Keith Harwood: "Those whom the Gods love grow young."
• Mick had to travel to Philadelphia with the tapes of this album for Keith to hear when Keith was at a drug clinic which forbade him to travel more than thirty miles outside of Cherry Hill, New Jersey.
• Reissued on EMI U.K. in March 1980.
• Rolling Stones Records released a promotional EP in the U.S. for LOVE YOU LIVE, which contained "If You Can't Rock Me," "Get Off of My Cloud," "Brown Sugar," "Jumpin' Jack Flash," and "Hot Stuff." The picture sleeve of this not-for-sale collector's item is made up of the black and white Polaroids of the Stones biting each other which were taken by Andy Warhol and which served as the basis for his LP cover art.
• No "s."

"LOVING CUP"
Written by: Jagger/Richards
Recorded by: The Rolling Stones
Release date: May 1972
Record label: Rolling Stones Records
Album: EXILE ON MAIN ST.
• Jimmy Miller—percussion.

"LOVING SACRED LOVING"/"WE GOT IT MADE"
1968 single by the End, produced by Bill, who cowrote the A side.

LUCE, PHILIP C.
Author of *The Stones.*

LUCIFER RISING
Film planned by Kenneth Anger, who cast Mick as Lucifer, and Keith as Beelzebub (Lucifer's glimmer twin). Anger felt that Keith, Anita, and Brian

were witches. The film was not made by the Stones because Mick didn't want to be *anyone's* Lucifer. Anger finally *did* film *Lucifer's Rising* with a Jimmy Page soundtrack.

LUDWIG, BOB C.
Mastered tapes of TATTOO YOU and STILL LIFE.

LUNA, DONYALE
Assistant to the fire-eater at "The Rolling Stones' Rock and Roll Circus."

LUNDSTROM, ASTRID
See Wyman, Astrid.

"LUXURY"
Written by: Jagger/Richards
Recorded by: The Rolling Stones
Release date: October 1974
Record label: Rolling Stones Records
Album: IT'S ONLY ROCK 'N' ROLL
• Nicky Hopkins—piano.

LYDON, MICHAEL
Journalist who accompanied the Stones on the 1969 U.S. tour and chronicled it in his book *Rock Folk.*

LYNN, TAMMI
Backup vocalist on "Let It Loose."

LYONS, GARY
Mixer of two tracks on TATTOO YOU.

MTV
America's twenty-four-hour, cable-TV music channel. In 1982 Mick (among other rock artists) did an "I Want My MTV" ad for commercial television stations. It was rumored that Mick wasn't paid for his MTV commercial, doing it for the good of rock 'n' roll.

MAALIMIN OF JOUJOUKA, THE
The Master Musicians of Morocco recorded by Brian for BRIAN JONES PRESENTS THE PIPES OF PAN album.

MAC "MUNICH"
Assistant engineer on IT'S ONLY ROCK 'N' ROLL.

MACALLISTER, KOOSTER
Assistant engineer on STILL LIFE.

MCALLESTER, DON
Photographer of LET IT BLEED album cover.

MCCRAE, GEORGE AND GWEN
Backup singers on MONKEY GRIP.

MCCUEN, JOHN
Nitty Gritty Dirt Band member, who plays on MONKEY GRIP.

MCDONALD, KATHI
Backup vocalist on "All Down the Line."

MCDONALD, PHIL
Engineer on BLACK AND BLUE.

MCFEE, JOHN
Fiddle and pedal steel guitar player on "What's the Point?"

MCGEE, CHUCK
Stones' equipment manager credited as part of the road crew on STILL LIFE.

MCGRATH, EARL
Former president of Rolling Stones Records; he left in 1980 to manage Jim Carroll.

MCKENNA, MICK
Assistant engineer on LOVE YOU LIVE.

MCLAGAN, IAN "MAC"
Original member of the Small Faces (see Faces, The), Ian played piano and organ on SOME GIRLS, organ on GIMME SOME NECK, electric piano and organ on 1 2 3 4, was a member of the touring New Barbarians, played keyboards on the Stones' 1978 and 1981 tours, and appeared on STILL LIFE and in the film *Let's Spend the Night Together.*

MCLAUGHLIN, JOHN
Guitarist whose work on Rolling Stones outtakes and demos surfaced on the METAMORPHOSIS album.

MCQUEEN, STEVE
Late American actor and sex symbol mentioned in "Star Star." The Stones sent him a prerelease tape of the song for approval. He okayed it.

MADAIO, STEVE
Horn player on 1 2 3 4.

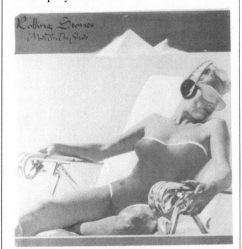

MADE IN THE SHADE
Artist: The Rolling Stones
Producer: The Glimmer Twins
Release date: June 1975
Record label: Rolling Stones Records

Tracks: 10
"Brown Sugar"
"Tumbling Dice"
"Happy"
"Dance Little Sister"
"Wild Horses"
"Angie"
"Bitch"
"It's Only Rock 'n' Roll"
"Doo Doo Doo Doo Doo (Heart-breaker)"
"Rip This Joint"
• 23rd U.S. album.
• 21st U.K. album.
• Released basically to coincide with the 1975 North American tour.
• Reissued by EMI U.K. in March 1980.

MADISON SQUARE GARDEN
GET YER YA-YA'S OUT was recorded at two shows, Nov. 27 and 28, 1969, at this New York City indoor arena. Leonard Bernstein and Jimi Hendrix were among those watching the show from behind the amps onstage. New York City's largest indoor concert hall, Madison Square Garden played host to the Stones on all their recent U.S. tours. Four million fans applied for tickets in the mail lottery held for the 1981 New York concerts.

MAGIC, BLUE
Backup vocalist on "If You Really Want to Be My Friend."

MAHONEY'S LAST STAND
1976 original film soundtrack album composed by Ron Wood and Ronnie Lane, released on Atlantic Records, U.K., for this Canadian film.

MALO, RON
Engineer at Chess Studios, Chicago, who worked with the Stones.

MAN WHO KILLED MICK JAGGER, THE
Brilliant 1979 novel by David Littlejohn about a graduate student and social misfit who sets out to murder "the idol of his generation."

MANASSAS
1972 LP by Stephen Stills' band of the same name, featuring Bill.

MANCHESTER ODEON
British concert hall where in October 1965, Keith was knocked unconscious for five minutes after a bottle thrown from the audience hit him on the head. He was taken offstage, but returned.

MANDEL, HARVEY
American guitarist, formerly of Canned Heat, Mandel played on "Memory Motel" and "Hot Stuff." Mick thought Mandel would be a great replacement for Mick Taylor, but Keith nixed it during the "Great Guitarists Hunt" of 1975.

MANDRAX
Name of Keith's yacht in Villefranche, France. He and Anita were accused of

having drugs on board the boat when they were living in France in 1972. Keith's fondness for the name Mandrax is proven by the fact that he also has a dog named Mandrax. Keith and Anita have been busted for possession of the drug Mandrax.

MANKOWITZ, GERED
Photographer who shot the Stones for the cover photos of DECEMBER'S CHILDREN, BIG HITS, GOT LIVE IF YOU WANT IT!, BETWEEN THE BUTTONS, SLOW ROLLERS, and MORE HOT ROCKS, for which he is also co-art director.

"MANNISH BOY"
Written by: London/McDaniel/Morganfield
Recorded by: The Rolling Stones
Release date: September 1977
Record label: Rolling Stones Records
Albums: LOVE YOU LIVE (live in Toronto)
SUCKING IN THE SEVENTIES (live)

MANSFIELD
Town in England where Bert Richards was hospitalized after being wounded in World War II. Keith and his mother joined him here until the war was over.

MANUEL, VIVIAN
Woman who claimed Mick slapped her across the face when she tried to give him a summons. She sued the Stones for $328,500, claiming their fans trampled her farmland during the 1969 concert at Altamont.

MAPLE LEAF GARDENS
Toronto stadium where the Stones performed for only fifteen minutes in April 1965. The police shut off the power, fearing a riot.

MARATHON MAN
Jerry Hall had a bit part in this film, but it landed on the cutting room floor.

MARDIN, ARIF
Record producer who arranged horns on "Melody."

MARKLE, GIL
Owner of Long View Farm.

MARKS, J.
Author of the book *Mick Jagger: The Singer Not the Song*.

MARKS, SARAH
Secretary at Rolling Stones Records in London.

MARLBOROUGH STREET MAGISTRATES COURT
Site of many of the Stones' drug bust sentencings.

MARQUEE CLUB
London club on Wardour Street in Soho run by Jack Berry. The Marquee organization was responsible for the National Jazz and Blues Federation Festival, which evolved into the still-blasting Reading Festival. Alexis Korner's Blues Incorporated had a Thursday night residency at the Marquee for most of 1962, with Mick often joining in on vocals. When, on July 12, Blues Incorporated were invited to perform live on the radio on BBC's "Jazz Club" show, the Rolling Stones—then Mick, Keith, Brian (still calling himself Elmo Lewis), Ian Stewart on piano, Dick Taylor on bass, with Mick Avory on drums—stood in for them, being the first official Rolling Stones gig. At this club in March 1971, the Stones filmed a farewell show (that's a farewell to the U.K., since they were moving to

France), "Ladies and Gentlemen, The Rolling Stones" (not the movie of the same name), which was aired in Europe. During the taping Keith argued with club owner Harold Pendleton, and swung his guitar at Pendleton's head. Keith missed being brought up on charges for this because he also missed Pendleton's head with his swing. Mick dedicated the song "Bitch" to Pendleton. In spring 1983, the Marquee celebrated its 25th anniversary and Bill, Charlie, and Ian Stewart joined Alexis Korner and others in a birthday jam.

MARRIOTT, STEVE
British pint-sized rocker, leader of the Small Faces and then Humble Pie, who was featured on "In Another Land," and considered for Stoneship during the "Great Guitarists Hunt" of 1975.

MARSEILLES
Mick was hospitalized after a concert in this French town in 1966 after he was hit in the head by a chair thrown at him onstage during the band's performance.

MARTHA AND THE VANDELLAS
Famous American girl group, best known for their hit "Dancing in the Streets." Keith has said that "Satisfaction" is based loosely on that song, though "Street Fighting Man" sounds more like it lyrically.

MARTIN, DEAN
Host of the U.S. TV show, "Hollywood Palace," which featured the Stones' first American TV appearance. (See "Hollywood Palace.")

MARTIN, LINDA
Author of *The Rolling Stones in Concert*.

MARTY WILDE AND THE WILDCATS
British band opening for the Stones on their January 1964 U.K. tour. Current chart-topper Kim Wilde is Marty's daughter.

MASKED MARAUDERS
1969 album by a Canadian band. A giant hoax, this album was rumored to have been made by a supergroup which contained Mick, in addition to Bob Dylan, John Lennon, Paul McCartney, George Harrison, and other notables.

MASON, DAVE
Played acoustic guitar on "F.U.C. Her" and also participated in Bill's band that performed on the Jerry Lewis Labor Day Telethon in 1979. He's also rumored to play on BEGGARS BANQUET.

MASTERS, VALERIE
Once used by Keith as a stage name.

MATTACKS, DAVE
Drummer on BILL WYMAN.

MATTHEWS, SHIRLEY
Sang backup vocals on "Fountain of Love."

MATTRESS SOUND
Ron's garage in Manderville Canyon, California, and site of early recording sessions for 1 2 3 4.

MAXIGASM
A Carlo Ponti film scheduled, but never shot, with the Rolling Stones in North Africa in 1968.

MAY, BARRY
Writer of the first article ever to appear about the Rolling Stones, April 1963, in the *Richmond and Twickenham Times*.

MAYALL, JOHN
British blues champion in whose band, the Blues Breakers, Mick Taylor grew to fame before joining the Stones (he followed Clapton and Peter Green in the lead guitarist slot). Brian rehearsed with him after leaving the Stones.

MAYPOLE PRIMARY SCHOOL
First school Mick attended.

MAYSLES, ALBERT AND DON (THE MAYSLES BROTHERS)
Directors of the film *Gimme Shelter*. The Stones felt the finished project was more a Maysles Brothers film than a Stones film.

MEAN STREETS
1973 Martin Scorsese film starring Robert De Niro in which "Tell Me" is heard.

MEEHAN, TONY
Former member of Cliff Richard and the Shadows, who, as a solo artist, opened for the Stones on their third British tour.

"MEET ME IN THE BOTTOM"
Song chosen by Bill for THE BLACK BOX compilation.

MEEVIWIFFEN, TONY
Rendered back-cover illustration for THEIR SATANIC MAJESTIES REQUEST.

"MELODY"
Written by: Jagger/Richards
Recorded by: The Rolling Stones
Release date: April 1976
Record label: Rolling Stones Records
Album: BLACK AND BLUE
• Arif Mardin—horn arrangement.
• Billy Preston—organ, piano, backup vocals.
• "Inspiration by Billy Preston."

MELODY MAKER
British weekly music paper. The Stones advertised in this paper for a bass guitarist in late 1962 and held the auditions at the Wetherby Arms. In addition to needing a bass player, the Stones needed an amplifier. And Bill was the bassist with the biggest amp. (See VOX AC-30.)

"MEMO FROM TURNER"
Written by: Jagger/Richards
Recorded by: Mick Jagger
Release date: September 1970

Record label: Warner Bros./Decca/ABKCO
Albums: PERFORMANCE STARRING JAMES FOX—MICK JAGGER
METAMORPHOSIS
Single: B/w "Natural Magic" (U.K. 11/70)
• Arranged and produced by Jack Nitzsche.
• Conducted by Randy Newman.
• The version on METAMORPHOSIS is different.

"MEMORY MOTEL"
Written by: Jagger/Richards
Recorded by: The Rolling Stones
Release date: April 1976
Record label: Rolling Stones Records
Album: BLACK AND BLUE
• Wayne Perkins—acoustic guitar.
• Harvey Mandel—guitar.
• Billy Preston—string synthesizer, backup vocals.
• Song was inspired by the real Memory Motel, located on Montauk Point, Long Island, New York. The motel has since closed.

MEMPHIS HORNS
Performers on the 1972 U.S. tour.

MERCEDES BENZ
In February 1976 Mick was admitted to a New York City hospital suffering from a respiratory infection, earlier rumored to be a drug overdose. Mick and girlfriend signed the hospital register as "Mercedes" and "Benz."

"MERCY MERCY"
Written by: Covay/Miller
Recorded by: The Rolling Stones
Release date: July 1965
Record label: London/Decca
Albums: OUT OF OUR HEADS (U.S.)
OUT OF OUR HEADS (U.K.)

METAMORPHOSIS
Artist: The Rolling Stones
Producer: Andrew Loog Oldham and Jimmy Miller
Release date: June 1975
Record label: Decca/ABKCO
Tracks: 16
"Out of Time"
"Don't Lie to Me" (Berry)
"Some Things Just Stick in Your Mind"*
"Each and Everyday of the Year"
"Heart of Stone"
"I'd Much Rather Be with the Boys" (Oldham/Richards)
"(Walking through the) Sleepy City"
"We're Wasting Time"*
"Try a Little Harder"
"I Don't Know Why" (Wonder/Riser/Hunter/Hardaway)
"If You Let Me"
"Jiving Sister Fanny"
"Downtown Suzie" (Wyman)
"Family"
"Memo from Turner"

"I'm Going Down" (Jagger/Richards/Taylor)
*On British pressing, not U.S. pressing.
• 22nd U.S. album.
• 22nd U.K. album.
• Because litigations forced the release of this record, it is nicknamed "Klein's Revenge." The Stones compiled an edition they would've preferred. Bill assembled the songs, for an LP to be called THE BLACK BOX and to be packaged with a booklet of old photos, press clippings, etc. The songs Bill chose were:
"Bright Lights, Big City"
"Cops and Robbers"
"I'd Much Rather Be with the Boys"
"Little Red Rooster" (live)
"Down the Road Apiece" (live)
"Let's Talk It Over"
"If You Let Me"
"Godzi"
"Panama Powder Room"
"Gold Painted Nails"
"Fanny Mae"
"Meet Me in the Bottom"
Instead, Klein chose demos and out-takes, hence musicians like Jimmy Page, John Paul Jones, John McLaughlin, Phil Spector, and a couple of Hollies and more appear, but no one's sure on which tracks.
• METAMORPHOSIS was researched and compiled by Al Steckler.
• Art direction—Al Steckler, Richard Roth.
• Graphics—Linda Guymon.
• Concept—Glenn Ross.
• A METAMORPHOSIS T-shirt was offered for sale on the paper record sleeve.
• NECROPHILIA was the original title of the album.
• Complex and semipoetic liner notes written by Andrew Loog Oldham.
• No "s."

METERS, THE
New Orleans–based band who started out backing Fats Domino, traveled to England with Dr. John, and opened some shows on the Stones' 1975 U.S. tour, 1976 European tour, and the 1981 U.S. tour.

MICHAEL KOHLHAAS—DER REBELL
1969 film starring David Warner in the title role, with Keith and Anita. An Oceanic film production; executive producers, Elliot Kastner and Jerry Gershwin; produced by Jerry Bick; directed by Volker Schlondorff.

MICK JAGGER AND BRIAN JONES AND THE ROLLING STONES
In the beginning the Stones were billed this way.

MICK JAGGER: EVERYBODY'S LUCIFER
Book by Anthony Scaduto, published

in 1974 by David McKay Co.; far from Mick's favorite book.

MICK JAGGER IN HIS OWN WORDS
Book compiled by Miles and published by Omnibus Press, U.K., 1982.

MICK JAGGER INTRODUCES EXCERPTS FROM EXILE ON MAIN ST.
1972 flexidisc which came free with an issue of the *New Musical Express*.

MICK JAGGER AS NED KELLY
1970 United Artists soundtrack LP for the film *Ned Kelly*, produced by Ron Haffkine, featuring Mick on "The Wild Colonial Boy."

MICK JAGGER AND THE ROLLING STONES
Unofficial name by which the Stones are often called. Bill has noted that this only happens in America.

MICK JAGGER: THE SINGER NOT THE SONG
Book by J. Marks, published by Curtis Books in the U.K. in 1974.

MICK TAYLOR
Mick's 1979 solo LP.

"MIDNIGHT RAMBLER"
Written by: Jagger/Richards
Recorded by: The Rolling Stones
Release date: November 1969
Record label: Decca/London
Albums: LET IT BLEED
　　　　GET YER YA-YA'S OUT (live)
　　　　HOT ROCKS
　　　　ROLLED GOLD
• The lyrics quote the exact words of Albert de Salvo ("The Boston Strangler") when confessing to the rape and murder of twenty-five-year-old

Beverly Samans.
• Mick prefers the live version on GET YER YA-YA'S OUT to the studio recording of this song. Keith also prefers the song live, because it can be longer.

"MIDNIGHT SPECIAL"
Song by Johnny Rivers that was Bill's least favorite song in 1965.

MIGHTY STONES MOBILE, THE
Nickname for the Rolling Stones Mobile Recording Studio.

"MIGHTY FINE TIME"
Written by: Bill Wyman
Recorded by: Bill Wyman
Release date: May 1974
Record label: Rolling Stones Records
Album: MONKEY GRIP
• Jackie Clark—guitar.
• Abigail Haness—backup vocals.
• Danny Kootch—guitar.
• Leon Russell—piano.
• Dallas Taylor—drums.
• Boneroo Horn Section—Peter Graves, Mark Colby, Ken Faulk, Neal Bonsanti.

MILES
Compiler of *Mick Jagger in His Own Words* and author of *The Rolling Stones: An Illustrated Discography*.

MILESTONES
Artist: The Rolling Stones
Producer: —Compilation album
Release date: January 1972
Record label: Decca
Tracks: 12
"(I Can't Get No) Satisfaction"
"She's a Rainbow"
"Under My Thumb"
"I Just Want to Make Love to You" (Dixon)
"Yesterday's Papers"
"I Wanna Be Your Man" (Lennon/McCartney)
"Time Is on My Side" (Meade/Norman)
"Get Off of My Cloud"
"Not Fade Away" (Petty/Hardin)
"Out of Time"
"She Said Yeah" (Jackson/Christy)
"Stray Cat Blues"
• 14th U.K. album.

MILLER, JIMMY
British record producer who had a major hit with the Spencer Davis Group's "Gimme Some Lovin'" and went on to produce the Stones' "Jumpin' Jack Flash." He worked with the Stones from 1968 through 1973, producing BEGGARS BANQUET, which he also engineered (along with "Eddie and Gene"); LET IT BLEED, on which he also plays percussion; STICKY FINGERS, on which he plays percussion, too; EXILE ON MAIN ST.; and GOATS HEAD SOUP, where he once again handles percussion chores.

MILLER, ROSE
See Taylor, Rose.

MILNE, A. A.
Author of *Winnie the Pooh* and owner of Cotchford Farm (later Brian's home), where he wrote the book.

MINZAH HOTEL, EL
Hotel in Tangiers, Morocco, where Brian, Anita, and Christopher Gibbs stayed in 1966. In 1967, fleeing the pressures of the Redlands bust, Brian, Anita, and Keith set out to drive there, stopping along the way when Brian ODed and had to be hospitalized in Toulon, France. After leaving Brian behind, Keith and the rest of the party (including driver Tom Keylock and friend Debra Dickson) were arrested for disorderly conduct but never charged in Barcelona.
When they finally arrived at El Minzah (minus Debra Dickson), they met up with Robert Fraser, Christopher Gibbs, and Mick and Marianne. Anita went back to Toulon to pick up Brian, bringing him back to El Minzah, where the couple fought and soon broke up for good, with Anita fleeing with Keith to London.
Brian returned to this hotel about a year later, with then-girlfriend Suki Potier and Christopher Gibbs. On this trip it was Suki who overdosed and had to be hospitalized.

"MISS AMANDA JONES"
Written by: Jagger/Richards
Recorded by: The Rolling Stones
Release date: January 1967
Record label: Decca/London
Albums: BETWEEN THE BUTTONS (U.K.)
        BETWEEN THE BUTTONS (U.S.)

"MISS YOU"
Written by: Jagger/Richards
Recorded by: The Rolling Stones
Release date: June 1978
Record label: Rolling Stones Records
Album: SOME GIRLS
Single: B/w "Faraway Eyes" (U.S./U.K. 5/78)
    Disco pressing: Eight-minute thirty-six-second version on twelve-inch disc (U.S./

U.K. 6/78)
• Ian "Mac" McLagan—piano.
• Mel Collins—sax.
• Sugar Blue—harmonica.
• The Stones "going disco" opened up a whole new audience for them.

"MR. SPECTOR AND MR. PITNEY CAME TOO"
Unreleased song recorded in February 1964.

MITCHELL, MITCH
Drummer of A. N. Other, though much more famous for being drummer for Jimi Hendrix. Mitchell rehearsed with Brian after he left the Stones.

MITCHELSON, MARVIN
American jet-set divorce lawyer who represented Marsha Hunt in her custody case against Mick and who also handled Bianca's divorce from the same man.

MOCAMBO, EL
Toronto club where the material that appears on side three of LOVE YOU LIVE was recorded during the trip Keith never should have made. The band played here for two nights, March 4 and 5, 1977, for an audience of 500 people each night. For their fee the band got half the bar money. The first night's take amounted to $371. The band loved performing here, feeling like they were back at the Crawdaddy.

MODELISTE, JOSEPH
Meter's drummer, formerly Dr. John's drummer, who toured with the New Barbarians and played on Ian McLagan's 1979 TROUBLEMAKER LP, which also featured Ron and Keith.

MOJOS, THE
British rock band, with drummer Aynsley Dunbar, who opened for the Stones on their fifth British tour in September/October 1964.

MOLLAND, JOEY
Badfinger, then Natural Gas guitarist who auditioned for the Stones during their "Great Guitarists Hunt" of 1975.

MOLLY HATCHET
Band which opened for the Stones during parts of their 1981 U.S. tour.

MONCK, CHIP
Edward Herbert Beregford Monck worked with Bill Graham in the late sixties San Francisco rock scene, handled "logistics" for the Stones' 1969 American tour, arranged the Stones' 1970 European and British tour, and designed stage and lighting for the Stones' Pacific tour in 1973.

"MONEY"
Written by: Gordy/Bradford
Recorded by: The Rolling Stones
Release date: January 1964
Record label: London/Decca
Albums: MORE HOT ROCKS
      NO STONE UNTURNED
EP: THE ROLLING STONES (U.K. 1/64)

MONEY, RONNY
Wife of British R-&-B-er Zoot Money, who met Brian at a memorial concert for Cyril Davies at London's Flamingo Club. The two became great platonic friends. Ronny got Brian started on marijuana, thinking it would combat all the pills he had been taking.

MONKEES, THE
American pop band and TV stars whose members Micky Dolenz, Peter Tork, and Mike Nesmith wore black armbands on stage during their 1967 British concert in sympathy for those devils, Mick and Keith, who were in jail.

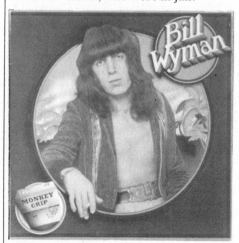

MONKEY GRIP
Artist: Bill Wyman
Producer: Bill Wyman
Release date: May 1974
Record label: Rolling Stones Records
Tracks: 9
"I Wanna Get Me a Gun"
"Crazy Woman"
"Pussy"
"Mighty Fine Time"
"Monkey Grip Glue"
"What a Blow"
"White Lightnin'"
"I'll Pull You Thro'"
"It's A Wonder"
• First solo album by a Rolling Stone.
• Dallas Taylor, Danny Kootch, and Joe Lala form the core of the album

and are assisted by nearly twenty guest musicians. (See individual songs for credits.) Horns arranged by Peter Graves and Bill.
• Engineered, mixed, and production-assisted—Howard Albert and Ron Albert.
• Mastered—Karl Richardson.
• Album design and artwork—Jimmy Wachtel, assisted by Amanda Flick.
• Photography—Bob Jenkins.
• Bill also did five promo films for the LP.

"MONKEY GRIP GLUE"
Written by: Bill Wyman
Recorded by: Bill Wyman
Release date: May 1974
Record label: Rolling Stones Records
Album: MONKEY GRIP
• Lowell George—guitar.
• Danny Kootch—guitar.
• Joe Lala—percussion.
• William Smith—piano.
• Dallas Taylor—drums, Guido.
• Betty Wright, George McCrae, Gwen McCrae—backup vocals.
• Boneroo Horn Section—Peter Graves, Mark Colby, Ken Faulk, Neal Bonsanti.

"MONKEY MAN"
Written by: Jagger/Richards
Recorded by: The Rolling Stones
Release date: November 1969
Record label: Decca/London
Album: LET IT BLEED
• Jimmy Miller—percussion.
• Nicky Hopkins—piano.

MONTEREY POP FESTIVAL
California music festival in the summer of 1967. Brian attended with Nico and Sheila Oldham (Andrew's wife) and can be seen in all his finery in an audience shot in the film *Monterey Pop*. Brian introduced the Jimi Hendrix Experience at the festival, calling Jimi "the greatest guitarist I've ever seen."

MONTREAL FORUM
Montreal, Canada, stadium where an anonymous bomber left a bomb near the equipment truck during the Stones' 1972 tour. No note was left, but the bomb did explode, not doing much damage.

MONTREUX, SWITZERLAND
Needing special care because of her drug problem, Anita entered a private hospital here to give birth to Dandelion in April 1972. Keith and Marlon stayed at the Metropole Hotel. The band flew in later to join the Richards family so the Stones could rehearse for their upcoming U.S. tour, secretly in a cinema.

MOODY BLUES
British group who played at some of the shows on the Stones' seventh British tour in September/October 1965.

"MOONLIGHT MILE"
Written by: Jagger/Richards
Recorded by: The Rolling Stones
Release date: April 1971
Record label: Rolling Stones Records
Album: STICKY FINGERS
• Jim Price—piano.
• Paul Buckmaster—string arrangement.
• Mick Taylor claims that he should have gotten credit for composing part of this song. Mick Jagger said he didn't do enough to warrant credit. Keith, in the end, wasn't even there when the song was recorded.
• "The Japanese Thing" was the original song title.

MOORE, STAN
Security chief for the Stones during their 1972 U.S. tour.

MORD UND TOTSCHLAG—(A DEGREE OF MURDER)

This 1966 film by German "new wave" director Volker Schlonderff, starring Anita Pallenberg as a waitress who murders her lover, with soundtrack by Brian Jones, was Germany's entry at the Cannes Film Festival that year.

MORE FAST GIRLS

One of the tentative titles for SOME GIRLS.

MORE HOT ROCKS (BIG HITS AND FAZED COOKIES)

Artist: The Rolling Stones
Producer: Andrew Loog Oldham with various songs produced by the Rolling Stones and Jimmy Miller.
Release date: December 1972
Record label: London
Tracks: 25
"Tell Me"
"Not Fade Away" (Petty/Norman)
"The Last Time"
"It's All Over Now" (B. & S. Womack)
"Good Times, Bad Times"
"I'm Free"
"Out of Time"
"Lady Jane"
"Sittin' on a Fence"
"Have You Seen Your Mother, Baby, Standing in the Shadow?"
"Dandelion"
"We Love You"
"She's a Rainbow"
"2000 Light Years from Home"
"Child of the Moon"
"No Expectations"
"Let It Bleed"
"What to Do"
"Money" (Gordy/Bradford)
"Come On" (Berry)
"Fortune Teller" (Neville)
"Poison Ivy" (Leiber/Stoller)
"Bye Bye Johnny" (Berry)
"I Can't Be Satisfied" (Waters)
"Long Long While"
• 19th U.S. album.
• Photography—Gered Mankowitz.
• Art direction—Gered Mankowitz and Fabio Nicoli.

• Cover concept—Lenne Allik.
• Album conceived by Al Steckler.
• Inner sleeve photos are from the BETWEEN THE BUTTONS photo sessions.
• Andrew Loog Oldham makes poet again on the liner notes.
• No "s."

MORRISON, JIM

"The Lizard King," American rock poet, and leader of the Doors, who died on July 3, 1971, exactly two years to the day Brian had died. Both were twenty-seven when they died.

MORRISON, VAN

Ultrapopular recording artist who plays alto sax, harmonica, and guitar on STONE ALONE.

MOST, MICKIE

Vocalist who appeared on the first Stones' U.K. tour in the fall of 1963. Trading in his voice for his ears, Mickie went on to become one of the biggest producers in sixties England with such clients as the Animals, Jeff Beck, Donovan, and Herman's Hermits, and later formed his own label, RAK.

"MOTHER'S LITTLE HELPER"

Written by: Jagger/Richards
Recorded by: The Rolling Stones
Release date: April 1966
Record label: Decca/London
Albums: AFTERMATH (U.K.)
    FLOWERS
    THROUGH THE PAST, DARKLY U.K
    THROUGH THE PAST, DARKLY U.S.
    HOT ROCKS
Single: B/w "Lady Jane" (U.S. 6/66)
• Brian plays twelve-string guitar.

MULDAUR, MARIA

American vocalist who performs two of the songs Bill composed for the film *Green Ice*.

"MUNICH HILTON"

SOME GIRLS outtake.

MURCIA, JOEY

Guitarist on "Crazy Woman."

MURRAY THE K

See Kaufman.

MUSCLE SHOALS STUDIOS

Recording studio in Alabama where the Stones recorded "Brown Sugar," "You Gotta Move," and "Wild Horses" in December 1969, all of which were released on STICKY FINGERS in 1971.

MUSICLAND

Recording studio in Munich, West Germany, where the Stones recorded IT'S ONLY ROCK 'N' ROLL and BLACK AND BLUE (except for the song "Melody").

MUSTIQUE

Island in the Caribbean where Mick owns five acres of land and is building a home, which, at Jerry Hall's insistence, will not contain a recording studio.

"MY GIRL"

Written by: Robinson/White
Recorded by: The Rolling Stones
Release date: June 1967
Record label: London/Decca
Albums: FLOWERS
    STONE AGE

"MY OBSESSION"

Written by: Jagger/Richards
Recorded by: The Rolling Stones
Release date: January 1967
Record label: Decca/London
Albums: BETWEEN THE BUTTONS (U.K.)
    BETWEEN THE BUTTONS (U.S.)

"MY ONLY GIRL"

Original title of "That Girl Belongs to Yesterday" before Gene Pitney rewrote the chorus with Mick and Keith.

"MY WAY OF GIVING"/"YOU'RE SO GOOD FOR ME"

1967 Chris Farlowe single produced by Mick.

MYERS, ALAN

Devo drummer who performs on Ron's "Wind Howlin' Through."

NET
Neuroelectric Therapy. (See Black box.)

NAFTALIN, MARK
Pianist best known for his work as a member of the great Paul Butterfield Blues Band. He performs on STONE ALONE.

NAGEL'S MAN
Keith's role in *Michael Kohlhaas—Der Rebel*, a film which stars Anita as Katrina.

NANKER PHELGE
Pseudonym the Stones used for group compositions. Nanker is the act of pushing up the tip of the nose and pulling down the skin under the eyes; Phelge is the last name of Stones' friend Jimmy, who lived with the band in Edith Grove. In 1965 the publishing rights to the Nanker Phelge songs were signed over to Allen Klein. (See Klein, Allen.)

NASH, GRAHAM
Member of the sixties pop group the Hollies, and later of Crosby, Stills & Nash, with and without Young. In February 1964 Nash was in the studio for the recording of the Stones' "Not Fade Away," "And the Rolling Stones Met Phil and Gene," "Mr. Spector and Mr. Pitney Came Too," and "Andrew's Blues." Some of his work with the Stones appears on METAMORPHOSIS.

NATIONAL FEDERATION OF HAIRDRESSERS
Wallace Scowcroft, the president of U.K. National Federation of Hair-dressers, in 1964, offered a free haircut to the next number-one group or artist on the pop charts, claiming the Stones as worst coiffed. Scowcroft told London's *Daily Mirror* that one of the Stones looks "like he's got a feather duster on his head."

NATIONAL JAZZ FEDERATION
The early Stones—Mick, Keith, Brian, Dick Taylor, and Ian Stewart—joined this organization to "network."

NEASDEN
North London suburb where Charlie was born. He was the only Stone raised in a "working class" background.

NECROPHILIA
Original title of METAMORPHOSIS, which was changed because Decca felt that it was in bad taste. Covers with that name were printed but never released.

NED KELLY
1970 color film released by United Artists; produced by Neil Hartley; directed by Tony Richardson. The film was based on the life of nineteenth-century Australian outlaw Ned Keily, starring Mick in the title role. Waylon Jennings sings the majority of the dozen Shel Silverstein composed songs, and Mick sings "The Wild Colonial Boy." For Mick this project was plagued with disasters. Filming was scheduled to begin on July 7, 1969. Because of Brian's recent death (July 3), Mick wanted to postpone the filming. But Neil Hartley threatened to sue Mick if he performed at Hyde Park (on July 5) and failed to show up in Australia. So Mick and Marianne Faithfull flew to Australia on time, causing them to miss Brian's funeral. Added to that, Marianne (who also had a role in the film) attempted suicide shortly after their arrival in Sydney. She was replaced by another actress, and Mick continued filming while Marianne lay in the hospital in a coma for about a week. To top it off, on August 18, 1969, Mick was accidentally shot during the filming. *Ned Kelly* premiered in July 1970 in

Glerowan, Australia, home of the real-life Ned Kelly.

"NEIGHBORS"
Written by: Jagger/Richards
Recorded by: The Rolling Stones
Release date: October 1981
Record label: Rolling Stones Records
Album: TATTOO YOU
Single: Flip of "Hang Fire"
    (U.S./U.K. 81)
• Mick wrote the lyrics for Keith, who has been thrown out of more than one apartment because of his penchant for playing music almost constantly and always too loud.
• The British spelling, "Neighbours," appears on the disc's label; the American spelling, "Neighbors," is on the album sleeve.
• The video for this song shows the Stones with a neighboring prostitute and a hacksaw murderer (both at work), among others. It was banned by MTV after a mass of audience complaints.
• Mick claims the video was filmed in his building.
• Also on the subject of neighbors—it was recently reported that Ron's New York neighbors complained about his all-night parties and loud music. When they threatened to have him evicted, Ron retaliated and bought the entire apartment building.

NELLCOTE
Keith's "white palace" villa on the beach in Villefranche, France, which he rented for $2,400 a week in 1971.

The Stones brought a mobile recording unit to Keith's house and also built a studio in his basement. All of the Stones, plus ladies, moved into the house, and Keith offended them when he gave each Stone a weekly bill for $200 rent during the recording of EXILE ON MAIN ST. The police had the house under observation the entire time Keith lived there, and while he and the rest of the Stones were recording in Jamaica, a warrant was issued for their arrests, claiming drug use in the house. All of the Stones testified that it was *Keith's* house and they were innocent of the charges.

Only Keith and Anita were arrested. In October 1971, all of Keith's guitars were stolen from this house.

NEUSTATTER, WALTER
Psychiatrist who the courts assigned to Brian to help him with his drug appeal. The doctor claimed that Brian's IQ was 133 and felt that time spent in jail would destroy him.

NEVILLE BROTHERS, THE
New Orleans–based band who opened some of the dates of the Stones' 1981 U.S. tour. Keith has artistic interest in their new album.

NEVISON, RON
Engineer on LOVE YOU LIVE.

NEW BARBARIANS, THE
Band formed by Ron to promote his GIMME SOME NECK LP, consisting of Ron and Keith on guitars, Ian McLagan on piano, Joseph Modeliste on drums, Bobby Keys on horns, and Stanley Clarke on bass. The band's first gig was at Oskawa Hall in Toronto in April 1979. The band—plus Stones—did two sets to fulfill Keith's requirement to do a benefit performance for the blind after his suspended sentence for heroin possession in 1977. The profits from the show benefited the Canadian National Institute for the Blind. After that performance Keith and Ron took the New Barbarians on the road for twenty concerts, promoting it by promising "and friends," all of

whom failed to show. Though Neil Young was credited with naming the band, he was among the absent.

NEW CHURCH
Band formed in 1969 by Alexis Korner and Danish blues singer Peter Thorup with Colin Hodgkinson on bass. Brian was anxious to join them, but Korner encouraged him to form his own band. New Church played with the Stones at their historic Hyde Park Concert in July 1969, two days after Brian's death.

"NEW FASHION, A"
Written by: Bill Wyman
Recorded by: Bill Wyman/S. Wyman
Release date: 1981
Record label: A & M
Album: BILL WYMAN
Single: B/w "Girls" (U.K. 1981)

NEW MUSICAL EXPRESS
This British weekly music paper hosts a yearly Pollwinner's Concert that features its readers' favorite artists and at which the Stones have often appeared. At the May 1968 concert at Wembley Stadium the Stones appeared *unannounced* and played three numbers. It was Brian's final live concert appearance. In 1974, *NME* listed the 100 all-time great albums and the Stones were noted six times, with STICKY FINGERS at #9, and LET IT BLEED, BEGGARS BANQUET, THE ROLLING STONES, EXILE ON MAIN ST., and GET YER YA-YA'S OUT all in the top sixty.

NEW YORK DOLLS, THE
Early-seventies New York City glitter band. Mick and Keith always felt that lead singer, David Johansen, was mimicking Mick, though David, in his currently successful solo career, is doing a better job at Eric Burdon. Former Dolls' lead guitarist, Johnny Thunders, spends his time giving Keith a run for the money for the standing-corpse-on-stage title.

NEWMAN, NANETTE
Backup vocalist on "Country Honk" and "You Can't Always Get What You Want."

NEWMAN, RANDY
American singer/songwriter who conducted the music on the *Performance* soundtrack album, including Mick's "Memo from Turner."

NEWMAN-JONES, TED
Custom designer of some of Keith's guitars. He traveled with the Stones during their 1972 U.S. tour as Keith's official guitar tuner.

NEWS OF THE WORLD
British newspaper. In May 1963, the Stones played a charity gig sponsored by this paper. In the February 5, 1967, edition of the paper an article was printed stating that Mick used LSD. That night Mick was televised on "The Eammon Andrews Show" denouncing the story and the paper, and the following morning Mick sued *News of the World* for libel. (It was really Brian that the reporter had spoken to, but he mistook him for Mick.) Mick and the rest of the Stones feel that the Redlands bust soon thereafter was set up by the newspaper in retaliation for Mick threatening to sue. The libel case was dropped.

NICARAGUA
Bianca's birthplace, where in December 1972 an earthquake erupted, killing thousands. Mick and Bianca went to Managua to look for Bianca's family. Her parents were safe, but the devastation moved Mick and Bianca witnessed to set up a benefit concert to raise money to help the earthquake victims. On January 18, 1973, the Stones held a benefit concert at the L.A. Forum.

NICOLI, FABIO
Co–art director of MORE HOT ROCKS album jacket.

"19TH NERVOUS BREAKDOWN"
Written by: Jagger/Richards
Recorded by: The Rolling Stones
Release date: February 1966
Record label: Decca/London
Albums: BIG HITS (U.S.)
BIG HITS (U.K.)
GOT LIVE IF YOU WANT IT! (live)

HOT ROCKS
ROCK 'N' ROLLING STONES
ROLLED GOLD

Singles: B/w "As Tears Go By" (U.K. 2/66)

B/w "Sad Day" (U.K. 2/66)

• Mick came up with the title for this song before he had either the music or the lyrics. He wrote the song around the title.

NIRVANA

New York Indian restaurant which features a sitar player entertaining the diners. One night in fall 1982, Woody took over Shyam Yudh's sitar for a set, with most of the patrons unaware that they were at an impromptu Stone (that's singular) concert.

NITZSCHE, JACK

Arranger at RCA's Hollywood studios when he first met the Stones. He played keyboards on some of the tracks on ROLLING STONES NO. 2 and ROLLING STONES, NOW! He plays organ, piano, harpsichord, and percussion on OUT OF OUR HEADS, performs on "Play with Fire," "Paint It, Black," DECEMBER'S CHILDREN, AFTERMATH, BEGGARS BANQUET, STICKY FINGERS, and arranged EMOTIONAL RESCUE. He also worked with the Stones when he was musical director of the *T.A.M.I. Show,* and composed and produced the soundtrack LP for *Performance.* He has since gone on to produce Mink Deville and Graham Parker and the Rumour, though concentrating on film work.

NIXON, RICHARD

Ex-president of the U.S. whose landing in Air Force One caused a delay of several hours in the Stones' chartered plane being able to leave New York's LaGuardia airport during their fall 1969 tour. In May 1972, the Stones' press office announced that the U.S. army had asked the Stones to do a benefit concert for President Nixon in his bid for reelection against Senator George McGovern. Perhaps they were inspired by the Stones' mention of Nixon and his wife, Pat, in the song "Rip This Joint," which was released that month.

"NO EXPECTATIONS"

Written by: Jagger/Richards
Recorded by: The Rolling Stones
Release date: August 1968
Record label: Decca/London
Albums: BEGGARS BANQUET
MORE HOT ROCKS
Single: Flip of "Street Fighting Man" (U.S. 8/68)

• This song was performed between takes by the Stones at their "Rock and Roll Circus."

"NO MORE FOOLIN'"

Written by: Bill Wyman
Recorded by: Bill Wyman
Release date: February 1976
Record label: Rolling Stones Records
Album: STONE ALONE
• Gregg Errico—drums.
• Mark Naftalin—piano.
• Bob Welch—guitar.
• Floyd Cooley—tuba.

NO REASON TO CRY

Eric Clapton album which Ron plays on.

NO STONE UNTURNED

Artists: The Rolling Stones
Producer: Compilation album
Release date: October 1973
Record label: Decca
Tracks: 12
"Poison Ivy" (Leiber/Stoller)
"The Singer Not the Song"
"Surprise Surprise"
"Child of the Moon"
"Stoned"
"Sad Day"
"Money" (Gordy/Bradford)
"Congratulations"
"I'm Moving On" (Snow)
"2120 South Michigan Avenue" (Nanker Phelge)
"Long Long While"
"Who's Driving Your Plane?"
• 19th U.K. album.

"NO USE IN CRYING"

Written by: Jagger/Richards
Recorded by: The Rolling Stones
Release date: October 1981
Record label: Rolling Stones Records
Album: TATTOO YOU
Single: Flip of "Start Me Up" (U.S./U.K. 1981)

A NOD'S AS GOOD AS A WINK...TO A BLIND HORSE

1972 Faces album featuring Ron.

NORTH WALES SHEEPDOG SOCIETY

Charlie was the president of this British organization.

"NOT FADE AWAY"

Written by: Petty/Hardin
Recorded by: The Rolling Stones
Release date: February 1964
Record label: Decca/London
Albums: ENGLAND'S NEWEST HIT MAKERS
BIG HITS (U.S.)
BIG HITS (U.K.)
GOT LIVE IF YOU WANT IT! (live)
MILESTONES
ROLLED GOLD
MORE HOT ROCKS
Singles: B/w "Little By Little" (U.K. 2/64)
B/w "I Wanna Be Your Man" (U.S. 3/64)

• This was the first single to make it on to the U.S. charts. Phil Spector (on maracas), Gene Pitney, and Graham Nash and Allan Clarke of the Hollies were in Regent Sound Studios when this song was recorded.

"NOW I'VE GOT A WITNESS"

Written by: Nanker Phelge
Recorded by: The Rolling Stones
Release date: April 1964
Record label: Decca/London
Albums: THE ROLLING STONES
ENGLAND'S NEWEST HIT MAKERS
• Ian Stewart—organ.
• This song is subtitled "Like Uncle Phil and Uncle Gene" in the U.K.

NOW LOOK

Ron Wood solo album released while he was on tour with the Stones in July 1975, but five months before the official announcement of his Stoneship. Keith plays guitar on two tracks and sings harmony on one; Mick Taylor is on guitar on one song.

"NUCLEAR REACTIONS"

Written by: Bill Wyman
Recorded by: Bill Wyman
Release date: 1981
Record label: A & M
Album: BILL WYMAN

O

OAKFIELD JUNIOR SCHOOL
School Bill attended.

OASIS FILM PRODUCTIONS
Supplier of the camel Ron is sitting on on the cover of 1 2 3 4.

ODE TO A HIGH-FLYING BIRD
Children's book Charlie wrote and illustrated in 1961. It's the story of a little bird, but it's really about jazz great Charlie Parker. The book was published in 1964.

ODENSE, DENMARK
While in concert here in March 1965, Mick got an electrical shock, causing him to fall into Brian, who fell into the always stationary Bill, who was knocked unconscious for a few minutes by a 220-volt shock.

"OFF THE HOOK"
Written by: Jagger/Richards
Recorded by: The Rolling Stones
Release date: November 1964
Record label: Decca/London
Albums: THE ROLLING STONES NO. 2
    THE ROLLING STONES, NOW!
    PROMOTIONAL ALBUM
Single: Flip of "Little Red Rooster"
    (U.K. 11/64)

OFFICIAL ROLLING STONES FAN CLUB, THE
Annabelle Smith was the first secretary of this club, formed in 1963.

"OH BABY (WE GOT A GOOD THING GOIN')"
Written by: Ozen
Recorded by: The Rolling Stones
Release date: February 1965
Record label: London/Decca
Albums: THE ROLLING STONES, NOW!
    OUT OF OUR HEADS (U.K.)
    ROCK 'N' ROLLING STONES

"OLD GLORY"
Song recorded by the Stones in 1969 but never released.

OLD RAINCOAT . . . , AN
1970 Rod Stewart album featuring Ron.

OLDHAM, ANDREW LOOG
This redheaded teenage whiz-kid (he was younger than any of the Stones) had worked for two of Britain's most famous exports—the Beatles and fashion designer Mary Quant, the latter of whom had stated that he could do anyone's job better than anyone else—before "discovering" the Stones on a tip from journalist Peter Jones. Oldham, with partner Eric Easton, saw the Stones perform at the Crawdaddy Club in April 1963 and had their signatures on a contract by the following day, allowing for the formation of Impact Sound to supervise the Stones' recording sessions. Cleverly playing on the fact that Decca A & R man Dick Rowe had rejected the Beatles, Oldham instigated a bidding war between Decca and other record labels, with Decca—and especially the Stones and Oldham—winning out in the end, with commitments to vast sums for recording, promotion, and royalties. Oldham produced the early Stones records, writing their LP liner notes, and creating the outlaw image that was so essential to separate the Stones from the hordes of British bands who scurried to make it after the Beatles' phenomenal worldwide success. He got rid of "sixth Stone" Ian Stewart because he felt his image wasn't right, convinced Jagger/Richards to become a songwriting team, and in 1965 signed the deal with Allen Klein—whereby Oldham would manage the Stones, and in business affairs, Klein would manage Oldham. To fill the spare time left over from controlling the destinies of "the world's greatest rock 'n' roll band," Oldham managed Marianne Faithfull and some not-so-successful mid-sixties British acts; produced the Andrew Loog Oldham Orchestra and Chorus, who recorded "classical" arrangements of pop hits in the production style of Oldham's idol, Phil Spector; and formed Immediate Records in 1966, with an artist roster that came to include Humble Pie and the Nice, among others.

In September 1967, in the middle of the sessions for THEIR SATANIC MAJESTIES REQUEST, Oldham and the Stones parted ways, though sixteen years later, it still remains a mystery as to whose idea this was. Two years later, in 1969, Immediate went bankrupt, and Oldham went to America. He next popped up as producer of Donovan's 1973 LP, ESSENCE TO ESSENCE, going on to produce STREET RATS for Humble Pie. Immediate Records was relaunched in the mid-seventies, and Oldham's first signing was Marianne Faithfull, the pretty girl whom he had made a star more than a decade earlier. In spring 1983 it was rumored that Oldham was busy both at the controls for Robert Gordon's new LP and writing a book about his life and times with the Rolling Stones. But for the past twenty years he has *always* been in the hearts and minds of all the "hip young malchick" managers (Malcolm McLaren, Jake Riviera, etc.), who with great flair, cunning, and sometimes success, aspire to be as famous as their groups.

they learned of Brian's death. In Brian's honor, and adhering to the adage "the show must go on," they kept on working.

OLYMPICS, THE
The Stones are reportedly negotiating to perform at the 1984 event to be held in Los Angeles.

"ON THE DEATH OF BRIAN JONES"
Poem by Jim Morrison.

"ON WITH THE SHOW'
Written by: Jagger/Richards
Recorded by: The Rolling Stones
Release date: November 1967
Record label: Decca/London
Album: THEIR SATANIC
        MAJESTIES REQUEST

100 CLUB
Small London club where the Stones played an unannounced show in June 1982 for four hundred people. They recorded their set.

"100 YEARS AGO"
Written by: Jagger/Richards
Recorded by: The Rolling Stones
Release date: August 1973
Record label: Rolling Stones Records
Album: GOATS HEAD SOUP
• Billy Preston—clavinet.

"ONE MORE TRY"
Written by: Jagger/Richards
Recorded by: The Rolling Stones
Release date: July 1965
Record label: London/Decca
Albums: OUT OF OUR HEADS (U.S.)
         STONE AGE

ONE PLUS ONE
One hundred–minute color film, directed by Jean-Luc Godard, produced by Michael Pearson and Iain Quarrier; executive producer, Eleni Collard. The movie, a Cupid Production, is a film of the Stones' recording sessions for "Sympathy for the Devil" and more. In the U.S. the film is called *Sympathy for the Devil.*

1234
Artist: Ron Wood

OLDHAM, HARRY
No relation to Andrew. Security guard at Manchester TV studio who turned the hoses on 200 screaming fans who were waiting for the Stones to arrive.

OLYMPIC STUDIOS
London recording studio where Andrew Oldham and Eric Easton first produced the Stones in May 1963, nine days after signing them. At their first session (engineered by Roger Savage) the Stones recorded their first single "Come On," in addition to "I Want to Be Loved," "Love Potion #9," and "Pretty Thing." They went on to record many albums here, including BETWEEN THE BUTTONS, THEIR SATANIC MAJESTIES REQUEST, BEGGARS BANQUET, LET IT BLEED (and JAMMING WITH EDWARD), and STICKY FINGERS, as well as the single "We Love You." Jean-Luc Godard filmed the Stones recording "Sympathy for the Devil" here in June 1968. During the filming the studio ceiling caught fire. On July 3, 1969, the Stones were recording here when

Producer: Ron Wood and Andy Johns
Release date: August 1981
Record label: Columbia
Tracks: 9
"1 2 3 4"
"Fountain of Love"
"Outlaws"
"Redeyes"
"Wind Howlin' Through"
"Priceless"
"She Was Out There"
"Down to the Ground"
"She Never Told Me"
• Charlie Watts, Nicky Hopkins, Ian McLagan, Bobby Womack, and many others, including Alan Myers of Devo, appear on this album. (See individual songs for credits.)
• Studio—Mattress Sound, Chateau Recorders, the Record Plant (Los Angeles).
• Mixed at Record Plant, Los Angeles.
• Engineer—Andy Johns, except for "Wind Howlin' Through," which was engineered by Tom Yuill.
• Assistant engineers—Eddie Delena, Ricky Delena, Kevin Eddy, Karrot Faye.
• Management—Michael Houchin.
• Cover photo—Bruce Burnside.
• Cover collage—David Peters.
• Design—Tony Lane.
• Liner notes—by Andy Johns, who requests that you don't let anyone tape your copy of the LP since "the label needs the money."
• Ron Wood did three self-portraits on the back cover and inside sleeve.

"1 2 3 4"
Written by: Ron Wood
Recorded by: Ron Wood
Release date: August 1981
Record label: Columbia
Album: 1 2 3 4
• Alvin Taylor—drums.
• Jim Keltner—percussion.
• Steve Madaio, Jim Horn, and Bobby Keys—horns.

ONLY LOVERS LEFT ALIVE
Novel by Dave Willis. In May 1966 Allen Klein purchased the film rights to this book for the Stones. Oldham had chosen this story because he found the plot of violent and rebellious youths taking over Britain to be the perfect subject matter for the Stones. Oldham and Klein planned to coproduce the movie, which Decca would finance, with the Stones getting $1 million. It was announced that the movie would go into production at MGM's Boreham Wood Studios in the fall of 1966, but this never came to be.

ONSLOW SECONDARY MODERN
Hatfield, England, school which Mick Taylor attended.

ONTARIO COURT OF APPEALS
Court that ruled in favor of Keith when his Toronto bust sentencing was appealed.

OOH LA LA
1973 Faces album featuring Ron.

OPIUM
Drug which Keith does not take. Yves St. Laurent perfume which features Jerry Hall in its advertisements.

ORBISON, ROY
American performer who toured Australia with the Stones in January 1965. Three thousand people ransacked the airport at Sydney when the tour plane landed.

OSLER, HUGH
Probation officer assigned to Keith after his Toronto drug bust conviction. In 1978 he admitted that he hadn't discussed Keith's use of drugs with him during the year that he was his probation officer.

OTIS, SHUGGIE
American infant prodigy who auditioned for the Stones during the "Great Guitarists Hunt" of 1975. Shuggie is Johnny Otis' son.

OUR OWN STORY BY THE ROLLING STONES
"Official" book written by Pete Goodman and published in November 1964.

OUT OF OUR HEADS (U.S.)
Artist: The Rolling Stones
Producer: Andrew Loog Oldham for Impact Sound
Release date: July 1965
Record label: London
Tracks: 12
"Mercy Mercy" (Covay/Miller)
"Hitch Hike" (Gaye/Stevenson/Paul)
"The Last Time"
"That's How Strong My Love Is" (Jamison)
"Good Times" (Cooke)
"I'm All Right" (Nanker Phelge)

"(I Can't Get No) Satisfaction"
"Cry to Me" (Russell)
"The Under Assistant West Coast Promotion Man" (Nanker Phelge)
"Play with Fire" (Nanker Phelge)
"The Spider and the Fly"
"One More Try"
• 4th U.S. album.
• Jack Nitzsche—organ, piano, harpsichord, percussion.
• Ian Stewart—organ, piano, harpsichord.
• Phil Spector—zoom bass.
• Studios—RCA, Hollywood; Chess, Chicago; London.
• Engineers—Dave Hassinger, RCA; Ron Malo, Chess; Glyn Johns, London.
• Arranged by the Rolling Stones.
• Cover—David Bailey.
• Liner notes—Andrew Loog Oldham.
• Stones first number-one album in the U.S.
• "Satisfaction" is listed without "(I Can't Get No)" on the cover and disc.
• No "s."

OUT OF OUR HEADS (U.K.)
Artist: The Rolling Stones
Producer: Andrew Loog Oldham
Release date: September 1965
Record label: Decca
Tracks: 12
"She Said Yeah" (Jackson/Christy)
"Mercy Mercy" (Covay/Miller)
"Hitch Hike" (Gaye/Stevenson/Paul)
"That's How Strong My Love Is" (Jamison)
"Good Times" (Cooke)
"Gotta Get Away"
"Talkin' 'Bout You" (Berry)
"Cry to Me" (Russell)
"Oh Baby (We Got a Good Thing Goin')" (Ozen)
"Heart of Stone"
"The Under Assistant West Coast Promotion Man" (Nanker Phelge)
"I'm Free"
• 3rd U.K. album.
• Ian Stewart—piano, organ, percussion.
• Jack Nitzsche—piano, organ, percussion.
• J. W. Alexander—percussion.

out of our heads
THE ROLLING STONES*

- Studio—Chess, Chicago; RCA, Hollywood.
- Engineers—Ron Malo, Chess; Dave Hassinger, RCA.
- First all-American engineered album the Stones recorded.
- No "s."
- Photography—Gered Mankowitz.
- Arranged by the Rolling Stones.
- Andrew Oldham plays the political poet on the LP's liner notes, with reference to "riots in downtown L.A. and war in uptown Viet Nam," advising "If the bomb does go off, make sure you get higher than the bomb."

"OUT OF TIME"
Written by: Jagger/Richards
Recorded by: The Rolling Stones
Release date: April 1966
Record label: Decca/London/ABKCO
Albums: AFTERMATH (U.K.)
FLOWERS
MILESTONES
MORE HOT ROCKS
METAMORPHOSIS
ROLLED GOLD
Single: B/w "Jiving Sister Fanny"
(U.K./U.S. 9/75)
- The version on METAMORPHOSIS is different from the earlier releases of this song.
- Chris Farlowe recorded this song in June 1966, produced by Mick, and it's the backing track of this version that appears on METAMORPHOSIS.

"OUTLAWS"
Written by: Ron Wood/J. Ford
Recorded by: Ron Wood
Release date: August 1981
Record label: Columbia
Album: 1 2 3 4
- Ian Wallace—drums.
- Nicky Hopkins—piano.
- Ian McLagan—organ.
- Anita Pointer—backup vocals.

"OVER YOU BABY"/"I'LL NEVER FALL IN LOVE AGAIN"
John Lee's Groundhogs single produced by Bill and Glyn Johns in 1965.

OVERTURE/COAST TO COAST
1974 Faces LP featuring Ron.

PAGE, JIMMY
Former lead guitarist of a small British quartet known as Led Zeppelin. Prior to his days in Led Zep and, before that, the Yardbirds, he was a studio musician who worked on Rolling Stones demos (which later surfaced on the METAMORPHOSIS album) and was also employed as house producer and arranger of Andrew Oldham's Immediate Records. He played lead guitar on Brian's soundtrack album for *A Degree of Murder.* In 1965, the Stones asked Page to join the band, planning to throw Brian out, but Page declined. In early 1975, Page jammed in the studio with Keith, recording a song called "Scarlet" with Rick Grech on bass, though it was highly unlikely that in the "Great Guitarists Hunt," Page would leave the then biggest band in the world—even for the Stones.

"PAIN IN MY HEART"
Written by: Neville

Recorded by: The Rolling Stones
Release date: January 1965
Record label: Decca/London
Albums: THE ROLLING STONES NO. 2
THE ROLLING STONES, NOW!
SLOW ROLLERS
EP: GOT LIVE IF YOU WANT IT! (live)

"PAINT IT, BLACK"
Written by: Jagger/Richards
Recorded by: The Rolling Stones
Release date: April 1966
Record label: London/Decca
Albums: AFTERMATH (U.S.)
BIG HITS (U.K.)
THROUGH THE PAST, DARKLY U.S.

STONE AGE
HOT ROCKS
ROLLED GOLD

Singles: B/w "Stupid Girl" (U.S. 4/66)

B/w "Long, Long While" (U.K. 5/66)

• This song started out as a prank when Bill was playing the organ in imitation of Eric Easton, who was once an organist in a cinema.
• Brian plays sitar on this track.
• "Don't ask me what the comma is in the title—that's Decca's." —Keith.
• Because of the above-mentioned comma, some critics felt this was a racist song. When Mick was asked what the song actually meant, he replied: "It means paint it black. '(I Can't Get No) Satisfaction' means I can't get no satisfaction."

PAISTE
Cymbal manufacturer which features Charlie's name in its advertisements.

PALACE OF CULTURE
Warsaw, Poland, site of the Rolling Stones' first performance behind the iron curtain in April 1967. Police used batons and tear gas on the 3,000 teenagers who tried to storm the concert.

PALLENBERG, ANITA
Keith's common-law wife and the mother of his two children, Marlon and Dandelion, Anita was born in Italy and educated in Germany. She was a model in Paris when she first met Brian—not Keith, Brian—and knew that she wanted to be with him. Three months later she traveled to London and met up with all the Stones, moving in with Brian, with Keith as a frequent houseguest. Anita wanted to be an actress and starred in the films *A Degree of Murder* and *Michael Kohlhaas—Der Rebel,* with parts also in *Barbarella* and *Performance.* Brian,

Keith, and Mick were all attracted to Anita, but she opted for her look-alike, Brian.

Finding life with Brian too violent, she eventually decided she'd be happier with Keith, who loved her also and could never understand why she stayed with Brian. Brian was devastated when Anita left him, and tried to get her back, blaming Keith for taking away his girlfriend. This personal friction between Keith and Brian also affected the band's situation and kept Brian even more isolated from everyone than he already was, but Anita and Keith stood firm in their commitment to each other. "Just because a chick *leaves* somebody to go with somebody else is no reason to feel guilty. It happens all the time. It could have been someone 12,000 miles away, but it *happened* to be the *guy* who stood on the *other* side of Mick onstage. And that's *that*," Keith has said.

Anita has been referred to as "the sixth Stone" (a title she shares with Ian Stewart, however), and her fascination with black magic and drugs have created a mystique as intriguing as that surrounding the Stones themselves. She was also the only "girl" any of the Stones would ever listen to. Anita and Keith, who were together from 1966, publicly parted ways in mid-1980, but as Keith said in a 1981 interview in *Rolling Stone:* "I don't consider myself separated from Anita or anything. She's still the mother of my kids. Anita is a great, great woman. She's a fantastic person. I love her. I can't *live* with her, you know?"

PAN
The goat-god. During a week-long festival in Pan's honor, Brian taped the Maalimin of Joujouka, as heard on his LP, BRIAN JONES PRESENTS THE PIPES OF PAN AT JOUJOUKA.

PAN AMERICAN DEVELOPMENT FOUNDATION
In May 1973 after the Stones' January benefit concert for the Nicaraguan earthquake relief fund, Mick and Bianca presented the U.S. senate with a check for $350,000 to help the victims of this disaster in Bianca's birthplace. The concert raised $200,000, and Mick personally donated $150,000. It was rumored that this "small donation" helped Keith get a working visa to tour the U.S.

"PANAMA POWDER ROOM"
Song chosen by Bill for THE BLACK BOX compilation.

"PARACHUTE WOMAN"
Written by: Jagger/Richards
Recorded by: The Rolling Stones
Release date: November 1968
Record label: London/Decca
Album: BEGGARS BANQUET
• The Stones performed this song in the "Rock and Roll Circus."

PARKER, LORD
Chief Justice of the London Appeal Court who dismissed the charge against Mick and Keith when they appealed their Redlands-bust sentencing. He also heard Brian's appeal after his first drug-bust sentencing (Courtfield).

PARKINSON, DALE
Lawyer who appeared at Tettenhall Staff Court on behalf of Mick, who had three driving charges against him. In November 1964, London's *Daily Express* quoted the lawyer as saying in defense of his client: "The Duke of Marlborough had longer hair than my client and he won some famous battles .... His hair was powdered, I think because of fleas—my client has no fleas."

PARSONS, GRAM
Member of the Flying Burrito Brothers, who recorded "Wild Horses" before the Stones released their version. Parsons was a close friend of Keith's and moved in with Keith and Anita after he left the Burritos. *Rolling Stone* reported in 1971 that a Keith and Parsons LP was in the works, but it never came out. Parsons' country playing had a strong influence on Keith, but others close to Keith reportedly resented their closeness. Parsons died of a drug overdose in California in 1973. Keith still has his white cowboy suit.

PASCAL
Percussionist on GOATS HEAD SOUP.

PASCHE, JOHN
Creator of the artwork for the GOATS HEAD SOUP inner sleeve.

PASSARO, ALAN
The Hell's Angel who was found "not guilty" in the stabbing death of Meredith Hunter, in a trial which finally ended in January 1971. (See Altamont.)

PAST ALL DISHONOR
Film set in the Civil War era. In 1982 Keith was rumored to have been cast in it. The rumors were later denied.

PATHÉ MARCONI, EMI STUDIOS
Paris, France, recording studio where the Stones recorded parts of SOME GIRLS, EMOTIONAL RESCUE, and TATTOO YOU.

PATTERSON, MEG
Scottish-born, California-based surgeon and inventor of the black box, she

numbers Keith among her patients. (See Black box.)

PAUL, GENE
Assistant engineer on BLACK AND BLUE.

"PEANUT BUTTER TIME"
Written by: Bill Wyman
Recorded by: Bill Wyman
Release date: February 1976
Record label: Rolling Stones Records

Album: STONE ALONE
- Danny Kortchmar—guitar.
- Dallas Taylor—drums.
- Nicky Hopkins—organ.
- Bob Welch—guitar.
- Mark Naftalin—piano.
- Guille Garcia—percussion.
- Ruth & Bonnie Pointer—backup vocals.

PEC VARP, LE
Villa in Switzerland where, rumor has it, Keith had his blood changed to get off heroin in 1973. Marshall Chess also was reported to have undergone "the cure," as performed by Florida M.D., Dr. Denber. In May 1975, Keith allegedly returned for a dose of blood that would pass U.S. inspection and allow the Stones to perform their scheduled American tour.

PEELLAERT, GUY
Artist whose book *Rock Dreams* includes paintings of the Stones. After it was published in 1974, Mick invited Guy to a Munich recording session to find inspiration for the Stones next LP cover, and he designed and painted the jacket for IT'S ONLY ROCK 'N' ROLL.

PEOPLE BAND, THE
1970 album by the People Band produced by Charlie.

PERFORMANCE
1970 film starring James Fox, Mick Jagger, and Anita Pallenberg, produced by Sanford Lieberson, and directed by Nicolas Roeg and Donald Cammell, based on a screenplay by Cammell. Warner Brothers released this film in which a criminal on the run (Fox) takes refuge in the home of a retired pop star, Turner (Jagger). Full of flashbacks, flash forwards, and every other kind of disorienting effect, *Performance* disturbingly examines what was felt to be decadence—bisexuality, drugs, mysticism—vs. what might have been the *true* decadence of the "real" world in its back-stabbing and gangsterlike business dealings. Now a cult classic, this film was not universally loved; indeed, there were a couple of years between the film's completion and its commercial release. Many people feel that Mick based his performance on Brian, and that Cammell actually had Brian's life-style in mind when he wrote the screenplay. While Anita and Mick filmed *Performance*, Keith stayed away, busying himself with work on LET IT BLEED, and it was rumored that Anita and Mick had a brief affair during the filming. Mick so hated the final version of the film that he refused to attend *Performance*'s premiere.

PERFORMANCE STARRING JAMES FOX —MICK JAGGER
Soundtrack LP from *Performance*. Mick sings "Memo from Turner" on the album, for which Randy Newman served as musical director. Jack Nitzsche produced and arranged it.

PERKINS, AL
Steel guitar player on "Torn and Frayed."

PERKINS, WAYNE
American guitarist who played on three tracks on BLACK AND BLUE and was a prime contender in the "Great Guitarists Hunt" of 1975. Marshall Chess unofficially announced that Perkins would assume Mick Taylor's Stoneship, but though Keith liked him (a rarity), the Stones decided they needed a British guitarist for the band. It was also felt that Perkins hadn't enough concert experience to handle touring demands.

PERKS, ANN
Bill's sister.

PERKS, DIANE
Bill's wife, who he married in October 1959. She gave birth to their only child, Stephen, in 1962, and the marriage ended in 1966, after she moved to South Africa to live with relatives. They were finally divorced in 1969.

PERKS, JOHN
Bill's brother.

PERKS, JUDY
Bill's sister.

Poster for the Rolling Stones 1970 European Tour created by John Pasche.

PHELGE, JIMMY
Printer who shared a tiny flat with Mick, Keith, and Brian at Edith's Grove. (See Nanker Phelge.)

PHILADELPHIA FURIES, THE
North American Soccer League team owned by Mick, along with Peter Frampton, Rick Wakeman, Paul Simon, and others.

PHILIPPE
Assistant engineer on SOME GIRLS.

PHILLIPS, H.
Pianist on "Infekshun."

PHILLIPS, JOHN
Leader of the Mamas and Papas during the sixties and eighties, who was helped out on his 1977 solo LP by Mick and Keith.

PICKETT, LENNY
Horn player and arranger on STONE ALONE.

PICTORIAL PRODUCTIONS
Mount Vernon, New York, studio where the set for THEIR SATANIC MAJESTIES REQUEST LP cover was built and photographed.

PIGALLE
Original title of SOME GIRLS, named after the "red light" district of Paris.

PIPER, CHRISTIAN
Painter of the Mick and Keith portraits for the covers of TATTOO YOU.

PITNEY, GENE
American singer who met the Stones on the TV show "Thank Your Lucky Stars." Mick and Keith wrote "My Only Girl" for Gene, who rewrote the chorus with their help and changed the name to "That Girl Belongs to Yesterday." He plays piano on "Little by Little" and on the unreleased "Andrew's Blues." Oldham encouraged Gene to try to help Brian write songs, but nothing ever came of this. Some of Gene's other work with the Stones is heard on METAMORPHOSIS.

"PLAY WITH FIRE"
Written by: Nanker Phelge
Recorded by: The Rolling Stones
Release date: February 1965
Record label: Decca/London
Albums: OUT OF OUR HEADS (U.S.)
　　　　BIG HITS (U.S.)
　　　　HOT ROCKS
　　　　SLOW ROLLERS
Single: Flip of "The Last Time" (U.K. 2/65) (U.S. 3/65)
• Recorded by Mick, Keith, and Phil Spector on acoustic guitar, with Jack Nitzsche on guitar and harpsichord after Oldham, Bill, Brian, and Charlie had fallen asleep in the studio.

PLAYBOY MANSION
Hugh Hefner's Chicago mansion, at

PERKS, KATHLEEN
Bill's mom, who was once employed as a factory worker.

PERKS, PAUL
Bill's brother.

PERKS, WILLIAM
Bill's real name. (See Wyman, Bill.)

PERKS, WILLIAM
Bill's father, a bricklayer.

PERRIN, LES
Stones' press agent from 1968 to 1973.

PESSIN, FRANCIS
Creator of the lettering for the LOVE YOU LIVE LP cover.

PETERS, DAVID
Creator of the collage for the LP cover of 1 2 3 4.

"PETROL"
Unreleased Stones song.

PETTET, JOANNA
Actress who lived in Brian's flat on Kings Road before he did. When the police busted Brian for possession of cannabis, which was found in a ball of yarn at the flat indMay 1968, Joanna testified that the ball of yarn had been left—without the drug—by her in the flat.

PETTY, TOM
American rock hero who visited the Stones in Paris in December 1982 while they were recording there.

PHANTOM, SLIM JIM
Stray Cat who drums on Bill's "Rio de Janeiro."

which the Stones stayed during their 1972 U.S. tour. Mick found there were just too many girls to handle there, though Bill had a grand time playing backgammon with Hefner.

"PLEASE GO HOME"
Written by: Jagger/Richards
Recorded by: The Rolling Stones
Release date: January 1967
Record label: Decca/London
Albums: BETWEEN THE BUTTONS (U.K.)
FLOWERS

PLUMMER, BILL
Upright-bass and bass player on EXILE ON MAIN ST.

POETS, THE
A Glasgow, Scotland, group managed by Andrew Oldham in the mid-sixties.

POINTER, ANITA
Backup vocalist on "Outlaws" and "She Never Told Me."

POINTER, RUTH AND BONNIE
Backup vocalists on STONE ALONE.

"POISON IVY"
Written by: Leiber/Stoller
Recorded by: The Rolling Stones
Release date: January 1964
Record label: Decca/London
Albums: SATURDAY CLUB
MORE HOT ROCKS
NO STONE UNTURNED
EP: THE ROLLING STONES (U.K. 1/64)
• The EP version differs from the SATURDAY CLUB version.
• "Poison Ivy" wasn't released in the U.S. until 1972 because it had been a major hit by the Coasters in America.

POLLACK, MALCOLM
Assistant engineer on STILL LIFE.

POND, P. P.
"Blues" name of Paul Jones, who went on to become the lead singer of Manfred Mann. Under this alias, Jones performed with that other Jones, "Elmo Lewis," who wanted him to be lead singer of the Stones.

POP, IGGY
America's perennial bad boy rocker who opened for the Stones in his home state, Michigan, during their 1981 U.S. tour, visited with the Stones in their Paris recording studio in December 1982, and dedicated his autobiography, *I Need More*, to Keith.

POPCORN—AN AUDIO-VISUAL THING
1970 film produced by Peter Ryan and directed by Peter Clifton, which features the Stones performing "2000 Light Years from Home" and "Jumpin' Jack Flash," in addition to clips of Otis Redding (doing "Satisfaction"), Joe Cocker, Traffic, Hendrix, and more.

POPWELL, "POPS"
Bassist on Ron's GIMME SOME NECK.

POST OFFICE
Where Keith had his first job—it lasted four days—during the 1961 Christmas season. He spent his paycheck on records for his mom.

POSTA, ADRIENNE
Singer to whose 1964 party Paul McCartney invited Marianne Faithfull and John Dunbar. It was here that Mick and Marianne first met.

POTIER, SUKI
Model who lived with Brian for a year and a half after he and Anita broke up. She accompanied Brian to Tangiers for his recording of the Joujouka musicians, took a drug overdose, and had to be hospitalized there. She was one of Brian's former girlfriends who attended his funeral. She recently died.

"POTTED SHRIMP"
EXILE ON MAIN ST. outtake.

POWER STATION STUDIOS
Recording studio where Bob Clearmountain mixed STILL LIFE.

PREACHERS
Mid-sixties band which was managed by Bill and contained Peter Frampton in his pre-Herd days and drummer Tony Chapman.

PRESTON, BILLY
American keyboardist who played organ on STICKY FINGERS; clavinet and piano on GOATS HEAD SOUP and IT'S ONLY ROCK 'N' ROLL; played piano, organ, and string synthesizer and sang backup vocals on BLACK AND BLUE; and played keyboards and sang backup vocals on LOVE YOU LIVE. He performed live with the Stones during their 1972

U.S. tour and their 1973 European tour, also performing his own opening sets. He performed during the 1975 Tour of the Americas, for which he was paid as a "half Stone," receiving $250,000 (the same as not-yet-Stone Ron Wood), as opposed to the "official" Stones who each received $450,000 for the tour. Billy's prospects for continuing with the Stones were a bit shaky, because he created so much audience excitement that the Stones found it hard to outshine him. When Preston showed up at the start of the 1976 European tour with his own soundman, Keith knew that Billy really considered himself the star. And that was *not* the way God planned it.

PRICE, JIM
American horn player who was brought to the attention of the Stones when he and Bobby Keys came to England to join Eric Clapton in a band which never materialized. Price toured with the Stones in 1972 (U.S.) and 1973 (Europe) and recorded with them on numerous occasions, including STICKY FINGERS (trumpet and piano), EXILE ON MAIN ST. (trumpet, trombone, and organ), and GOATS HEAD SOUP (horns).

"PRICELESS"
Written by: Ron Wood/Bobby Womack
Recorded by: Ronnie Wood
Release date: August 1981
Record label: Columbia
Album: 1 2 3 4
• Carmine Appice—drums.
• Jay Davis—bass.
• Robin Le'Mesurier—guitar.
• Nicky Hopkins—piano.
• Clydie King—backup vocals.
• Arranged by Rod Stewart.

PRINCE
Minnesota-based flash rocker who opened for the Stones in Los Angeles during their 1981 tour.

PRINCESS MARGARET
One of the Stones' most royal fans, she accompanied the band during their 1972 U.S. tour before falling for disco and John Travolta later that decade. As Mick said, "It's not my fault if Princess Margaret turns up. I can't kick her out. Well, I suppose I could, but. . . ."

PRIORY NURSING HOME
Hospital where Brian was admitted twice during his first two drug busts in 1967. The second time he was at Priory, Linda Lawrence and Suki Potier visited him, Linda bringing along their son, Julian, to cheer Brian up.

"PRODIGAL SON"
Written by: Rev. Robert Wilkins
Recorded by: The Rolling Stones
Release date: November 1968

Record label: London/Decca
Albums: BEGGARS BANQUET
PROMOTIONAL ALBUM

PROMOTIONAL ALBUM, THE
(The actual title of this LP is THE ROLLING STONES. It's listed here and is listed under individual tracks as THE PROMOTIONAL ALBUM to avoid confusion with so many other LPs and EPs of the same original name.)
Artist: The Rolling Stones
Producer: Andrew Loog Oldham/The Rolling Stones/Jimmy Miller
Release date: October 1969
Record label: London/Decca
Tracks: 14
"Route 66" (Troup)
"Walking the Dog" (Thomas)
"Around and Around" (Berry)
"Everybody Needs Somebody to Love" (Russell/Burke/Wexler)
"Off the Hook"
"Suzie Q" (Hawkins/Lewis/Broad-water)
"I'm Free"
"She Said Yeah" (Jackson/Christy)
"Under My Thumb"
"Stupid Girl"
"2000 Man"
"Sympathy for the Devil"
"Prodigal Son" (Rev. Robert Wilkins)
"Love in Vain" (Payne)
• This was a special radio promo album pressed in a limited edition and not for sale to the public. It was intended to be a "program aid" to disc jockeys since it covered the two "greatest hits" LPs and also included the yet-to-be-released "Love in Vain." Two hundred copies were shipped to the U.K. for journalists, since there was no commercial radio there at the time.

PROMOTONE B.V.
The Stones' Holland-based holding company formed for the Stones by Prince Loewenstein.

"PUSSY"
Written by: Bill Wyman
Recorded by: Bill Wyman

Release date: May 1974
Record label: Rolling Stones Records
Album: MONKEY GRIP
Single: Flip of "White Lightnin'"
(U.S./U.K. 1/74)
• Byron Berline—country fiddle.
• Jackie Clark—guitar.
• Peter Graves—trombone.
• Joe Lala—percussion.
• John McCuen—banjo.
• Dallas Taylor—drums.

PUSSYCATS
1974 Harry Nilsson LP which Mick is rumored to perform on.

PUTTIN' ON THE STYLE
1977 Lonnie Donegan album featuring Ron.

QUAGLINO'S
St. James, London, restaurant which hosted the post-concert party for the "Wembley Supergig" concert featuring Crosby, Stills, Nash & Young, Joni Mitchell, the Band, and others playing to an audience of 75,000 at Wembley Football Stadium in September 1974. Bianca was escorted to the party by none other than ace Face Ron Wood, while hubby Mick was thousands of miles away in Nassau in the Bahamas at a party for Stevie Wonder.

QUARRIER, IAIN
Producer of *One Plus One*, who added the complete sequence of the recording

session of "Sympathy for the Devil" to the film against director Godard's wishes.

"QUARTER TO THREE, A"
Written by: Guida/Anderson/Barge/Royster
Recorded by: Bill Wyman
Release date: February 1976
Record label: Rolling Stones Records
Album: STONE ALONE
Single: B/w "Soul Satisfying"
(U.S./U.K. 4/76)
• Dallas Taylor—drums, percussion.
• Bob Welch—guitar.
• Guille Garcia—percussion.
• Van Morrison—alto sax.
• Mark Naftalin—piano.
• Ruth & Bonnie Pointer—backup vocals.

QUEEN ELIZABETH HALL
London concert hall where Mick Taylor performed in Mike Oldfield's *Tubular Bells* in June 1973.

Ringmaster Mick, with Brian, Bill, Eric Clapton, Marianne Faithfull and assorted performers at "The Rolling Stones' Rock and Roll Circus."

RCA STUDIOS
Hollywood, California, recording studio where the Stones worked during their first U.S. tour in 1964. They felt that they needed to record in America to get the proper sound for their records. With engineer Dave Hassinger, they recorded most of THE ROLLING STONES NO. 2, 12 x 5, and THE ROLLING STONES, NOW! In December 1965, they recorded "19th Nervous Breakdown," "Mother's Little Helper," and several LP tracks at RCA.

RAFFAELLI, RON
Cover photographer of HOT ROCKS.

RAINBOW CONCERT
1973 Eric Clapton album featuring Ron.

RAINDROP PRODUCTIONS
Bill Graham's company which handled the staging for the Stones' 1981 and 1982 tours.

"RAINY DAY WOMEN NUMBERS 12 AND 35"
Bob Dylan song which was put on the stereo as the police were leaving Redlands after busting Mick, Keith, and friends. The perfectly timed lyric sang out, "everybody must get stoned," as the bobbies made their exit.

RAIT, GORDON
Employee at Rolling Stones Records, U.K., and at the Rolling Stones Mobile Unit.

RAMRODS, THE
Cheltenham band in which Brian played alto sax before he and Pat Andrews left for London.

RAY, NICHOLAS
Director of *Rebel without a Cause*. The Stones tried to get him to direct *Back, Behind, and in Front*, but the deal fell through when Mick met him and didn't like him.

REA, CHRIS
Guitarist on "Visions."

READY, STEADY, GO!
Compilation album released in January 1964 by Decca Records, to which the Stones contributed "Come On" and "I Wanna Be Your Man." Other artists on the album included the Big 3, Brian Poole, and the Rockin' Berries, among others. Though both Stones songs had previously been available as singles, both the Stones and Andrew Oldham thought it was important to be associated with this ultrapopular British TV rock show, which the Stones appeared on many times.

REBENNACK, MAC
(See John, Dr.)

REBOP
Percussionist on GOATS HEAD SOUP.

RECORD MIRROR
The first music publication to publish a major article about the Stones, in April 1963. (See Jones, Peter, and Jopling,

Norman.) Keith and Mick's photos were on the cover, and Brian was upset that his picture wasn't included.

RECORD PLANT (LOS ANGELES), THE
Recording studio where parts of 1 2 3 4 were recorded and the album was mixed.

RECORD PLANT (NEW YORK), THE
Recording studio where EMOTIONAL RESCUE was mixed.

RECORD PLANT REMOTE, THE
Recording equipment used by Bob Clearmountain and David Hewitt to record STILL LIFE.

RED LION, THE
London club which was once run by Glyn Johns and where Giorgio Gomelsky first saw the Stones performing.

"REDEYES"
Written by: Ronnie Wood
Recorded by: Ronnie Wood
Release date: August 1981
Record label: Columbia
Album: 1 2 3 4
• Inspired by Mick Jagger.
• Charlie Watts—drums.
• Nicky Hopkins—piano.

REDLANDS
Country home in West Wittering, England, which Keith bought in early 1966 for £20,000. It was built in the fifteenth century and has a moat around it. A few months after he purchased Redlands, Keith bought the cottage across the road for an additional £5,000. (See Arrests, for the famous Redlands bust of 1967.) In 1968, the Stones recorded at Redlands, with Jimmy Miller producing and Glyn Johns engineering. They recorded "Still a Fool," "Hold On, I'm Coming," and "Rock Me Baby," all of which were never released. The house was badly damaged in a fire in July of 1973, and again in mid-1982. (Keith wasn't home at the time of the second fire.) Redlands, coincidentally, was the name Keith and Anita registered under at the Harbour Castle Hotel in Toronto in 1977, making that name—after Keith's—the most famous drug-bust-related title in Stonedom.

REED, JIMMY
One of Mick and Brian's blues idols. When Brian became bored playing guitar, he went on to play the harmonica Reed-style.

"REELIN' AND ROCKIN'"
Chuck Berry song on the demo tape Little Boy Blue and the Blue Boys sent to Alexis Korner. The Stones also recorded this song in 1964, but it was never released.

REES-MOOG, WILLIAM
Editor of the *London Times*, who wrote

the editorial "Who Breaks a Butterfly on a Wheel?"

REG KING
1971 Reg King LP on which Mick Taylor plays.

REGAN, KEN/CAMERA 5
Photographer of STILL LIFE LP sleeve.

REGENT SOUND
London studio where the Stones recorded their first album in 1964, in addition to subsequent tracks.

REGGAE
1974 Herbie Mann LP featuring Mick Taylor.

REID, TERRY
Brilliant young British guitarist and groupies' delight (his father accompanied him on tour to fight off the girls), who opened for the Stones during their U.S. tour in 1969. He and his band played a set at Mick and Bianca's wedding reception in 1971. Not having been heard from since the late seventies when he released a couple of folksy-type LPs, Reid may regret having turned down that other brilliant young British guitarist, Jimmy Page, when he asked Reid to join Led Zep as lead singer. When Reid said no, he recommended that Page call Robert Plant, so we all owe him one!

REIFENSTAHL, LENI
Photographer whose photo spread on the Jaggers was published in the *London Sunday Times* in October 1974.

"RESPECTABLE"
Written by: Jagger/Richards
Recorded by: The Rolling Stones
Release date: June 1978
Record label: Rolling Stones Records
Album: SOME GIRLS
Single: B/w "When the Whip Comes Down" (U.K. 9/78)
• Mick comments on Bianca's meeting with presidential son, Jack Ford, at the White House in the lyrics to this song.

REX
The only police dog on the Isle of Wight. The August 14, 1964, edition of London's *Daily Express* carried a story of his adventures labeled: "It's All Over Now for Rex," stating how he patrolled the stage at the Douglas Ballroom as the Stones played for 7,000 fans. After twenty minutes, the noise affected him and he began to snarl viciously at the crowd *and* the Stones.

REYNOLDS, "SNAKE"
Assistant engineer on EMOTIONAL RESCUE.

RICHARD, KEITH
Stage name which Keith Richards used for quite some time. Andrew Oldham

had decided to drop Keith's "s" in hopes that fans would think he was related to British heartthrob (from the mid-fifties onward and still going strong . . .) Cliff Richard. Once the Stones came into their own decision-making power, Keith decided to return to his original "s," and the name appears both ways, all over, to this day.

RICHARDS, DANDELION (ANGELA)
Daughter of Keith and Anita, born April 17, 1972. She spent most of her childhood living with Keith's mother because Keith and Anita traveled so frequently.

RICHARDS, DAVE
Assistant engineer on BLACK AND BLUE. No relation.

RICHARDS, DORIS
Keith's mother. During World War II, Doris drove a van for a bakery; after the war she sold washing machines. She played ukelele and bought Keith his first guitar after he had borrowed a classmate's and found that he could play it. She and Keith are very close, though she has often wondered aloud to the press why her son didn't grow up "normal."

RICHARDS, HERBERT (BERT)
Keith's dad. He was wounded in the service during World War II and worked for General Electric after the war. Keith wasn't close to his father while he was growing up, and they were estranged until quite recently. Bert joined the Stones on tour in 1982, and he was quite an attraction in the audience for Prof. Ron Wood's "speaking" debut. (See Learning Annex.)

RICHARDS, MARLON
Keith and Anita's son, born August 10, 1969. He has been touring with the Stones since infancy.

Bert, Marlon & Keith.

RICHARDS, KEITH

Born: December 18, 1943
The following is reprinted from a fact sheet sent to American fans in spring 1964:

KEITH RICHARDS
REAL NAME Keith Richards.
BIRTHPLACE Dartford. Kent.
BIRTHDATE 18. 12. 43.
HEIGHT 5'10".
WEIGHT 10st.
COLOUR OF EYES Brown.
COLOUR OF HAIR Black.
PARENTS' NAMES Doris/Bert.
BROTHERS/SISTERS None.
PRESENT HOME Hampstead.
INSTRUMENTS PLAYED Guitar.
WHERE EDUCATED Dartford Technical School, Sidcup Art.
MUSICAL EDUCATION Self-taught.
ENTERED SHOW BUSINESS AT: 18.
FIRST PUBLIC APPEARANCE Marquee.
TV DEBUT "Thank Your Lucky Stars."
RADIO DEBUT "Saturday Club."
DISC LABEL Decca.
HOBBIES Sleeping.
FAVOURITE SINGERS Shirelles, Crystals.
FAVOURITE COLOUR Black.
FAVOURITE FOOD Chicken.
FAVOURITE DRINK Orange Juice.
FAVOURITE COMPOSERS Goffin/King.
LIKES Boats, High-heel boots.
DISLIKES Crosseyes, Policemen.
[Authors' note: So can you imagine how Keith feels about policemen who look at him crosseyed, something that's been happening for more than twenty years. . . .]
TASTE IN MUSIC R & B/Country.
PERSONAL AMBITION Rich and Happy.
PROFESSIONAL AMBITION To be at no. 1.

At the age of two, Keith Richards could sing in perfect pitch. It's all been downhill since then. Keith Richards IS the Rolling Stones.

"I don't really have that much to say, I mean, if you want to talk about the Rolling Stones, you should talk to Keith, who, I think, embodies the whole Rolling Stones image. . . ."

—Charlie Watts, 1973

"He was born my brother by accident by different parents."

—Mick Jagger, 1978

"I had always understood that, in the Stones, Keith was the most important—and, I think, in the beginning, I was always in love with Keith much more than anyone else, as a fan. . . . He's the epitome of the Romantic hero. . . . He's turned into Count Dracula now. . . ."

—Marianne Faithfull

"I was scared shitless of Keith for years. The way he looked was so fuckin' evil. . . ."

—Andy Johns

"Classic naughty schoolboy."

—Charlie Watts

"What I love most of all is playing with this band onstage 'cause that's when it's best."

—Keith Richards

"In every other band everyone follows the drummer. That's the standard way of doing things. Our band follows the rhythm guitarist."

—Bill Wyman

KEITH RICHARDS

"It would be ridiculous for me to cut a solo album because it would only sound like the Stones without Mick singing."

—Keith Richards

"What would I have become if I hadn't joined the Stones? A layabout—but a very high-class one."

—Keith Richards, 1964

"I gave up drugs when the doctor told me I had six months to live. I mean, if you're gonna get wasted, get wasted elegantly."

—Keith Richards, August 1974

"I only ever get ill when I give up drugs."

—Keith Richards, October 1974

"I reconciled myself to what I was years ago. I'm not gonna last forever. I'm changing my image, I'm finally getting my teeth fixed."

—Keith Richards, 1974

"Images linger on like shadows. People still see me as the junkie-fiend-rebel . . . top of the death list."

—Keith Richards, 1981

"I've got no preoccupation with death whatsoever."

—Keith Richards, 1974

"Keith puts reality into the Stones. Junk or no junk, it's the only *reality."*

—Jack Nitzsche

RICHARDS, TARA (JO JO GUNNE)
Keith and Anita's child. Born in Switzerland on March 26, 1976, he died when he was only ten weeks old.

RICHARDSON, KARL
Mastered tapes for MONKEY GRIP.

RICHMOND AND TWICKENHAM TIMES
Local newspaper, which was the first to write about the Stones, reviewing their gig at the Crawdaddy Club in April 1963. (See May, Barry.)

RICHMOND JAZZ AND BLUES FESTIVAL
The Stones played at the fourth annual British festival after they returned from their first American tour.

RICK DANKO
1978 album by ex-Band member, featuring Ron.

"RIDE ON BABY"
Written by: Jagger/Richards
Recorded by: The Rolling Stones
Release date: June 1967
Record label: London
Album: FLOWERS
• This song was originally recorded by Chris Farlowe in October 1966 and produced by Mick.

"RIDE ON BABY"
Written by: Bill Wyman
Recorded by: Bill Wyman/S. Wyman
Release date: 1981
Record label: A & M
Album: BILL WYMAN
• Brian Setzer—guitar.
• Stephen Wyman—synthesizer.

RIGHTEOUS BROTHERS
American "blue-eyed soul" duo who opened for the Stones during their spring 1965 U.S. tour.

"RIO DE JANEIRO"
Written by: Bill Wyman
Recorded by: Bill Wyman
Release date: 1981
Record label: A & M
Album: BILL WYMAN
Single: Flip of "(Si Si) Je Suis Un Rock Star" (U.S./U.K. 81)
• Slim Jim Phantom—drums.

"RIP THIS JOINT"
Written by: Jagger/Richards
Recorded by: The Rolling Stones
Release date: May 1972
Record label: Rolling Stones Records
Albums: EXILE ON MAIN ST.
MADE IN THE SHADE
• Dick and Pat Nixon are mentioned in the lyrics.

RIPPLE RECORDS
Bill's record label, with an artist roster of himself and Terry Taylor.

"ROAD RUNNER"
Song recorded by the Stones in early 1963 at their first session with Glyn Johns, but never released.

ROAD TO FREEDOM
1973 Alvin Lee album featuring Ron.

ROBERT FROSSET CIRCUS
Circus which loaned the Stones clowns, acrobats, and a fire-eater for the "Rock and Roll Circus."

ROBERTS, E. H.
Headmaster of Grove Park Grammar School at Wrexham, who, in April 1965, condemned parents who allowed their children to wear "Rolling Stones corduroy" trousers to school. (The birth of "Rolling Stones Clothes"?)

ROBERTSON, GEOFF
Author of the play *The Trials of Oz*.

ROBINSON, JIMMY
Assistant engineer on STONE ALONE.

ROCK CITY
1973 film produced and directed by Peter Clifron, comprised of clips of such artists as Eric Burdon and the Animals, Steve Winwood, Hendrix, Pink Floyd, Rod and the Faces, and more. The Stones perform "We Love You," "2000 Light Years from Home," and "Have You Seen Your Mother, Baby, Standing in the Shadow?"

"ROCK ME BABY"
Song the Stones recorded but never released.

ROCK 'N' ROLLING STONES
Artist: The Rolling Stones
Release date: October 1972
Record label: Decca
Tracks: 12
"Route 66" (Troup)
"The Under Assistant West Coast Promotion Man" (Nanker Phelge)
"Come On" (Berry)
"Talkin' 'Bout You" (Berry)
"Bye Bye Johnny" (Berry)
"Down the Road Apiece" (Raye)
"I Just Wanna Make Love to You" (Dixon)
"Everybody Needs Somebody to Love" (Russell/Burke/Wexler)
"Oh, Baby (We Got a Good Thing

Goin')" (Ozen)
"19th Nervous Breakdown"
"Little Queenie" (Berry)
"Carol" (Berry)
• 17th U.K. LP.

ROCK 100
Book by David Dalton and Lenny Kaye, published by Grosset and Dunlap in 1977, the cover of which is a photo of the Stones.

ROCK RADIO AWARDS
Syndicated U.S. radio listeners' poll-type show. The fifth annual broadcast in 1983 was hosted by Ron.

ROCKET 88
Boogie woogie band formed in the late 1970s by Ian Stewart, with Charlie Watts, Jack Bruce, Alexis Korner, and others. They gig sporadically at small clubs, and released an album, ROCKET 88, in 1981, produced by Stewart.

ROCKET 88
1981 LP by Rocket 88 featuring Charlie.

"ROCKS OFF"
Written by: Jagger/Richards
Recorded by: The Rolling Stones
Release date: May 1972
Record label: Rolling Stones Records
Album: EXILE ON MAIN ST.

ROD STEWART, FACES, AND KEITH RICHARDS
Film of a Rod Stewart and the Faces concert with Keith joining the band for a couple of tunes during their 1974 London performance.

ROGAN, ALAN
On loan from the Who, guitar technician responsible for the care and feeding of all the guitars used by Keith, Ron, Bill, and Mick during their 1981-82 tour. He is credited as a member of the road crew on STILL LIFE.

ROGERS, ROY
Keith's childhood idol.

ROLLED GOLD (THE VERY BEST OF THE ROLLING STONES)
Artist: The Rolling Stones
Release date: November 1975
Record label: Decca
Tracks: 28
"Come On" (Berry)
"I Wanna Be Your Man" (Lennon/McCartney)
"Not Fade Away" (Petty/Hardin)
"Carol" (Berry)
"It's All Over Now" (B. & S. Womack)
"Little Red Rooster" (Dixon)
"Time Is on My Side" (Meade/Norman)
"The Last Time"
"(I Can't Get No) Satisfaction"
"Get Off of My Cloud"
"19th Nervous Breakdown"
"As Tears Go By" (Jagger/Richards/Oldham)

"Under My Thumb"
"Lady Jane"
"Out of Time"
"Paint It, Black"
"Have You Seen Your Mother, Baby, Standing in the Shadow?"
"Let's Spend the Night Together"
"Ruby Tuesday"
"Yesterday's Papers"
"We Love You"
"She's a Rainbow"
"Jumpin' Jack Flash"
"Honky Tonk Women"
"Sympathy for the Devil"
"Street Fighting Man"
"Midnight Rambler"
"Gimmie Shelter"
• 23rd U.K. LP.
• ROLLED GOLD was compiled by Stones chronicler Roy Carr and Decca employee Alan Fitter.
• The LP was originally scheduled for Christmas 1974, as a three-record boxed set called THE ESSENTIAL ROLLING STONES, but the METAMORPHOSIS negotiations delayed it, eventually causing the change in concept and title.

ROLLED GOLD VOL. 2
1981 Decca double-album Stones compilation featuring twenty tracks all available elsewhere.

"ROLLIN' STONE BLUES"
Muddy Waters song from which the Stones took their name.

ROLLIN' STONES, THE
Name the band came up with the day before their first gig at the Marquee Club in 1962. The "g" at the end of "Rollin'" was added later on.

ROLLING STONE MAGAZINE
Mick was a major shareholder in the British edition of this paper. He wanted to be involved in editorial content and day-to-day activities, but because he didn't have the time, the British edition ceased to exist in November 1969. Meanwhile, back in America, negative reviews by the biweekly publication of the SOME GIRLS album and 1978 U.S. concerts caused the Stones to ban

Rolling Stone reporters from attending their concerts. They threw Chet Flippo off their tour, refusing to give any more interviews to *Rolling Stone.* In the September 21, 1978 issue of *Rolling Stone,* publisher Jann Wenner wrote an editorial retraction of Paul Nelson's negative review of SOME GIRLS. Eventually relations were re-established with the magazine.

ROLLING STONES, THE
"I hope they don't think we're a rock 'n' roll outfit."
    —Mick Jagger, 1963

The World's Greatest Rock 'n' Roll Band. (See A to Z, this book.)

ROLLING STONES (EP), THE
Artist: The Rolling Stones
Producer: Impact Sound/Eric Easton
Release date: January 1964
Record label: Decca
Tracks: 4
"Bye Bye Johnny" (Berry)
"Money" (Gordy Jr./Bradford)
"You Better Move On" (Alexander)
"Poison Ivy" (Leiber/Stoller)

ROLLING STONES, THE
Artist: The Rolling Stones
Producer: Andrew Loog Oldham and Eric Easton for Impact Sound
Record label: Decca
Release date: April 1964
Tracks: 12
"Route 66" (Troup)
"I Just Want to Make Love to You" (Dixon)
"Honest I Do" (Reed)
"I Need You Baby (Mona)" (McDaniels)
"Now I've Got a Witness (Like Uncle Phil and Uncle Gene)" (Nanker Phelge)
"Little by Little" (Phelge/Spector)
"I'm a King Bee" (Moore)
"Carol" (Berry)
"Tell Me (You're Coming Back)"
"Can I Get a Witness" (Holland/Dozier/Holland)
"You Can Make It if You Try" (Jarrett)
"Walking the Dog" (Thomas)
• lst U.K. LP.

• Studio—Regent Sound, London.
• Photography—Nicholas Wright.
• Oldham believed that the Stones had such a thoroughly defined image long before they had a musical identity, and was so positive that the record-buying public was just waiting for the LP, he removed everything but the band's photo and the Decca logo from the front cover. No names, no words.
• Oldham's liner notes, on the other hand, did have a lot to say. Here appeared his now legendary words, "The Rolling Stones are more than just a group—they are a way of life," for the first time.
• The LP sold 100,000 copies.

ROLLING STONES, THE
Book edited by David Dalton, published in the U.K. by Star Books, 1975; and in the U.S. by Quick Fox Books, 1979.

ROLLING STONES, THE
Rolling Stone magazine's compilation of their best articles on the Stones, published by Straight Arrow in 1975.

ROLLING STONES AMERICAN FAN CLUB
Group whose membership was 80,000 by the fall of 1964, even though the Stones hadn't had a major hit in America yet.

ROLLING STONES AMERICAN TOUR 1972
Double album, with Stevie Wonder's set included, which the Stones wanted to release on Rolling Stones Records. They were stopped by Decca Records and Allen Klein, who said that they owned the rights to "Honky Tonk Women," "Jumpin' Jack Flash," and "Satisfaction," all of which were included on the album.

ROLLING STONES BEER
In 1973, the Stones planned to market their own brand of beer. They were looking for the highest brewery bid to set their plan in motion when the idea was dropped.

ROLLING STONES CLOTHES
A line of children's sportswear that Mick has threatened to spring on the world in 1984.

ROLLING STONES: AN ILLUSTRATED DISCOGRAPHY, THE
Book following the Stones' recorded career, compiled by Miles, and published by Omnibus Press, U.K., 1981.

ROLLING STONES: AN ILLUSTRATED RECORD, THE
Roy Carr's album-sized history of the Stones, published in 1976 by Harmony Books, New York. Sadly, now out of print.

ROLLING STONES IN CONCERT, THE
Book written by Linda Martin and published by Colour Library Books, U.K., 1982.

ROLLING STONES IN THEIR OWN WORDS, THE

Book of quotes compiled by David Dalton and Mick Farren, published by Omnibus Press, U.K., 1980.

ROLLING STONES: THE FIRST TWENTY YEARS, THE

History written and edited by David Dalton and published by Alfred A. Knopf, New York, in 1981.

ROLLING STONES: THE LAST TOUR, THE

Book consisting of photos by Philip Kamin and text by Peter Goddard, chronicling the Stones' 1981 U.S. tour. Published in 1982 by Beaufort Books, Inc., New York.

ROLLING STONES MOBILE UNIT, THE

Known as the "Mighty Stones Mobile," this recording studio-on-wheels is a thirteen-foot-high, thirty-two-foot-long air-conditioned truck. The Stones used this when they recorded parts of STICKY FINGERS, EXILE ON MAIN ST., BLACK AND BLUE, SOME GIRLS, and EMOTIONAL RESCUE. In the May 29-June 3, 1971, issue of Britain's *Melody Maker,* the Stones placed an ad for anyone interested in renting their Mobile, advising them to contact Stella in the Stones office for details. Ian Stewart is now in charge of the Mobile Unit.

ROLLING STONES MONTHLY BOOK, THE

Fan magazine published by Beat Publications, U.K. The first issue came out on June 10, 1964. It consisted of articles about and photos of the Stones, and was published monthly for two and a half years, folding after its thirtieth issue in November 1966.

ROLLING STONES NO. 2, THE

Artist: The Rolling Stones
Producer: Andrew Loog Oldham for Impact Sound
Release date: January 1965
Record label: Decca
Tracks: 12
"**Everybody Needs Somebody to Love**" (Russell/Burke/Wexler)

"**Down Home Girl**" (Leiber/Butler)
"**You Can't Catch Me**" (Berry)
"**Time Is on My Side**" (Meade/Norman)
"**What a Shame**"
"**Grown Up Wrong**"
"**Down the Road Apiece**" (Raye)
"**Under the Boardwalk**" (Resnick/Young)
"**I Can't Be Satisfied**" (Waters)
"**Pain in My Heart**" (Neville)
"**Off the Hook**"
"**Suzie Q**" (Hawkins/Lewis/Broadwater)
• 2nd U.K. LP.
• Jack Nitzsche—piano.
• Ian Stewart—piano, organ.
• Studios—Chess, Chicago; RCA, Hollywood; Regent, London.
• Engineers—Ron Malo, Dave Hassinger.
• Arranged by the Rolling Stones.
• Cover photo—David Bailey.
• Andrew Oldham wrote the liner notes to this during his Anthony Burgess/*A Clockwork Orange*-influenced period, referring to the "Stones, a new groupie who like wild and good. Their music is Berry-chuck." There was no comment on Andrew's artistry from the "hip malchicks who prance the street," aka the Stones.
• "s."

ROLLING STONES, NOW!, THE

Artist: The Rolling Stones
Producer: Andrew Loog Oldham for Impact Sound
Release date: February 1965
Record label: London
Tracks: 12
"**Everybody Needs Somebody to Love**" (Russell/Burke/Wexler)
"**Down Home Girl**" (Leiber/Butler)
"**You Can't Catch Me**" (Berry)
"**Heart of Stone**"
"**What a Shame**"
"**Mona (I Need You Baby)**" (McDaniels)
"**Down the Road Apiece**" (Raye)
"**Off the Hook**"
"**Pain in My Heart**"
"**Oh Baby (We Got a Good Thing Goin')**" (Ozen)

"**Little Red Rooster**" (Dixon)
"**Surprise, Surprise**"
• 3rd U.S. LP.
• Jack Nitzsche—piano, Nitzsche-phone.
• Ian Stewart—piano.
• Ian Stewart is credited on the back cover with playing organ on "Time Is on My Side," which is *not* on the album.
• Studio—Chess, Chicago; RCA, Hollywood; Regent Sound, London.
• Engineers—Ron Malo, Dave Hassinger.
• Arranged by the Rolling Stones.
• Cover photo—David Bailey.
• The liner notes are the same as those for THE ROLLING STONES NO. 2.
• "s."

ROLLING STONES ON TOUR, THE

Book published in 1978 by Dragon's Dream, consisting of photos by Annie Leibovitz and Christopher Sykes, with text by Terry Southern.

"ROLLING STONES: PAST AND PRESENT"

Twelve-hour radio special broadcast by 275 U.S. radio stations in October 1982.

ROLLING STONES RECORDS

The Stones' own record label, started in 1971. In spring of that year, the

Stones signed with Kinney National (Warner Communications) to distribute Rolling Stones Records through its Atlantic Records division. Andy Warhol designed the corporate tongue logo, and "Brown Sugar," the label's first single, was released on April 13, followed a couple of weeks later by

STICKY FINGERS, the label's first LP. Marshall Chess, son of the founder of Chess Records, was brought in to head the label. In the mid-seventies he was replaced by Earl McGrath, and in 1980 Art Collins assumed the vice-presidency of the company. Though the Stones have always been on their own roster, other artists have come and gone, including Bill Wyman as solo artist, and Peter Tosh. In February 1977, Rolling Stones Records contracted to have EMI license its product everywhere but in the U.S., and many Rolling Stone Record albums have been re-released in the U.K. since. In August 1983 the Rolling Stones signed with CBS effective 1985 when all their other contracts will expire. The deal reportedly requires the Stones to supply four albums in exchange for a figure somewhere between twenty and twenty-five million dollars.

"ROLLING STONES' ROCK AND ROLL CIRCUS, THE"
Filmed on December 10 and 11, 1968, this extravaganza, produced by Mick and directed by Michael Lindsay-Hogg, was intended to be a BBC-TV special to promote the BEGGARS BANQUET album. It turned into a never-aired multimedia event with the Who, Eric Clapton, John and Yoko, Mitch Mitchell, Jethro Tull, Taj Mahal, Marianne Faithfull, acts from the Robert Frossett Circus (including clowns, a fire-eater, and acrobats), plus the Stones. The tickets were distributed through the Rolling Stones Fan Club and *New Musical Express*. The audience was given colorful hats and ponchos to add to the circus motif. The stage was set up like a three-ring circus with the Stones and other guests dressed the part. With Mick as ring-master the show began. Highlights included Jethro Tull, Keith dressed as a dandy, complete with top hat and monocle, assisting the fire-eater, Marianne Faithfull performing "Something Better," the supergroup A. N. Other (Keith, John, Eric, Mitch Mitchell, and Yoko) performing a Beatles song, and the Who. The Stones didn't hit the stage until well after midnight, and by that time most of the audience had already left. The Stones (with Rocky Dijon on bongos) performed "Route 66," "Confessin' the Blues," and "Jumpin' Jack Flash," to warm up the loyal few who had waited. And when the cameras started to roll the Stones did two more versions of "Jumpin' Jack Flash," "Parachute Woman" three times, and "You Can't Always Get What You Want." After a break they played "Yonder's Wall," "Walkin' Blues," and "No Expectations," ending the show with "Sympathy

for the Devil" and "Salt of the Earth"—the finale, which the audience (including the Who and John, Yoko, and Eric) joined in on. At 6 A.M. everyone went home.

The Stones weren't satisfied with the finished project, admitting that everything was good—except their set. Fans are still waiting to see this show, particularly because it was Brian's last performance as a Stone. It was reported in 1982 that the soundtrack will be released by ABKCO Records in the near future; Allen Klein denies this.

ROLLING STONES SONGBOOK, THE
1966 LP by the Andrew Oldham Orchestra which features ten Rolling Stones songs, eight of which are Jagger/Richards or Nanker Phelge compositions, plus Oldham's "Theme for a Rolling Stone." Various Stones are rumored to perform on various tracks, but they go uncredited.

"ROLLING STONES STORY, THE"
BBC Radio One special aired in April 1973.

ROLLINS, SONNY
Saxophone player who performs uncredited on three tracks on TATTOO YOU.

ROMEO, MAX
Backup vocalist on "Dance." In 1981, Romeo released an LP entitled HOLDIN' OUT MY LOVE TO YOU, which featured Keith. Shanachie Records, who released the LP, used a poster of Keith, a photo of Keith on the back cover of the LP, and a sticker on the front cover to promote the reggae artist's album. Keith sued the label, and the poster, photo, and sticker were discontinued.

RONETTES, THE
American female singing trio who opened for the Stones on their first headlining British tour in January 1964. On a personal note, Mick and Keith both fancied Ronnie (later Mrs. Phil Spector); Keith got her, and Mick wound up with sister Estelle.

RONSTADT, LINDA
American singer who performed "Tumbling Dice" on stage with the Stones in Tucson, Arizona, during their 1978 tour. Mick was renting her Los Angeles home in August 1978, causing rumors of an affair between the two.

ROOSTERS, THE
An R & B band formed in 1962 by Brian and Paul Jones. By January 1963, *neither* Jones was a member, though Tom McGuinness, who would later play with Paul Jones in Manfred Mann, and Eric Clapton, who would later take over the world, made up two-fifths of the Roosters line-up.

ROSE, JANE
Administrative assistant at Rolling Stones Records, New York.

ROSETTI
Brand name of Keith's first guitar. It cost ten pounds.

ROSS, DIANA
Superstar singer who threw a party for the Stones before their 1975 Los Angeles concert. Celebrities came out in force for the party and some even stayed long enough to watch the Stones. Raquel Welch and Liza Minnelli were among those who attended the show, but they were not amused when Mick threw a bucket of water on them.

ROSS, GLENN
Credited with graphic "concept" of METAMORPHOSIS.

ROSS, MICHAEL
Art director, designer, and co-conceiver (with Bill) of the BILL WYMAN LP cover.

ROTH, RICHARD
Co-art director of METAMORPHOSIS LP cover.

"ROTTEN ROLL"
Unreleased song recorded by the Stones, Paris, 1977.

ROUGH MIX
1977 LP by Pete Townshend and Ronnie Lane featuring Charlie.

ROUNDHOUSE
Concert arena in London where the Stones gave their "farewell" performance on March 14, 1971, before leaving England to move to the south of France.

"ROUTE 66"
Written by: Troup
Recorded by: The Rolling Stones
Release date: April 1964
Record label: Decca/London
Albums: THE ROLLING STONES
    ENGLAND'S NEWEST HIT MAKERS
    DECEMBER'S CHILDREN
    PROMOTIONAL ALBUM
    ROCK 'N' ROLLING STONES

EP: GOT LIVE IF YOU WANT IT! (live)
• Performed by Stones as a warm-up at the "Rock and Roll Circus."

ROWE, DICK
Decca Records A & R man, famous for turning down the Beatles. Andrew Oldham wisely played on this sore spot and scored a record-breaking

record deal for his new boys, the Rolling Stones.

ROWLANDS, BRUCE
Drummer on "(Si Si) Je Suis Un Rock Star."

ROYAL ALBERT HALL
London concert hall where the Stones saw the Beatles perform in 1963. When Brian was mobbed by fans who mistook the long-haired Stone for a Beatle, he realized in a flash that he wanted to be a famous pop star. During the Stones' eighth tour of Britain, their September 23, 1966, concert here was recorded for the GOT LIVE IF YOU WANT IT! LP.

ROYAL CANADIAN MOUNTED POLICE
Officers who busted Keith in his hotel suite at the Harbour Castle Hotel on February 28, 1977. They found almost an ounce of heroin and cocaine on the premises.

ROYSTON BALLROOM, BECKENHAM
Scene of the dance where Bill met his future wife, Diane, in the late fifties.

"RUBY TUESDAY"
Written by: Jagger/Richards
Recorded by: The Rolling Stones
Release date: January 1967
Record label: London/Decca
Albums: BETWEEN THE BUTTONS (U.S.)
    FLOWERS
    THROUGH THE PAST, DARKLY U.K.
    THROUGH THE PAST, DARKLY U.S.
    HOT ROCKS
    ROLLED GOLD
    SLOW ROLLERS
Single: Flip of "Let's Spend the Night Together" (U.S./U.K. 1/67)
• The album version of this song is slightly longer than the single version.
• Brian plays recorder on the song.

RUDGE, PETER
Tour manager for the Stones' 1972, 1975, and 1978 American tours and for the 1977 appearance in Toronto.

RUDIES, THE
British reggae band that played at Mick and Bianca's wedding reception.

RUISLIP MANOR
School which Ron attended, scoring an "A" level in art.

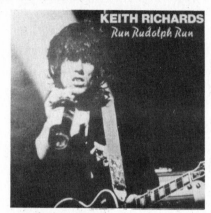

"RUN RUDOLPH RUN"
Written by: Keith Richards
Recorded by: Keith Richards
Release date: December 1978
Record label: Rolling Stones Records
Album: None
Single: B/w "The Harder They Come" (U.S./U.K. 12/78)
• This single was reissued in November 1979.
• Keith hoped to reissue it every Christmas season, but consistently forgets.
• Informed sources say the backup musicians on this song are Ron, Charlie, and Ian McLagan. Keith, who might be the *most* informed source in this matter, credits Ian Stewart and Canadian drummer Mick Driscoll.

RUNDGREN, TODD
Wizard and true star who was a member of the group which Bill put together to perform on the 1979 Muscular Dystrophy Labor Day Telethon. Todd and Bill are both managed by Eric Gardner.

RUSSELL, ETHAN
Cover and liner photographer of THROUGH THE PAST, DARKLY; he also took liner photos for GET YER YA-YA'S OUT and accompanied the Stones on their 1969 U.S. tour.

RUSSELL, LEON
Eternal rocker, best known for his work with Joe Cocker/Mad Dogs and Englishmen, who plays piano and arranged the horns on "Live with Me," and also performs on MONKEY GRIP. Bill and Charlie appear on his 1970 LP, LEON RUSSELL.

RYLE, JOHN
Deputy literary editor of London's *Sunday Times*, who is receiving approximately $75,000 for writing Mick's autobiography with him. They're at work right now!

Early line-up with "the sixth Stone," Ian Stewart on maracas.

S

S.S. SEA PANTHER
Allen Klein's yacht, where the Stones stayed for three days in June 1966 when they were in the U.S., holding a press conference on board.

STP
Nickname for the Stones Touring Party, 1972 U.S. tour.

S.T.P: A JOURNEY THROUGH AMERICA WITH THE ROLLING STONES
Robert Greenfeld's book on the Stones' 1972 U.S. tour, published by E.P. Dutton, U.S., 1974.

STP NEWSLETTER
Daily newsletter published during the Stones' 1972 U.S. tour.

SACHS, DR. ALBERT
Physician who performed the autopsy on Brian at Queen Victoria Hospital, reporting drowning, drugs, and liver degeneration.

"SAD DAY"
Written by: Jagger/Richards
Recorded by: The Rolling Stones

Release date: February 1966
Record label: London/Decca
Album: NO STONE UNTURNED
Singles: Flip of "19th Nervous Break-
down" (U.S. 4/73)
B/w "You Can't Always Get
What You Want" (U.K. 4/73)
• This song took seven years after its U.S. release to come out in the U.K.

SAGE, BARRY
Assistant engineer on SOME GIRLS.

SAINT ANNE CHAPEL, ST. TROPEZ, FRANCE
Site of Mick and Bianca's wedding, May 12, 1971, which was attended by scores of rock luminaries.

ST. GEORGE'S HOSPITAL
British hospital where Brian was treated in December 1967, after collapsing under the strain of his drug busts and criminal charges.

ST. JOSEPH'S CONVENT SCHOOL
Reading, England, school which Marianne Faithfull was attending when she first met Mick.

ST. LAURENT, YVES
French fashion designer whose clothes Bianca modeled for London's *Daily Mirror,* July 1973. The YSL fragrance, Opium, features Jerry Hall in its

advertising. Does Mick own stock in the company?

ST. MARK'S BAR AND GRILL
Greenwich Village "bistro"—the pink place—where the indoor sequence of the promo film for "Waiting on a Friend" was shot.

ST. MARY'S HOSPITAL
Paddington, England, hospital where Marsha Hunt had Mick's baby, Karis, in November 1970. Mick took them both home from the hospital.

ST. PAUL, MINNESOTA
After the show at this stop on the 1978 tour, Bill fell off the stage when he leaned against a curtain he mistakenly thought was covering a wall. He chipped a bone in his left hand, had a swollen wrist, a scalp cut, and was unconscious for five minutes. Bill couldn't fall off stage *during* the show because he never moves while performing.

ST. REGIS HOTEL, NEW YORK CITY
Fashionable hotel where Mick's twenty-ninth birthday party was held on July 26, 1972, after the last show of their American tour at Madison Square Garden. Ahmet Ertegun hosted the bash and invited 500 guests, including Zsa Zsa Gabor, Woody Allen, Dick

Cavett, Truman Capote, and Dylan. Muddy Waters and Count Basie and his Orchestra performed.

"SALT OF THE EARTH"
Written by: Jagger/Richards
Recorded by: The Rolling Stones
Release date: November 1968
Record label: Decca/London
Album: BEGGARS BANQUET
• Keith sings the first verse, which is the first time his voice is heard singing solo on record.
• Stones performed this song, with the Who, at the finale of the "Rock and Roll Circus," with John Lennon, Yoko Ono, and Eric Clapton joining in on the last chorus.

SAMUELSOHN, BRAD
Assistant engineer on EMOTIONAL RESCUE.

SAN BERNARDINO, CALIFORNIA
First stop on the Rolling Stones' first tour of the U.S.—probably agreed upon because it is, indeed, on "Route 66."

SAN REMO SONG FESTIVAL
Mick attended this festival in Italy with Marianne Faithfull. Mick claimed that on the way home to London he purchased—from a vending machine at the airport—the pills he had with him when he was busted at Redlands.

SANCHEZ, TONY
Author of *Up and Down with the Rolling Stones*. The Stones appreciated his efforts at procuring drugs for them more than his literary prowess.

SANGSTER, ROBERT
World's richest racehorse owner, whose estimated wealth is $850 million. His relationship with Mick's lady, Jerry Hall, in the fall of 1982 caused press speculation, in the form of newspaper headlines, daily radio broadcasts, and the cover of *People* magazine, that Mick and Jerry were through. Jerry announced that she and the forty-six-year-old Australian would be getting married as soon as he divorced his wife, but before Mick could even date every blonde in Paris, the two were reconciled. (See Schifano, Mario. This is a recurring theme.)

SANTA BARBARA MACHINEHEAD
Group composed of Ron Wood, Jon Lord, Twink, and Kim Gardner, whose recorded efforts appear on the Immediate Records 1968 compilation, BLUES ANTHOLOGY VOL. 3.

SANTANA
Carlos Santana's rock/jazz band who opened for the Stones at Altamont, their benefit at the Los Angeles Forum, and in Michigan on their 1981 U.S. tour.

"SATISFACTION"
See "(I Can't Get No) Satisfaction."

SATURDAY CLUB
Compilation album released by Decca in January 1964, with the Stones contributing "Poison Ivy" and "Fortune Teller." Other artists appearing on the album are Dave Berry, the Tornadoes, Jet Harris, and Tony Meehan. "Saturday Club" was a BBC radio show on which the Stones appeared.

"SATURDAY NIGHT LIVE"
Mick made a surprise though well-rumored appearance to join then RSR-artist Peter Tosh in song in December of 1978. The entire Stones appeared on "Saturday Night Live" on the opening show of the 1978 season when New York City's mayor, Ed Koch, hosted the show. Mick, Ron, and Charlie appeared in comedy sketches, and the band performed two numbers.

SAVAGE, ROGER
Engineer on the first session Oldham and Easton produced in May 1963, at Olympic Studios. The Stones recorded "Come On," "I Want to Be Loved," "Love Potion No. 9," and "Pretty Thing."

"SAVE ME"
GOATS HEAD SOUP outtake.

SAVILLE THEATRE
London theater where the Stones played two shows the week after Altamont.

SAVLOV, RICHARD
Man killed, along with his friend, Mark Farger, at Altamont when a car plowed into their campsite hours after the concert was over.

SCADUTO, ANTHONY
Author of *Mick Jagger: Everybody's Lucifer*. Mick refused to cooperate and asked the other Stones not to talk to Scaduto either.

SCARFE, GERALD
British cartoonist famous in Pink Floyd circles as the creator of *The Wall* creatures and in Beatles circles as the man Jane Asher married instead of Paul McCartney. He created the larger-than-life dummies of the Stones which comedians Peter Cook and Dudley Moore used in a skit on the

"Saturday Night at the London Palladium" TV show. At the show's finale, the dummies were brought out onto the Palladium's revolving stage in place of the Stones who refused to join the rest of the evening's entertainers in waving good-night to the audience.

SCHATZBERG, JERRY
Photographer who took photos for the U.S. and U.K. AFTERMATH sleeves, in addition to the legendary photo of the Stones which graced the cover of the American single of "Have You Seen Your Mother, Baby, Standing in the Shadow?"; it featured the Stones in drag posing on New York's Park Avenue. The new Stones' identities for the day were: Bill—Penelope; Keith—Molly; Mick—Sarah; Charlie—Millicent; and Brian—Flossie. The Stones, made up and in heels, then went to a bar for a drink.

SCHER, PAULA
Art director of STILL LIFE album cover.

SCHIFANO, MARIO
Millionaire film director with whom Marianne Faithfull had an affair in order to make Mick jealous while he was in America in 1969. Mick went back to Marianne so she'd break up with Schifano, and then Mick left Marianne.

SCHLITZ
The beer that "rocked America" with corporate sponsorship of the Who's 1982 farewell tour. In 1983, Aerosmith turned down the company's offers, and rumors now have it that in an attempt to find a Steven Tyler look-alike, Schlitz is negotiating with the Stones for 1984.

SCHNEIDER, RONNIE
Head of Stones Promotions Ltd., a company which ran the 1969 U.S. tour. He quit working for his uncle, Allen Klein, to start Stones Promotions.

"SCHOOLBOY BLUES"
Acceptable retitle for "Cocksucker Blues," it was used in the play *The Trials of Oz*.

SCOTCH OF ST. JAMES'S
London club where the Stones' deal with Allen Klein was arranged. Also Brian punched Anita in the nose here because she said something nasty about Brian's relationship with Ronny Money.

SCOTT, DEBBY
A waitress at the London club Blases, who met Brian at another club, the Speakeasy, and went out with him for about a year, on and off. In the spring of 1968, an hour after Debby had left Brian at the Imperial Hotel, he was busted and blamed her for the incident.

SEARS POINT RACEWAY
Original site for what became Altamont, located north of San Francisco. Sears Point asked for thousands of dollars in escrow against damages, and their parent company, Filmways Corporation, demanded film distribution rights. Ronnie Schneider refused, and Filmways upped their fee to $100,000. The Stones were forced to move everything to Altamont Speedway and, in January 1970, sued Sears Point Raceway for £4.5 million for fraud and breach of contract because the Raceway forced them to move the concert at the last minute.

Mick n' Schlitz.

SEEFF, NORMAN
Photographer who did layout and design of EXILE ON MAIN ST. album jacket. He also photographed and directed the twelve scenes of "The Fall from Exile on Main St." which were included with the album on a series of postcards.

"SEND IT TO ME"
Written by: Jagger/Richards
Recorded by: The Rolling Stones
Release date: June 1980
Record label: Rolling Stones Records
Album: EMOTIONAL RESCUE
Single: Flip of "She's So Cold" (U.S./ U.K. 1980)

SETZER, BRIAN
Stray Cat who plays guitar on Bill's "Ride On Baby."

"SEVEN DAYS"
Written by: Bob Dylan
Recorded by: Ron Wood
Release date: May 1979
Record label: CBS
Album: GIMME SOME NECK
Single: B/w "Come to Realize" (U.K. 8/79)
• Keith—backup vocals.
• Mick Fleetwood—drums.

7-TEASE
1975 Donovan LP featuring Bill on one track.

"SEVENTEEN"
Written by: Bill Wyman
Recorded by: Bill Wyman
Release date: 1981
Record label: A & M
Album: BILL WYMAN
Single: Flip of "Come Back Suzanne" (U.K. 1981)
• Bob Wiczling—drums.

SEVENTH HEAVEN
Poetry book written by Patti Smith, published by Telegraph Books, U.S., 1972. Dedicated to Mickey Spillane and Anita Pallenberg, it contains the poem "Marianne Faithfull." Anita is also a character in Smith's poem "Girl Trouble."

SHABOO ALL-STARS
Band led by Matt "Guitar" Murphy who Keith jammed with on the stage of New York's Trax club in February 1981, performing "Johnny B. Goode" for half an hour.

"SHADES OF ORANGE"/"LOVING SACRED LOVING"
1968 single by the End produced by Bill. Charlie plays tabla on the flip side.

"SHAKE YOUR HIPS"
Written by: Moore
Recorded by: The Rolling Stones
Release date: May 1972
Record label: Rolling Stones Records
Album: EXILE ON MAIN ST.
• Bill Plummer—upright bass.
• Ian Stewart—piano.

"SHAME, SHAME, SHAME"
Recorded by the Stones in Rotterdam during the "Great Guitarists Hunt" of 1975 but never released.

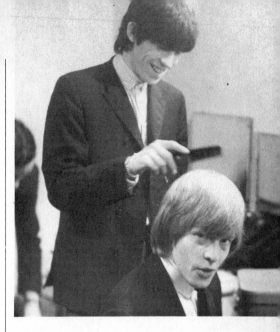

SHAMPOO, MR.
Name Brian was called by the rest of the Stones.

"SHATTERED"
Written by: Jagger/Richards
Recorded by: The Rolling Stones
Release date: June 1978
Record label: Rolling Stones Records
Albums: SOME GIRLS
         SUCKING IN THE SEVENTIES
         STILL LIFE (live)
Single: B/w "Everything Is Turning to Gold" (U.S./U.K. 6/78)
• What the authors will be if this book doesn't sell.

"SHE NEVER TOLD ME"
Written by: Wood/Ford
Recorded by: Ron Wood
Release date: August 1981
Record label: Columbia
Album: 1 2 3 4
• Charlie Watts—drums.
• Jim Keltner—percussion.
• Jimmy Haslip—bass.
• Ian McLagan—keyboards.
• Nicky Hopkins—keyboards.
• Waddy Wachtel—guitar.
• Anita Pointer—backup vocals.

"SHE SAID YEAH"
Written by: Roderick/Christy/Jackson
Recorded by: The Rolling Stones
Release date: September 1965
Record label: Decca/London
Albums: OUT OF OUR HEADS (U.K.)
         DECEMBER'S CHILDREN
         PROMOTIONAL ALBUM
         MILESTONES

"SHE SMILED SWEETLY"
Written by: Jagger/Richards
Recorded by: The Rolling Stones
Release date: January 1967
Record label: London/Decca
Albums: BETWEEN THE BUTTONS (U.S.)
         BETWEEN THE BUTTONS (U.K.)

"SHE STILL COMES AROUND"
Country song which Keith recorded in Toronto; it remains unreleased.

- Cover photography—Gered Mankowitz.
- Typography—The Studio.

SMALL FACES
(See Faces, The.)

SMITH, DUANE
Pianist on "Crazy Woman" and "I'll Pull You Thro."

SMITH, JON
Assistant engineer on EMOTIONAL RESCUE.

SMITH, WILLIAM
Pianist on "Monkey Grip Glue."

SNAKES AND LADDERS—THE BEST OF THE FACES
LP on which Ron Wood is featured. He also did the cover art.

SOME GIRLS
Artist: The Rolling Stones
Producer: The Glimmer Twins
Release date: June 1978
Record label: Rolling Stones Records
Tracks: 10
"Miss You"
"When the Whip Comes Down"
"Just My Imagination" (Whitfield/Strong)
"Some Girls"
"Lies"
"Far Away Eyes"
"Respectable"
"Before They Make Me Run"
"Beast of Burden"
"Shattered"
- 26th U.S. album.
- 26th U.K. album.

- Ian "Mac" McLagan—piano and organ.
- Mel Collins—sax.
- Sugar Blue—harmonica.
- See individual songs for other guest musicians' credits.
- Studio—EMI Studios, Paris, and The Rolling Stones Mobile Unit.
- Engineer and mixing—Chris Kimsey (except on "Before They Make Me Run," engineered by Dave Jordan).
- Assistant engineers—Barry Sage, Ben King, Philippe.
- Mastered by Ted Jensen/Sterling Sound.
- Cover concept and design—Peter Corriston.
- The Stones recorded forty-two songs before deciding on the above ten.

• The LP is basically about New York.
• Various famous people (including Raquel Welch) tried to stop the LP's release because their photos were on the cover. Only Lucille Ball's request caused a change in the U.S. artwork.
• Ron gave Mick guitar lessons so that his performances on "Respectable," "Lies," and "When the Whip Comes Down" would be better.
• Tentative titles included DON'T STEAL MY GIRLFRIEND.
• *"Why is this the title? Because we couldn't remember their fucking names."* —Keith.
• "s" on cover and actual disc; no "s" on lyric sheet.

"SOME GIRLS"
Written by: Jagger/Richards
Recorded by: The Rolling Stones
Release date: June 1978
Record label: Rolling Stones Records
Album: SOME GIRLS
• Sugar Blue—harmonica.
• Atlantic Records tried to get the Stones to change the line about "black girls," but the Stones refused.

SOME GIRLS
Female names mentioned in Rolling Stones songs:
Angie
Dietrich
Cathy
Candy
Little Susie
Lucy
Negrita
Fanny
Lady Jane
Lady Anne
Marie
Jezebel
Melody
Rosie
Hannah
Amanda
Wendy
Pat
Ruby Tuesday
Virginia

SOME GIRLS
The following women have been romantically linked with one or more Stones throughout the years, but their tenure as Stones' girls was not sufficient to merit a separate entry. Beyond the individual entries and this listing the remainder of the Stones' liaisons remain nameless.

Natasha Fraser—Lady Antonia Fraser's seventeen-year-old daughter, who Mick was going out with in 1981.

Cornelia Guest—New York's number-one debutante partied with Mick in 1982.

Pattie Harrison—Ron Wood was the first person Pattie slept with when she decided to cheat on her husband, George. (George didn't mind. He started dating Krissie Wood.)

Margot, Mary, Renne—Stones' traveling groupies in the film *Cocksucker Blues.*

Linda McCartney—spent time with Mick from 1964 onward. She wrote an article in a teen magazine about her night with Mick Jagger and is rumored to be "the divorcee in New York City" in "Honky Tonk Women."

Nikki and Tina—pair who lived with Brian after Anita left him for Keith.

Uschi Obermeier—German model who both Mick and Keith had a brief affair with at about the same time. She seemed to like Keith better but left both of them when a modeling assignment came up.

Valerie Perrine—blond actress who dated Mick in 1982.

Gwynne Rivers—daughter of artist Larry Rivers, who recently celebrated her eighteenth birthday with Mick's help.

Blandy Uzielli—Mick dated her in 1982.

Victoria Vicuna—young Venezuelan model Mick dated in 1982 and brought to Paris to console him while Jerry Hall was away.

"SOME THINGS JUST STICK IN YOUR MIND"
Written by: Jagger/Richards
Recorded by: The Rolling Stones
Release date: June 1975
Record label: Decca
Album: METAMORPHOSIS (U.K. only)
• This is one of the two songs that do not appear on the American pressing of METAMORPHOSIS.

"SOMETHING HAPPENED TO ME YESTERDAY"
Written by: Jagger/Richards
Recorded by: The Rolling Stones
Release date: January 1967

Record label: London/Decca
Albums: BETWEEN THE BUTTONS (U.S.)
BETWEEN THE BUTTONS (U.K.)
• Brian plays sax on this track.

SONGS OF THE ROLLING STONES
1976 LP manufactured by Allen Klein's ABKCO Records with excerpts from 30 Klein-controlled Jagger/Richards compositions. It was used as a sampler for music publishers, and is a favorite Stones collector's item.

"SOON FORGOTTEN"
Unreleased song recorded by Mick, Keith, Brian, Tony Chapman, and Ian Stewart in October 1962.

"SOUL SATISFYING"
Written by: Bill Wyman
Recorded by: Bill Wyman
Release date: February 1976
Record label: Rolling Stones Records
Album: STONE ALONE
Singles: Flip of "A Quarter to Three" (U.S./U.K. 4/76)
Flip of "Apache Woman" (U.S./U.K. 9/76)
• Dallas Taylor—drums.
• Danny Kortchmar—guitar.
• Dr. John—electric piano.
• Terry Taylor—guitar.
• Albhy Galuten—synthesizers.
• Jackie Clark—guitar.
• Paul Harris—organ.
• Guille Garcia—percussion.
• Ruth and Bonnie Pointer—backup vocals.
• Robert Greenidge—steel drums.

"SOUL SURVIVOR"
Written by: Jagger/Richards
Recorded by: The Rolling Stones
Release date: May 1972
Record label: Rolling Stones Records
Album: EXILE ON MAIN ST.

SOUND CITY
London music store where Ron "acquired" his first bass in 1967 when Jeff Beck decided there couldn't be two guitarists in his band and Ron was asked to change instruments. He paid for it five years later.

SOUND PACKAGING CORPORATION
Manufactured the jackets and sleeves of the STICKY FINGERS LP.

SOUTHERN LINE
The train on which Mick and Keith were reunited in 1960 after having known each other as children. Mick was carrying records by Chuck Berry, Little Walter, and Muddy Waters; Keith was carrying a guitar.

SOUTHERN, TERRY
Writer of the text for *The Rolling Stones on Tour.*

SOVIET UNION, THE
In June 1975 the Stones became the first rock band to get record royalties from the Soviet Union.

SNEIDERMAN, MR.

Known by various aliases including "King" and "Britton," he was labeled "Mr. X." by the press during the Stones' Redlands-bust trial. Sneiderman, who briefly worked for Keith, was accused by Keith and Mick of being a plant for the *News of the World* and setting up the drug bust. Although he had drugs on him, he wasn't arrested that night, and two days later he had left the country. A warrant was issued, but he hasn't been seen since.

SPECTOR, PHIL

Legendary American record producer and creator of the "Wall of Sound." He helped out on some Stones' recording sessions—starting when he and Gene Pitney visited the Stones in the studio in 1963. (See individual songs for listings.) Andrew Oldham idolized him and attempted Spector's creative approach in his work with his own Andrew Loog Oldham Orchestra, creating orchestrated versions of then modern-day hits.

SPEDDING, CHRIS

British guitar virtuoso mentioned as possible Mick Taylor replacement during the "Great Guitarists Hunt" of 1975.

SPENCER DAVIS GROUP

Steve Winwood's alma mater, who opened for the Stones during their September/October 1965 British tour.

"SPIDER AND THE FLY, THE"

Written by: Nanker Phelge
Recorded by: The Rolling Stones
Release date: July 1965
Record label: London/Decca
Albums: OUT OF OUR HEADS (U.S.)
STONE AGE

SPRINGER, ALEX

West German publisher who owned a skyscraper overlooking the Berlin Wall. In October 1969 it was rumored that the Stones would be giving a concert on top of the building. Thousands of fans gathered and police were called to disperse the crowd. Fifty people were arrested.

"STAR STAR"

Written by: Jagger/Richards
Recorded by: The Rolling Stones
Release date: August 1973
Record label: Rolling Stones Records
Albums: GOATS HEAD SOUP
LOVE YOU LIVE (live in Paris)
TIME WAITS FOR NO ONE
• Ian Stewart—"jangles."
• This song was remixed for the U.S. LP.
• The song was originally entitled "Starfucker." Ahmet Ertegun and Atlantic Records were adamant about not releasing it. Mick wouldn't budge either, but after the album sat for

months unreleased, a title change was made, leaving the lyrics intact.
• No matter what the title, the song was banned on BBC radio.
• In defense of the song's original title, Mick says, "If girls can do that, I can certainly write about it, because it's what I see."
• When performed in concert during the 1975 U.S. tour, a fifteen-foot phallus balloon rose from the stage. In San Antonio, Texas, the vice squad threatened to arrest the band if the balloon came up. The Stones didn't use it that show.

STARART

Book designed and edited by Debby Chesher, published by Starart Productions Limited, Alberta, Canada, 1979, featuring thirty-three pages of black and white and color reproductions of Ron's paintings and drawings.

"STARFUCKER"

See "Star Star."

STARGROVES

Mick's forty-acre sixteenth-century country manor in Berkshire, England, which was originally Oliver Cromwell's military headquarters. The Rolling Stones Mobile Unit was brought here for work on STICKY FINGERS, and other bands have used these facilities, including Led Zep, who recorded PHYSICAL GRAFFITI here. In 1978 Mick put the estate up for sale, asking half a million dollars for it.

STARR, RINGO

Ex-Beatle who performed in the group Bill arranged for the Jerry Lewis Labor Day Telethon in 1979.

"STAR-SPANGLED BANNER"

The American national anthem, the Jimi Hendrix recording of which was used as the forty-four-second outro to STILL LIFE.

"START ME UP"

Written by: Jagger/Richards
Recorded by: The Rolling Stones
Release date: October 1981
Record label: Rolling Stones Records
Albums: TATTOO YOU
STILL LIFE (live)
Single: B/w "No Use in Crying"
(U.S./U.K. 1981)
• This song was used as the introductory music for tennis star Guillermo Vilas during John McEnroe's 1983 "Tennis Over America Tour."

STATION HOTEL

Location of the Crawdaddy Club in London.

STECKLER, AL

Researched and compiled META-MORPHOSIS, also receiving co-art directing credits for the album. He also "conceived" MORE HOT ROCKS.

STEEL BAND ASSOCIATION OF AMERICA

One hundred West Indian steel drummers who played before the Stones hit the stage during their Tour of the Americas, 1975.

STEELE, TOMMY

British pop star whose beach house in Ocho Rios, Jamaica, was rented by Keith and Anita in November 1972 during the GOATS HEAD SOUP sessions, so that Anita and Bianca, who fought constantly, could be separated.

STERN

When the Stones performed in Germany in 1982, Mick was on the cover of both *Stern* and *Der Speigel* (the German equivalents of America's *Time* and *Newsweek*).

STERN, NEIL

Cinandre hairdresser who did Bill's hair for the cover of STONE ALONE.

STEVE THOMAS ASSOCIATES

Designers of GET YER YA-YA'S OUT LP cover.

STEVENS PSYCHIATRIC CENTER

Keith and Anita were treated at this Pennsylvania clinic after their Canadian drug bust.

STEWART, IAN

"The sixth Stone," Ian has been involved with the Stones or nucleus thereof since answering Brian's ad for musicians in *Jazz News*. He recorded a three-song demo with Mick, Keith, Brian, and Tony Chapman in 1962 (see Curly Clayton Sound Studio), and for more than twenty years he has appeared on almost every Stones recording (see individual album and song listings) and tour. In the early days, he was the only Stone with a driver's license, hence serving as band chauffeur. When Andrew Oldham decided that he didn't like Stewart's looks and that six members were too many for the band, he dismissed him, though Ian stayed on as road manager. When Brian left the Stones, he asked Ian to join a new group he was forming, but Ian turned him down. Ian is now in charge of the Rolling Stones Mobile Unit, when he isn't recording or touring with the Stones. In the late seventies he formed Rocket 88, a boogie woogie group which performs sporadically, releasing an album, ROCKET 88, in 1981 featuring Ian, Charlie Watts, Jack Bruce, and Alexis Korner.

STEWART, ROD

Britain's blond bombshell. Stewart's departure from the Faces to pursue a solo career made Ron realize that he was no longer tied to the band, and gave him the freedom to leave and become a Rolling Stone. Rod arranged "Priceless" on Ron's 1 2 3 4 album.

"STEWED AND KEEFED"

Unreleased recording, 1964.

STICKY FINGERS

Artist: The Rolling Stones
Producer: Jimmy Miller
Release date: April 1971
Record label: Rolling Stones Records
Tracks: 10

"Brown Sugar"
"Sway"
"Wild Horses"
"Can't You Hear Me Knocking"
"You Gotta Move" (McDowell)
"Bitch"
"I Got the Blues"
"Sister Morphine"
"Dead Flowers"
"Moonlight Mile"
• 16th U.S. album.
• 13th U.K. album.
• Guest musicians include Ian Stewart, Bobby Keys, Nicky Hopkins, Ry Cooder, Billy Preston, and half a dozen more (see individual songs for credits).
• Studios—Olympic Studios, London; Rolling Stones Mobile; Muscle Shoals Studio, Alabama.
• Engineers—Glyn Johns, Andy Johns.
• Assistant engineers—Chris Kimsey, Jimmy Johnson.
• Cover concept/photography—Andy Warhol.
• Album design/graphics—Craigbrauninc.
• Jackets/sleeves—Sound Packaging Corporation.
• This was the first album released on Rolling Stones Records.
• This was the first album Mick Taylor plays on, though many songs date from the Muscle Shoals session in 1967.
• This was the first Rolling Stones album to sell "a million" in the U.S. alone.
• Warhol's sleeve design was extremely

controversial. Spanish Atlantic Records refused to release it. They changed the cover, and while they were at it, substituted "Let It Rock" for "Sister Morphine."
• STICKY FINGERS was a working title for BEGGARS BANQUET though it was never intended to be the actual title. It was also intended to be the original title of the album that became LET IT BLEED a year and a half earlier.
• This album was re-released on EMI U.K. in March 1980.
• No "s."

"STILL A FOOL"

Song recorded by the Stones in 1968 but never released.

STILL LIFE (AMERICAN CONCERT 1981)

Artist: The Rolling Stones
Producer: The Glimmer Twins
Release date: June 1982
Record label: Rolling Stones Records
Tracks: 12

"Take the A Train" (Strayhorn)
"Under My Thumb"
"Let's Spend the Night Together"
"Shattered"
"Twenty Flight Rock" (Ned Fairchild)
"Going To A Go Go" (Robinson/Tarplin/Moore/Rogers)
"Let Me Go"
"Time Is on My Side" (Meade/Norman)
"Just My Imagination" (Whitfield/Strong)
"Start Me Up"
"(I Can't Get No) Satisfaction"
"Star-Spangled Banner"

• 30th U.S. album.
• 32nd U.K. album.
• Ian Stewart—piano.
• Ian McLagan—keyboards.
• Ernie Watts—saxophone.
• Recorded by—Bob Clearmountain and David Hewitt with the Record Plant remote.
• Mixed by—Bob Clearmountain at Power Station Studios.
• Assistant engineers—Malcolm Pollack, Barry Bongiovi, Larry Alexander, Phil Gitomer, Kooster MacAllister, David "DB" Brown.
• Mastered by—Robert C. Ludwig/Masterdisk.
• Photography—Michael Halsband, Ken Regan/Camera 5.
• Art Direction—Paula Scher.
• Front cover painting—Kazuhide Yamazaki.
• Road crew—Alan Rogan, Chuck McGee, Rob Davis.
• "s" on sleeve; "s" on disc varies from song to song.

STILLS, STEPHEN

Mick and Keith stayed at his home when the Stones were in California for their 1969 U.S. tour. Stills played at the St. Tropez jam session in honor of Mick's wedding. In the early seventies, it was rumored that Bill and Stills would form a band together.

STONE AGE

Artist: The Rolling Stones
Producer: Andrew Loog Oldham
Release date: April 1971
Record label: Decca
Tracks: 12

"Look What You've Done" (Morganfield)
"It's All Over Now" (B. & S. Womack)
"Confessin' the Blues" (Brown/McShann)
"One More Try"
"As Tears Go By" (Jagger/Richards/Oldham)
"The Spider and the Fly" (Nanker Phelge)
"My Girl" (Robinson/White)
"Paint It, Black"
"If You Need Me" (Pickett/Bateman/Sanders)
"The Last Time"
"Blue Turns to Grey"
"Around and Around" (Berry)

• 12th U.K. album.
• Studios—RCA, Hollywood; Chess, Chicago; Olympic, London.
• Decca Records released this after the Stones left the label.
• This album was disclaimed by the Stones in full-page ads in the British music press headlined "BEWARE!" and claiming that the Stones didn't know it was going to be released and in the band's opinion it was "below the standard we try to keep up, both in choice of content and cover design." The cover was a parody of the banned graffiti sleeve artwork which Decca rejected for BEGGARS BANQUET.
• Decca, to their credit, had four tracks which hadn't previously been available in Britain, making the album a necessity for Stones fans, instead of a rehash: "Look What You've Done," "Blue Turns to Grey," "One More Try," and "My Girl."

STONE ALONE

Artist: Bill Wyman
Producer: Bill Wyman
Release date: February 1976
Record label: Rolling Stones Records
Tracks: 12

"A Quarter to Three" (Guida/Anderson/Barge/Royster)
"Gimme Just One Chance"
"Soul Satisfying"
"Apache Woman"
"Every Sixty Seconds"
"Get It On"
"Feet" (Kortchmar)
"Peanut Butter Time"
"Wine & Wimmen"
"If You Wanna Be Happy" (Guida/Guida/Royster)
"What's the Point"
"No More Foolin'"

• Dallas Taylor—drums; Danny Kortchmar—guitars; and more than three dozen other musicians (see individual song listings for credits).
• All horns by—Mick Gillette, Steve (The Doctor) Kupka, Lenny Pickett, Emilio Castillo. Additional horns by Craig Dentweiler.
• Engineers—Gary Kjellgren, Howard Albert, Ron Albert.
• Assistant engineers—John Henning, Jimmy Robinson, Neil Hausman.
• Mixing—Tom Dowd, Gary Kjellgren, Bill Wyman (except "Apache Woman" mixed by Anita Wexler and Tom Moulton).
• Mastering—Dennis King.
• Photos—Bill King.
• Cover concept, set design, makeup—Pierre Laroche.
• Title lettering—Larry Laslo.
• Production assistants—Howard Albert and Ron Albert for Fat Albert Productions/Gary Kjellgren.
• For Cinandre—Neil Stern.

"STONED"

Written by: Nanker Phelge
Artist: The Rolling Stones
Release date: November 1963
Record label: Decca
Album: NO STONE UNTURNED

Single: Flip of "I Wanna Be Your Man" (U.K. 11/63)
• The first few hundred pressings of the single misspelled the title as "Stones."

STONES, THE
Book by Philip C. Luce, published by Howard Baker, Ltd., 1970.

STONES IN THE PARK
Documentary of the Stones' July 5, 1969, Hyde Park Concert, produced by Jo Durden Smith and Leslie Woodhead for Granada Films and shown on British television in September of that year.

STONES PROMOTIONS, LTD.
A company, headed by Ronnie Schneider, which ran the 1969 U.S. tour.

"STOP BREAKING DOWN"
Written by: Traditional, arranged by Jagger/Richards//Wyman/Taylor/Watts
Recorded by: The Rolling Stones
Release date: May 1972
Record label: Rolling Stones Records
Album: EXILE ON MAIN ST.
• Ian Stewart—piano.

"STORY OF OUR TIME—BRIAN JONES, THE ROLLING STONE, A"
BBC radio special aired in March 1971, in which Brian's father blamed Anita and Keith for Brian's death, saying that Anita's leaving him killed Brian.

"STRAY CAT BLUES"
Written by: Jagger/Richards
Recorded by: The Rolling Stones
Release date: November 1968
Record label: London/Decca
Albums: BEGGARS BANQUET
GET YER YA-YA'S OUT (live)
MILESTONES
• Mick claims that he took the sound for this song from the Velvet Underground song "Heroin."
• When performed during the U.S. tour in 1969, Mick changed the age in the lyrics from fifteen to thirteen.

STRAY CATS, THE
Keith saw this U.S. rockabilly band perform at London's Venue and invited them to his house for a jam, which lasted for four days. The Stray Cats opened for the Stones on a few dates of their 1981 U.S. tour, and Bill has claimed that the band is "the Rolling Stones of the 1980s."

Ron with Stray Cats Brian Setzer and Slim Jim Phantom and a member of Rainbow at the Rock Radio Awards.

STREATHAM
Town where Bill and his wife lived before Bill quit his job to be a full-time Stone.

"STREET FIGHTING MAN"
Written by: Jagger/Richards
Recorded by: The Rolling Stones
Release date: November 1968
Record label: Decca/London
Albums: BEGGARS BANQUET
THROUGH THE PAST, DARKLY U.K.
THROUGH THE PAST, DARKLY U.S.
GET YER YA-YA'S OUT (live)
HOT ROCKS
GIMME SHELTER
ROLLED GOLD

Singles: B/w "No Expectations" (U.S. 8/68)

B/w "Surprise, Surprise" (U.K. 7/70)

1972 U.K. maxi-single with "Everybody Needs Somebody to Love" and "Surprise, Surprise"

• The first British single was released two years after Decca deemed the song "subversive."

• The song was about the student riots in Paris in 1968, though it was also thought to be about the riots in August of that year which took place at the Democratic Presidential Convention in Chicago. It was banned by some U.S. radio stations, which felt that it could incite further riots. This pleased Mick, who told London's *Evening Standard:* "The last time they banned one of our records in America it sold a million." The original picture sleeve, showing demonstrators being beaten by police, was also banned.

• Brian plays tamboura and sitar.

STROMBERG, GARY

Press agent for the Stones during their 1972 U.S. tour and the 1973 European tour.

STUDIO, THE

Typographers for SLOW ROLLERS LP jacket.

STUDIO 54

"In" New York disco which served as Mick's home away from home in the Big Apple. Keith always found it a terrible waste of an elegant opera house and visited there rarely—to see Chuck Berry in February 1980 and to see James Brown two months later.

STUDIO 51

Ken Coyler's jazz club off of Charing Cross Road in London where the Stones had a Sunday afternoon residency and where they rehearsed before leaving on their first tour of Britain, headlined by the Everly Brothers. Andrew Oldham brought Lennon and McCartney into the back room of Studio 51 after finding them wandering the streets following a Variety Club luncheon at the Savoy Hotel. Using Keith's guitar and Bill's bass, John and Paul wrote "I Wanna Be Your Man" for the Stones in about fifteen minutes.

"STUPID GIRL"
Written by: Jagger/Richards
Recorded by: The Rolling Stones
Record label: Decca/London
Albums: AFTERMATH (U.K.)
AFTERMATH (U.S.)
PROMOTIONAL ALBUM
Single: Flip of "Paint It, Black" (U.S. 4/66)

SUCCESS
Early eighties film starring Jeff Bridges as an unsuccessful businessman and husband whose luck changes after he takes "lessons" from Corrine, a prostitute played by Bianca Jagger. It was released commercially in 1983.

SUCKING IN THE SEVENTIES

SUCKING IN THE SEVENTIES
Artist: The Rolling Stones
Producer: The Glimmer Twins
Release date: May 1981
Record label: Rolling Stones Records
Tracks: 10
"Shattered"
"Everything Is Turning to Gold" (Jagger/Richards/Wood)
"Hot Stuff"
"Time Waits for No One"
"Fool to Cry"
"Mannish Boy" (London/McDaniel/Morganfield)
"When the Whip Comes Down" (live)
"If I Was a Dancer (Dance Part 2)"
"Crazy Mama"
"Beast of Burden"
• 28th U.S. album.
• 30th U.K. album.

"SUMMER ROMANCE"
Written by: Jagger/Richards
Recorded by: The Rolling Stones
Release date: June 1980
Record label: Rolling Stones Records
Album: EMOTIONAL RESCUE

SUN, MOON AND HERBS
1971 Dr. John album on which Mick sings backup vocals on all but one of the album's eight tracks.

"SUNDAY NIGHT AT THE LONDON PALLADIUM"
British TV show which featured the Stones performing "Let's Spend the Night Together" in February 1967. The band refused to participate in a corny skit and also caused a public outcry by refusing to join the rest of the cast onstage at the end of the show to wave good-bye to the audience. (See Scarfe, Gerald, who saved the day for the London Palladium.)

SUNSET SOUND, HOLLYWOOD
Studio where EXILE ON MAIN ST. was mixed.

SUPERSTARS IN FILM CONCERT
1971 film produced and directed by Peter Clifton featuring the Stones performing "Have You Seen Your Mother, Baby, Standing in the Shadow?" in addition to footage of Ike and Tina Turner, the Animals, Donovan, Ten Years After, John and Yoko, Arthur Brown, and others.

SUPREMES, THE
American female trio, with lead singer Diana Ross, who appeared in the *T.A.M.I. Show* with the Stones.

"SURPRISE, SURPRISE"
Written by: Jagger/Richards
Recorded by: The Rolling Stones
Release date: May 1964
Record label: London/Decca
Albums: FOURTEEN
THE ROLLING STONES, NOW!
NO STONE UNTURNED
Single: Flip of "Street Fighting Man" (U.K. 7/70)
Maxi-single in U.K. with "Everybody Needs Somebody to Love" and "Street Fighting Man" (U.K. 1972)

"SUZIE Q"
Written by: Broadwater/Lewis/Hawkins
Recorded by: The Rolling Stones
Release date: October 1964
Record label: London/Decca
Albums: 12 x 5
THE ROLLING STONES NO. 2
PROMOTIONAL ALBUM

"SWAY"
Written by: Jagger/Richards
Recorded by: The Rolling Stones
Release date: April 1971
Record label: Rolling Stones Records
Album: STICKY FINGERS
Single: Flip of "Wild Horses" (U.S. 6/71)

• Nicky Hopkins—piano.
• Paul Buckmaster—string arrangements.

"SWEET BLACK ANGEL"
Written by: Jagger/Richards
Recorded by: The Rolling Stones
Release date: April 1972
Record label: Rolling Stones Records
Album: EXILE ON MAIN ST.
Single: Flip of "Tumbling Dice" (U.S./U.K. 4/72)
• The song is supposedly about black militant Angela Davis.
• Amyl Nitrate—marimbas.
• Jimmy Miller—percussion.
• The title is mistakenly listed as "Black Angel" on the LP sleeve.

"SWEET VIRGINIA"
Written by: Jagger/Richards
Recorded by: The Rolling Stones
Release date: May 1972
Record label: Rolling Stones Records
Album: EXILE ON MAIN ST.
• Ian Stewart—piano.
• This song was banned by some radio stations because Mick sings the word "shit."
• When performing this in concert, the Stones try to do an acoustic version.

SWINGING BLUE JEANS
British quartet who opened for the Stones during their January 1964 U.K. tour and parts of their February/March 1964 tour.

SWITZERLAND
Peace-loving nation where Keith's teeth come from.

SYDNEY
Name of the cat that Mick and Chrissie Shrimpton had; also the city in Australia where Marianne Faithfull attempted suicide by taking an overdose of sleeping pills.

SYKES, CHRISTOPHER
Photographer who, along with Annie Leibovitz, took the photos in the book *The Rolling Stones on Tour.*

"SYMPATHY FOR THE DEVIL"
Written by: Jagger/Richards
Recorded by: The Rolling Stones
Release date: November 1968
Record label: London/Decca
Albums: BEGGARS BANQUET
PROMOTIONAL ALBUM
GET YER YA-YA'S OUT (live)
HOT ROCKS
GIMME SHELTER
ROLLED GOLD
LOVE YOU LIVE (live in Paris)
• The entire evolution of this song in the recording studio was captured in the film *One Plus One.*
• Stones performed this song at their "Rock and Roll Circus."

SYMPATHY FOR THE DEVIL
U.S. title for the film *One Plus One.*

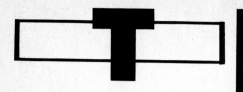

T

T.A.M.I. SHOW

(Teen Age Music International.) One hundred ten-minute black and white movie filmed at the Santa Monica Civic Auditorium in October 1964. Produced by Lee Savin, directed by Steve Binder, with executive producer William Sargeant, Jr., it was released by Electronovision/Screen Entertainments. The Stones appeared in the show along with Chuck Berry, James Brown and his Famous Flames, Marvin Gaye, Gerry and the Pacemakers, Lesley Gore, Jan and Dean, Billy J. Kramer and the Dakotas, Smokey Robinson and the Miracles, the Supremes, and the Beach Boys. The Stones performed "Around and Around," "Off the Hook," "Time Is on My Side," "It's All Over Now," "I'm All Right," and in the jam at the end of the show. When shown in the movies, the *T.A.M.I. Show* was entitled *Gather No Moss*.

TDK

Cassette tape company, which, to the dismay of record companies which are against home-taping, sponsored the Stones' 1982 European tour.

TAILOR AND CUTTER

British trade magazine which in March 1965 made a public plea to the Stones to "save tie makers" from financial ruin, citing the Stones for "disregard of proper clothes for proper occasions." *Tailor and Cutter* felt a word from the number-one artists in the top-twenty charts might lead the youth of Britain to wear ties. At least one of the Stones mended his ways, for Mick made the publications' Hot Hundred Best Dressed Men's list in 1971.

TAJ MAHAL

Performer at "The Rolling Stones' Rock and Roll Circus."

"TAKE THE A TRAIN"

The famous recording by Duke Ellington and his Orchestra of this Billy Strayhorn composition serves as the twenty-seven-second intro to the STILL LIFE album.

"TAKE IT OR LEAVE IT"

Written by: Jagger/Richards
Recorded by: The Rolling Stones
Release date: April 1966
Record label: Decca/London
Albums: AFTERMATH (U.K.)
FLOWERS
SLOW ROLLERS

"TALKIN' 'BOUT YOU"

Written by: Chuck Berry
Recorded by: The Rolling Stones
Release date: September 1965
Record label: Decca/London
Albums: OUT OF OUR HEADS (U.K.)
DECEMBER'S CHILDREN
ROCK 'N' ROLLING STONES

"TALL AND SLENDER BLONDES"

EMOTIONAL RESCUE outtake.

TANDEM HIGHWAY

In 1980 it was announced that Mick was going to star in this film about a rock star whose wife commits suicide, leaving him to raise their six-year-old son, who he takes on the road with him.

TAPANAINEN, TAPANI

Assistant engineer on BLACK AND BLUE, IT'S ONLY ROCK 'N' ROLL, and LOVE YOU LIVE.

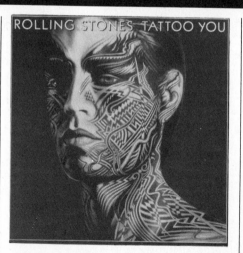

TATTOO YOU

Artist: The Rolling Stones
Producer: The Glimmer Twins
Release date: October 1981
Record label: Rolling Stones Records

Tracks: 11
"Start Me Up"
"Hang Fire"
"Slave"
"Little T & A"
"Black Limousine" (Jagger/Richards/Wood)
"Neighbors"
"Worried about You"
"Tops"
"Heaven"
"No Use in Crying"
"Waiting on a Friend"
• *"I got fed up with writing all those credit lists out and everyone wants one* above *the other one, and then I don't remember who is playing. Everyone got paid anyway."* —Mick.
• Sonny Rollins plays sax on three tracks, uncredited.
• Nicky Hopkins plays piano on one track, uncredited.
• Pete Townshend sings backup on "Slave," uncredited.
• Studio—EMI, Paris; Nassau, Bahamas.
• Associate producer and engineer—Chris Kimsey for Wonder Knob, Ltd.
• Mixed by Bob Clearmountain and Gary Lyons.
• Paintings—Christian Piper.
• Art director—Peter Corriston.
• Mastering—Bob Ludwig/Masterdisk.
• This album entered the U.K. charts at number two; the same month it was number one in the U.S.
• Mick Taylor sued the Stones for royalties.

TAVERN ON THE GREEN
New York's Central Park restaurant

where the Stones held a press conference to announce the release of their film *Let's Spend the Night Together* in January 1983.

TAYLOR, ALVIN
Drummer on 1 2 3 4.

TAYLOR, CHLOE
Daughter of Mick and Rose Taylor, born on January 6, 1971.

TAYLOR, DALLAS
Well-known American session drummer who played with Crosby, Stills, Nash & Young, and on STONE ALONE and MONKEY GRIP.

TAYLOR, DICK
Bass player who was a member of Little Boy Blue and the Blue Boys and, later, the Stones. He went to Dartford Grammar School with Mick and in 1960 attended Sidcup Art School with

Keith. Taylor played at the Stones' historic first gig at the Marquee Club on July 12, 1962, but left the band to pursue studies at the Royal College of Art. After the Stones hit it big, Taylor formed the band, the Pretty Things.

TAYLOR, LIONEL
Mick Taylor's father, who was an aircraft worker while Mick was growing up.

TAYLOR, MARILYN
Mick Taylor's sister.

TAYLOR, MICHAEL
Mick Taylor's real name.

TAYLOR, ROSE MILLER
Wife of Mick Taylor. She was living with him when he was a Stone, and had his baby, Chloe, before they married. Their marriage took place right after Mick Taylor left the Stones, but it didn't last long.

TAYLOR, MICK

Born: January 17, 1948

Mick Taylor, a teenage blues fanatic and guitarist who worked as an artist's engraver, belonged to a band called the Gods when he was asked to sub for one night for an ailing Eric Clapton in John Mayall's Blues Breakers. Clapton eventually left Mayall, as did his replacement, Peter Green (to form Fleetwood Mac), at which point Mayall decided that Taylor was *finally* old enough to be a Blues Breaker. A couple of years later, Taylor decided he wanted to play more than just the blues and left Mayall.

After the Stones decided that Brian could no longer remain a band member, Ian Stewart suggested that they contact Taylor. Mick spoke to John Mayall, who had no negative words for the guitarist, so Mick gave him a call. A few weeks later—having given Taylor a week "to think about it"—it was announced on June 13, 1969, that Mick Taylor would indeed become an official Stone, replacing Brian Jones. He made his debut as a Stone at the free Hyde Park Concert on July 5, 1969, which, ironically, served as a memorial to Brian.

Due to touring pressures and other hazards of the rock 'n' roll life, Mick Taylor quit the Stones five years later, in December 1974, the day the band was to enter the studio for the recording of BLACK AND BLUE. Marshall Chess urged him to stay since the Stones were scheduled to tour the U.S. in 1975, but Taylor declined. He joined the Jack Bruce Band briefly, while every other known guitarist on the planet competed for his former Stones' slot. Taylor has boasted about his being "the only guitarist to leave the Stones alive"; though he may be breathing, with the exception of numerous guest spots on other artists' LPs, a little-heard solo effort in 1979, a guest appearance with his former band, the Stones, in Kansas City in December 1981, and a 1982 club tour, back with John Mayall, his musical career has been virtually dead.

"I just assume I was the best guitarist available at the time."

—Mick Taylor, 1969

"I loved Mick Taylor for his beauty. He was technically really great. But he was shy, maybe like Charlie and I."

—Bill Wyman, 1975

"The Stones ain't gonna end just because a guitar player dies or leaves."

—Keith Richards

TAYLOR, TERRY
Bill's "favorite guitarist" and the first artist signed to Bill's own record company, Ripple Records. Bill plans to produce his album. Taylor was the guitarist in The End and Tucky Buzzard. He plays guitar and slide guitar on STONE ALONE, and on BILL WYMAN he plays guitar and sings backup vocals.

"TELL ME BABY"
Song the Stones recorded in 1964 but never released.

"TELL ME (YOU'RE COMING BACK)"
Written by: Jagger/Richards
Release date: April 1964
Record label: Decca/London
Albums: THE ROLLING STONES
ENGLAND'S NEWEST HIT MAKERS
BIG HITS (U.S.)
MORE HOT ROCKS
Single: B/w "I Just Want to Make Love to You" (U.S. 6/64)
• Ian Stewart—piano.
• This is one of the first songs Mick and Keith wrote that the Stones recorded.

TENCH, BOB
Jeff Beck vocalist who went on to play guitar with Hummingbird and Streetwalker. He was a contender in the "Great Guitarists Hunt" of 1975.

TERRY, GEORGE
Slide guitarist on "Crazy Woman" and guitarist on "I'll Pull You Thro'."

"(THANK YOU) FOR BEING THERE"
"Song" Brian gave to New York music columnist Al Aronowitz. After Brian's death, Aronowitz gave the song to Donovan, who was living with Brian's ex-lover Linda Lawrence and Brian and Linda's son, Julian.

"THANK YOUR LUCKY STARS"
British show on which the Stones made their television debut the day their first single "Come On" was released, June 7, 1963. Oldham insisted that the Stones dress up Beatle-like in matching checked jackets for the broadcast, a Rolling Stones first and last.

THANK YOUR LUCKY STARS, VOLUME TWO
Compilation album released by Decca in September 1963, with the Stones supplying "Come On." The Bachelors, Brian Poole, and Mickie Most (as a vocalist!) contributed.

"THAT GIRL BELONGS TO YESTERDAY"
Jagger/Richards composition which was recorded by Gene Pitney and entered the U.S. charts before the Stones were ever heard of in America.

THAT'LL BE THE DAY
Film soundtrack for which Ron played on Billy Fury's tracks with Keith Moon and Graham Bond.

"THAT'S HOW STRONG MY LOVE IS"
Written by: Jamison
Recorded by: The Rolling Stones
Release date: July 1965
Record label: London/Decca
Albums: OUT OF OUR HEADS (U.S.)
OUT OF OUR HEADS (U.K.)

"THAT'S THE WAY GOD PLANNED IT"
1969 Billy Preston song featuring Keith on guitar.

THEAR, ROD
Assistant engineer on IT'S ONLY ROCK 'N' ROLL.

THEE
Mid-sixties Decca recording artists managed by Reg King, Andrew Oldham's chauffeur.

THEIR SATANIC MAJESTIES REQUEST
Artist: The Rolling Stones
Producer: The Rolling Stones
Release date: November 1967
Record label: London/Decca
Tracks: 10
"Sing This All Together"
"Citadel"
"In Another Land" (Wyman)
"2000 Man"
"Sing This All Together (See What Happens)"
"She's a Rainbow"
"The Lantern"
"Gomper"
"2000 Light Years from Home"
"On with the Show"
• 11th U.S. album.
• 7th U.K. album.
• Nicky Hopkins (piano) and Steve Marriott play on "In Another Land."
• Studios—Olympic, London; Bell Sound, London.
• Engineer—Glyn Johns.
• Arranged by The Rolling Stones.
• Design and photography—Michael Cooper.
• Back cover illustration—Tony Meeviwiffen.
• The cover photo was built by the Rolling Stones, Michael Cooper, and "Artchie" at Pictorial Productions,

Mount Vernon, New York.
• It was the first 3-D album cover. The psychedelic sleeve cost $25,000.
• John, Paul, George, and Ringo can be seen as flower blooms in the foreground in response to the Beatles mentioning Rolling Stones on their SGT. PEPPER album cover.
• This was the first album the Stones recorded without Oldham. He came to the studio while they were recording, but he left because they were playing poorly, which they intentionally did just to get rid of him.
• This was the last Stones album Brian contributed to, although he didn't like the psychedelic music they were doing.
• This album took almost a full year to record, during difficult times: four drug busts and two trials.
• The album's original title was COSMIC CHRISTMAS, then HER SATANIC MAJESTY REQUESTS AND REQUIRES. Mick feels it should have been called TOO LONG IN LONDON.
• "s" on cover; no "s" on disc.

THEY ALL LAUGHED
1981 Peter Bogdanovich film featuring Patti Hansen as a chain-smoking New York cab driver romantically involved with Ben Gazzara. After the filming Keith bought Patti the taxi she drove in the movie.

"365 ROLLING STONES (ONE FOR EACH DAY OF THE YEAR)"/"OH, I DO LIKE TO SEE ME ON THE 'B' SIDE"
1964 record by the Andrew Loog Oldham Orchestra. Charlie and Bill co-composed the B side with Oldham and play respectively drums and bass on it.

"THINK"
Written by: Jagger/Richards
Recorded by: The Rolling Stones
Release date: April 1966
Record label: Decca/London
Albums: AFTERMATH (U.K.)
AFTERMATH (U.S.)
• Chris Farlowe recorded a version of this song in January 1966 which was produced by Jagger, Richards, and Oldham and was a number-one U.K. hit before the Stones version was released.

THIRD EAR BAND
Performers at the Hyde Park Concert in 1969.

THOMAS, PATRICIA
Woman whose name was listed on the back cover of the ENGLAND'S NEWEST HIT MAKERS LP as contact for Americans interested in starting Rolling Stones Fan Clubs in 1964.

THOMPSON, DONALD
Headmaster of Woodloods Comprehensive School in Coventry, England, who suspended eleven boys in May

1964 for having hair "long and scruffy like the Stones." He said the boys could return to school if their hair was "neat like the Beatles."

THOROGOOD, FRANK
Builder who lived with Janet Lawson, a nurse, in the guest apartment at Cotchford Farm. He was there the night of Brian's death and helped Anna Wohlin drag Brian out of the pool.

"THROUGH THE LONELY NIGHTS"
Written by: Jagger/Richards
Recorded by: The Rolling Stones
Release date: July 1974
Record label: Rolling Stones Records
Single: Flip of "It's Only Rock 'n' Roll" (U.S./U.K. 7/74)
• Rumor has it that Jimmy Page plays on this song.

THROUGH THE PAST, DARKLY (BIG HITS VOL. 2) (U.K.)
Artist: The Rolling Stones
Producer: The Rolling Stones/Andrew Loog Oldham/Jimmy Miller
Release date: September 1969
Record label: Decca
Tracks: 12
"Jumpin' Jack Flash"
"Mother's Little Helper"
"2000 Light Years From Home"
"Let's Spend the Night Together"
"You Better Move On" (Alexander)
"We Love You"
"Street Fighting Man"
"She's a Rainbow"
"Ruby Tuesday"
"Dandelion"
"Sittin' on a Fence"
"Honky Tonk Women"
• 9th U.K. album.
• Cover and liner photos—Ethan Russell.
• It boasts an octagon-shaped record cover.
• Dedicated to Brian:
"Brian Jones (1943-1969)
When this you see, remember me
and bear me in your mind
Let all the world say what they may,
Speak of me as you find"
• "s."

THROUGH THE PAST, DARKLY (BIG HITS VOL. 2) (U.S.)
Artists: The Rolling Stones
Producers: The Rolling Stones/Jimmy Miller/Andrew Loog Oldham
Release date: September 1969
Record label: London
Tracks: 11
"Honky Tonk Women"
"Ruby Tuesday"
"Jumpin' Jack Flash"
"Paint It, Black"
"Street Fighting Man"
"Have You Seen Your Mother, Baby, Standing in the Shadow?"
"Let's Spend the Night Together"
"2000 Light Years from Home"
"Mother's Little Helper"
"She's a Rainbow"
"Dandelion"
• 13th U.S. album.
• Remainder of details are the same as on the British album of the same name.

THROUGH THE YEARS
1972 John Mayall LP featuring Mick Taylor.

THUNDERBIRDS, THE
Original name of Ron's first band, The Birds.

"TILL THE NEXT GOODBYE"
Written by: Jagger/Richards
Recorded by: The Rolling Stones
Release date: October 1974
Record label: Rolling Stones Records
Album: IT'S ONLY ROCK 'N' ROLL
• Nicky Hopkins—piano.

"TIME IS ON MY SIDE"
Written by: Meade/Norman
Recorded by: The Rolling Stones
Release date: September 1964
Record label: London/Decca
Albums: 12 x 5
    THE ROLLING STONES NO. 2
    BIG HITS (U.S.)
    BIG HITS (U.K.)
    GOT LIVE IF YOU WANT IT! (live)
    HOT ROCKS
    MILESTONES
    GIMME SHELTER
    ROLLED GOLD
    SLOW ROLLERS
    STILL LIFE (live)

Singles: B/w "Congratulations" (U.S. 9/64)
    Flip of "Twenty Flight Rock" (U.S./U.K. 6/82) (live)
• The single version is different than the early album versions.
• Keith claims to think about Brian whenever he plays this song.
• This song appears on more albums than any other song by the Stones.

TIME IS ON MY SIDE
Original title of *Let's Spend the Night Together* film.

TIME WAITS FOR NO ONE: ANTHOLOGY 1971-1977
Artist: The Rolling Stones
Producer: The Glimmer Twins and Jimmy Miller
Release date: May 1978
Record label: Rolling Stones Records
Tracks: 10
"Time Waits for No One"
"Bitch"
"All Down the Line"
"Dancing with Mr. D"
"Angie"
"Star Star"
"If You Can't Rock Me/Get Off of My Cloud"
"Hand of Fate"
"Crazy Mama"
"Fool to Cry"
• 27th U.K. album.

"TIME WAITS FOR NO ONE"
Written by: Jagger/Richards
Recorded by: The Rolling Stones
Release date: October 1974
Record label: Rolling Stones Records
Albums: IT'S ONLY ROCK 'N' ROLL
    TIME WAITS FOR NO ONE
    SUCKING IN THE SEVENTIES
• Nicky Hopkins—piano.

TIN MAN WAS A DREAMER, THE
1973 Nicky Hopkins LP featuring Mick Taylor.

TIN SOLDIER, THE
Movie co-written by Mick and Gene Taft, about a rock star who finds a thirteen-year-old boy—who turns out to be his son—on his doorstep. Filming of *The Tin Soldier* is underway now, with Malcolm McDowell in the starring role.

"TO KNOW HIM IS TO LOVE HIM"/"THERE ARE BUT FIVE ROLLING STONES"
1964 single produced by Andrew Loog Oldham. The A side is by Cleo; the B side is by the Andrew Oldham Orchestra. The Stones play on the A side.

TODAY'S POP SYMPHONY
1966 LP by the Aranbee Pop Symphony Orchestra under the direction of Keith Richards, produced by Keith. This "new conception of today's hits in classical style" featured ten sixties hits including the Jagger/Richards compositions "Play with Fire," "Mother's Little Helper," "Take It or Leave It," and "Sittin' on a Fence."

TOMMY
1975 soundtrack LP for the Who movie featuring Ron.

TONIGHT LET'S ALL MAKE LOVE IN LONDON
1967 film directed, produced, and written by Peter Whitehead, and distributed by Lorrimer Films. The Stones are seen performing "Lady Jane" in the film, and the 1968 soundtrack album features an interview with Mick but no Stones performances.

"TOPS"
Written by: Jagger/Richards
Recorded by: The Rolling Stones
Release date: October 1981
Record label: Rolling Stones Records
Album: TATTOO YOU

"TORN AND FRAYED"
Written by: Jagger/Richards
Recorded by: The Rolling Stones
Release date: May 1972
Record label: Rolling Stones Records
Album: EXILE ON MAIN ST.
• Al Perkins—steel guitar.
• Jim Price—organ.

TORONTO BUST
See Arrests.

TOSH, PETER
Reggae singer signed to Rolling Stones Records, who opened for the Stones on their 1978 U.S. tour. On some of the shows, Mick sang a duet with him on stage during his song "Don't Look Back." Mick also turned up when Peter Tosh appeared on "Saturday Night Live." Tosh recorded three albums on Rolling Stones Records. Keith has recorded an unreleased album with Tosh and his band.

"TOSS THE COIN"
Song recorded by the Stones in 1969 but never released.

TOUR OF THE AMERICAS
Official title for the Stones' 1975 U.S. tour.

TOWNSHEND, PETE
Rumored to be backup vocalist on "Wild Horses" and on TATTOO YOU. In honor of Mick's fortieth birthday, the Who leader wrote a not-so-touching tribute in the *London Times*.

"TRACKS OF MY TEARS"
Miracles hit which the Stones recorded in 1965 but never released.

TRAFFIC
Steve Winwood's group, slated to perform at "The Rock and Roll Circus," but because they couldn't appear, the Who took their place.

TRAMWAY MUSEUM SOCIETY
Brian was a member of this Cheltenham organization which was "dedicated to restoring old trams."

"TRAVELLIN' MAN"
EXILE ON MAIN ST. outtake.

TRIALS OF OSCAR WILDE, THE
An adaptation starring Mick as Wilde, Keith as the Marquess of Queensbury, and Marianne Faithfull as Bosie was used as the Stones' promo film for their single "We Love You." It was banned by the BBC, but it was shown in the U.S. and Germany. Peter Whitehead directed it.

TRIALS OF OZ, THE
Play by Geoff Robertson which incorporated the Stones song "Schoolboy Blues."

TRIDENT STUDIOS
London recording studio where the Stones mixed the live tapes of their Madison Square Garden show, 1969. Footage of this can be seen in the film *Gimme Shelter*.

TRIUMPH
Make of the motorcycle Brian crashed into a grocery store window near Cotchford Farm in 1969. He was admitted to the hospital under an alias to avoid publicity.

TROPICAL DISEASES
Working title for EXILE ON MAIN ST. The name derived from the extreme heat and humidity in the basement of Keith's French villa where the band recorded it.

TROPICANA, THE
Las Vegas nightclub which offered the Stones £10,000 to perform there for a week in 1974. The Stones turned down the offer.

TROUBLEMAKER
1979 Ian McLagan album featuring Ron and Keith.

TROY, DORIS
Backup vocalist on "You Can't Always Get What You Want." She also sang at Mick and Bianca's wedding reception.

TRUDEAU, MARGARET
Official Rolling Stones Joke Book, entry one:
Did you hear that the Trudeaus are putting down a new patio. Guess who laid the Stones?

Wife of Canadian Prime Minister Pierre Trudeau, who was extremely friendly with Mick or Ron or Mick *and* Ron during the Stones Canadian fiasco of 1977. When the Stones left Canada she followed Mick or Ron or Mick *and* Ron to New York, after making the offer of caring for Marlon Richards should Keith and Anita wind up in jail. Marlon was one man who definitely turned her down.

TRUTH
1968 Jeff Beck Group album featuring Ron on bass.

"TRY A LITTLE HARDER"
Written by: Jagger/Richards
Recorded by: The Rolling Stones
Release date: June 1975
Record label: Decca/ABKCO
Album: METAMORPHOSIS

"TRY ME"
James Brown song which the Stones recorded in 1965 but never released.

"TUBULAR BELLS"
Mick Taylor participated in the first public performance of Mike Oldfield's modern classic at Queen Elizabeth Hall in London in June 1973.

TUCKY BUZZARD
1971 album by the band Tucky Buzzard. It was produced by Bill and featured Mick Taylor on two tracks.

TUCKY BUZZARD
1973 LP by Tucky Buzzard. Produced by Bill, who plays on it, this album is different than the 1971 LP of the same name, above.

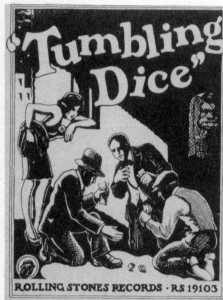

"TUMBLING DICE"
Written by: Jagger/Richards
Recorded by: The Rolling Stones
Release date: April 1972
Record label: Rolling Stones Records
Albums: EXILE ON MAIN ST.
   MADE IN THE SHADE
   LOVE YOU LIVE (live in Paris)
Single: B/w "Sweet Black Angel" (U.S./U.K. 4/72)
• Clydie King and Vanetta Fields— backup vocals.
• Originally this music, with different lyrics, was called "Good Time Women."

"TURD ON THE RUN"
Written by: Jagger/Richards
Recorded by: The Rolling Stones
Release date: May 1972
Record label: Rolling Stones Records
Album: EXILE ON MAIN ST.
• Bill Plummer—upright bass.

TURNER
Mick's character in *Performance*.

12 X 5
Artist: The Rolling Stones
Producer: Andrew Loog Oldham for Impact Sound
Release date: October 1964
Record label: London
Tracks: 12
"Around and Around" (Berry)
"Confessin' the Blues" (McShann/ Brown)
"Empty Heart" (Nanker Phelge)
"Time Is on My Side" (Meade/Norman)
"Good Times, Bad Times"

"It's All Over Now" (B. & S. Womack)
"2120 South Michigan Avenue" (Nanker Phelge)
"Under the Boardwalk" (Resnick/ Young)
"Congratulations"
"Grown Up Wrong"
"If You Need Me" (Bateman/Pickett)
"Suzie Q" (Broadwater/Lewis/ Hawkins)
• 2nd U.S. album.
• Studio—Chess, Chicago.
• Engineer—Ron Malo.
• Cover photo—David Bailey.
• Arranged by the Rolling Stones.
• "s."

"TWENTY FLIGHT ROCK"
Written by: Fairchild
Recorded by: The Rolling Stones
Release date: June 1982
Record label: Rolling Stones Records
Album: STILL LIFE (live)
Single: B/w "Time Is on My Side" (U.S./U.K. 6/82) (live)

"2120 SOUTH MICHIGAN AVENUE"
Written by: Nanker Phelge
Recorded by: The Rolling Stones
Release date: August 1964
Record label: Decca/London
Albums: 12 x 5
   NO STONE UNTURNED
EP: FIVE BY FIVE (U.K. 8/64)
• 2120 South Michigan Avenue is the Chicago address of Chess Records.

$21,273.00
Amount of money spent on Mick's wardrobe for the 1975 Tour of the Americas. The clothing included fashions by Giorgio di Sant' Angelo, Fernando Sanchez, and Mary McFadden.

TWICE AS MUCH
British duo managed by Andrew Oldham, who recorded the Jagger/ Richards composition "Sittin' on a Fence" before the Stones' version came out in Britain. The Stones' rendition had already been released in the U.S. Twice As Much included David Skinner, who reappeared in the 1979 lineup of Roxy Music.

"2000 LIGHT YEARS FROM HOME"
Written by: Jagger/Richards
Recorded by: The Rolling Stones
Release date: November 1967
Record label: London/Decca
Albums:
  THEIR SATANIC MAJESTIES REQUEST
  THROUGH THE PAST, DARKLY (U.K.)
  THROUGH THE PAST, DARKLY (U.S.)
  MORE HOT ROCKS
Single: Flip of "She's a Rainbow" (U.S. 11/67)
• Brian plays mellotron on this, one of the few songs that Keith likes on the album.

"2000 MAN"
Written by: Jagger/Richards
Recorded by: The Rolling Stones
Release date: November 1967
Record label: London/Decca
Albums:
  THEIR SATANIC MAJESTIES REQUEST
  PROMOTIONAL ALBUM

TWO WEEKS IN SEPTEMBER
1966 movie which French sex symbol/ actress Brigitte Bardot asked the Stones to appear in with her. They turned her down because they were doing their own film at the time. They were referring to one of the five or six films that were always in the talking stages during that period, none of which ever made it to celluloid.

TYLER'S CROFT MODERN SCHOOL
London school which Charlie attended.

UB-40
Band who opened some of the shows on the Stones 1982 European tour.

UCLA
University of California at Los Angeles where students studying for music degrees in 1968 were required to study the music of the Rolling Stones for their "important contribution."

"UNDER ASSISTANT WEST COAST PRO- MOTION MAN, THE"
Written by: Nanker Phelge
Recorded by: The Rolling Stones
Release date: May 1965
Record label: London/Decca
Albums: OUT OF OUR HEADS (U.S.)
   OUT OF OUR HEADS (U.K.)
   ROCK 'N' ROLLING STONES
Single: Flip of "(I Can't Get No) Satisfaction" (U.S. 5/65)
• The single version is a different version than the one on the album.
• The song is a jibe at George Sherlock, the London Records promo man who accompanied the Stones on their first American tour.

"UNDER MY THUMB"
Written by: Jagger/Richards
Recorded by: The Rolling Stones
Release date: April 1966
Record label: Decca/London
Albums: AFTERMATH (U.K.)
        AFTERMATH (U.S.)
        GOT LIVE IF YOU WANT IT! (live)
        PROMOTIONAL ALBUM
        HOT ROCKS
        MILESTONES
        GIMME SHELTER
        ROLLED GOLD
        STILL LIFE (live)
• The Stones resurrected this song, which caused sexist furor at its initial release, during their 1981-82 tour to prove they could still be aggravating.

"UNDER THE BOARDWALK"
Written by: Resnick/Young
Recorded by: The Rolling Stones
Release date: October 1964
Record label: London/Decca
Albums: 12 x 5
        THE ROLLING STONES NO. 2
        SLOW ROLLERS

UNHEALTH, MR.
Keith's nickname.

UNIT 4 PLUS 2
Band that opened for the Stones during part of their seventh British tour, September 1965. They had a major American hit with their record, "Concrete and Clay."

UP AND DOWN WITH THE ROLLING STONES
Book by Tony Sanchez, published by William Morrow & Co., 1979, in the U.S. The book was not released in England.

VADIM, ROGER
Film director who served as a witness at Mick and Bianca's wedding ceremony at the town hall in St. Tropez.

VALENCIA
Spanish town where Keith and Anita first decided "Let's Spend the Night Together," on the way to Morocco while Brian was in the hospital.

VAN HALEN
America's heavy metal kings, who opened for the Stones in Orlando, Florida, during their 1981 U.S. tour.

VAN HAMERSVELD, JOHN
Designer and layout artist for EXILE ON MAIN ST. LP jacket and postcards.

Mick with Stevie Ray

VIDAL, GORE
Author of the book *Kalki,* to which Mick bought the film rights. He's working on a screenplay, with Hal Ashby slated to direct.

"VISIONS"
Written by: Bill Wyman
Recorded by: Bill Wyman
Release date: 1981
Record label: A & M
Album: BILL WYMAN
• Chris Rea—guitar.

VITALE, JOE
Almost-Wings drummer who plays piano, drums, R.M.I. on STONE ALONE.

VOLVO MASTERS TOURNAMENT
Tennis championship match held at New York's Madison Square Garden in January 1983. Keith attended and visited John McEnroe "backstage." When challenged, Keith reportedly said that he'd play tennis against McEnroe, "only if he plays with a guitar." Further on the topic of tennis, a couple of years ago, Keith said: "When I was a junkie I used to be able to play tennis with Mick, go into the toilet for a quick fix, and still beat him."

VOX AC-30
The amplifier to which Bill owes his Stoneship. (See *Melody Maker.*)

VOX AMPLIFIERS
The Stones, perched upon or holding (depending on size) these amps, gave "thumbs up" approval to Vox in a 1963 endorsement ad for the speaker company.

W

WAAF-FM
Worcester, Massachusetts, radio station which gave away 300 tickets to the Stones' "secret" gig at Sir Morgan's Cove prior to the start of the U.S. tour in September 1981.

WHBI
New York radio station for which Keith did a commercial for Earl Chin's reggae show in 1982.

WACHTEL, JIMMY
Designer and artist of the MONKEY GRIP LP cover.

WACHTEL, WADDY
Session guitarist who's worked with dozens of artists from the Kootch/ Keltner band, *Attitudes,* to Warren Zevon, and plays on "She Never Told Me."

VARIETY OF ANNOYANCES, A
Tentative title of a book of anecdotes about "life on the road" written by Rod Stewart, illustrated by Ron.

VASHTI
Mid-sixties Decca recording artist managed by Andrew Oldham.

VAUGHAN, STEVIE RAY
Possibly the most-talked about guitarist of the '80's (so far), most notably for his work for and subsequent split with David Bowie. Vaughan, with his band, Double Trouble, was discovered in a Dallas, Texas, club by the bar-hopping team of Jagger and Richards. They flew the band to New York to play a private party, though a proposed recording contract with Rolling Stones Records never came through.

VEE, BOBBY
American pop singer who opened for the Stones during their first U.S. tour.

VELVET UNDERGROUND
American cult group who Brian introduced to Nico, who became their singer. Mick got the idea for "Stray Cat Blues" from their song, "Heroin."

"VENTILATOR BLUES"
Written by: Jagger/Richards/Taylor
Recorded by: The Rolling Stones
Release date: May 1972
Record label: Rolling Stones Records
Album: EXILE ON MAIN ST.

VESSUVIO CLUB
Tottenham Court Road, London, club which was decorated like an Arab tent—except for the photos of the Stones on its walls. It was run by Tony Sanchez and a partner, possibly as a front for Mick and Keith who hated being overcharged in other clubs. It opened on Mick's twenty-fifth birthday, July 26, 1968, with the Stones, Paul McCartney, and John Lennon in attendance.

Stones waiting at St. Marks Bar and Grill.

"WAIT FOR ME"/"I DON'T WANNA HURT YOU"

1967 single by the Warren Davis Monday Band produced by Bill, who cowrote the A side.

"WAITING ON A FRIEND"

Written by: Jagger/Richards
Recorded by: The Rolling Stones
Release date: October 1981
Record label: Rolling Stones Records
Album: TATTOO YOU
Single: B/w "Little T & A" (U.S./U.K. 81)

"(WALKIN' THRU THE) SLEEPY CITY"

Written by: Jagger/Richards
Recorded by: The Rolling Stones
Release date: June 1975
Record label: Decca/ABKCO
Album: METAMORPHOSIS

"WALKING THE DOG"

Written by: Thomas
Recorded by: The Rolling Stones
Release date: April 1964
Record label: Decca/London
Albums: THE ROLLING STONES
ENGLAND'S NEWEST HIT MAKERS
PROMOTIONAL ALBUM

"WALL OF NOISE"

What the early Stones' sound was called, in a takeoff on Phil Spector's "Wall of Sound."

WALLACE, IAN

Former King Crimson drummer who performs on three cuts on 1 2 3 4.

WALLER, MICKY

Jeff Beck drummer who rehearsed with Brian after he left the Stones.

WALLY HEIDER MOBILE

Unit which recorded the Madison Square Garden, N.Y. shows in 1969 which became GET YER YA-YA's OUT.

WALSH, JOE

James Gang and Eagles guitarist who plays on three tracks of STONE ALONE.

WARHOL, ANDY

Superstar artist and foremost proponent of pop art in the sixties, Warhol created the Rolling Stones red tongue logo, conceived of the controversial STICKY FINGERS record sleeve and took the photo for that LP cover, did the artwork for the cover of LOVE YOU LIVE, and painted a famous portrait of Mick. The Stones used his Montauk Point, New York, beach house for their rehearsals before the 1975 Tour of the Americas.

WARM SLASH

1971 Tucky Buzzard album produced by Bill.

WARNER, BOBBY

Assistant engineer on LOVE YOU LIVE.

WARWICK AIRPORT

Rhode Island airport where in July 1972 Keith, Mick, Marshall Chess, and Robert Frank were arrested after Keith tried to hit a photographer and everyone joined the scuffle. They were bailed out by Boston mayor Kevin White.

WASSERMAN, PAUL

Rolling Stones press representative, who started with the band during their 1975 Tour of the Americas.

WATERS, MUDDY

Blues legend and all-time Stones idol whose song "Rollin' Stone Blues" gave the band their name. He attended a "rent" party at Brian's flat on Pressbury

WATTS, CHARLIE

Born: June 2, 1941

The following is reprinted from a fact sheet sent to American fans in spring 1964:

CHARLIE WATTS

REAL NAME Charles Robert Watts.
BIRTH DATE 2. 6. 41.
BIRTHPLACE London.
HEIGHT 5'8".
WEIGHT 10st.
EYES Blue.
HAIR Brown.
PARENTS' NAMES Mr. & Mrs. Watts.
BROTHERS/SISTERS Linda.
HOME Wembley, Middlesex.
INSTRUMENTS Drums.
MUSICAL EDUCATION A good one.
ENTERED SHOW BUSINESS AT: 18.
FIRST APPEARANCE Marquee, Oxford Street.
BIGGEST BREAK IN CAREER Joining the Stones.
TV DEBUT "Thank Your Lucky Stars."
RADIO DEBUT "Saturday Club."
HOBBIES Women.
FAVOURITE SINGERS/ARTISTS Sammy Davis Jr., Greco, Picasso.
FAVOURITE COLOUR Red and Black.
FAVOURITE FOOD Good.
FAVOURITE BAND So many.
FAVOURITE DRINK Tea.
FAVOURITE CLOTHES Good.
FAVOURITE COMPOSER George Russel, Gil Evans.
MISC. LIKES Girls, clothes.
MISC. DISLIKES None.
TASTE IN MUSIC Good.
PERSONAL AMBITION Be successful.
PROFESSIONAL AMBITION To be at no. 1.
WHERE EDUCATED Tylers Croft, Harrow Art College.

The stable back-beat of the Rolling Stones got his first drum kit in his early teens at a cost of twelve pounds. He studied art, drummed for Alexis Korner's Blues Incorporated, and worked at an advertising agency before giving it all up to join the Stones in January 1963. He loves sports, collects antique guns, is interested in American Civil War history, has been married to the same woman for nineteen years, wears gorgeous shoes, never gets into trouble, and is one hell of a drummer!

"If someone asks me a direct question, I give a direct answer. Anyway, it's becoming a tradition that beat-group drummers shouldn't be the greatest talkers."

—Charlie Watts

"… a deadpan, dog-faced boy…"

—Bill Wyman

"Charlie's always there, but he doesn't always want to let everybody know. There's very few drummers like that."

—Keith Richards

"After all, Charlie's not really a Stone, is he? Mick, Keith, and Brian, they're the big bad Rolling Stones."

—Shirley Watts, 1969

"Everybody thinks Mick and Keith are the Rolling Stones. If Charlie wasn't doing what he's doing on drums, that wouldn't be true at all. You'd find out that Charlie Watts is the Stones."

—Keith Richards, 1980

Road, contributing to this early Stone's upkeep, and on a much grander scale performed at Mick's twenty-ninth birthday party at the St. Regis Hotel in New York City. By then, all the Stones could pay their own rents. Muddy Waters died on April 30, 1983.

WATERS, ROGER
Pink Floyd's genius-in-residence, but, more importantly, Ian Stewart's golf partner.

WATKINS
The brand-name of Bill's first amplifier. His Vox AC-30 was more important though.

WATTS, CHARLES
Charlie's father, who worked as a parcels truck driver at King's Cross Railway Station.

WATTS, ERNIE
Sax player on STILL LIFE.

WATTS, LILLY
Charlie's mother.

WATTS, LINDA
Charlie's sister, a beautician, who did Charlie's hair when he first became famous.

WATTS, SERAFINA
Daughter of Charlie and Shirley Watts, Serafina was born on March 18, 1968, but had to wait until 1982 to accompany the Stones on tour, which she recently did through Britain and Europe. Serafina has the distinction of being the only Rolling Stones child who dwells with a married couple who happen to be her parents.

WATTS, SHIRLEY
A sculptress, Shirley married Charlie in October 1964, a marriage which remained a secret for some time, even to Charlie's fellow Stones. She is the mother of Serafina.

WATTS, TONY
Compiler of SLOW ROLLERS.

"WE ALL GET OLD"
Written by: Ron Wood
Recorded by: Ron Wood
Release date: May 1979
Record label: CBS
Album: GIMME SOME NECK
• Charlie Watts—drums.
• "Pops" Popwell—bass.
• Ian McLagan—organ.

"WE HAD IT ALL"
EMOTIONAL RESCUE outtake, with Keith on lead vocal.

"WE LOVE YOU"
Written by: Jagger/Richards
Recorded by: The Rolling Stones
Release date: August 1967
Record label: Decca/London
Albums:
THROUGH THE PAST, DARKLY (U.K.)

Shirley, Charlie, Mick, and Chrissie Shrimpton shopping on London's Portobello Road, 1965.

MORE HOT ROCKS
ROLLED GOLD
Single: B/w "Dandelion" (U.S./U.K. 8/67)
• John Lennon and Paul McCartney—backup vocals.
• The Stones recorded this song to thank the fans who supported Mick and Keith during the Redlands bust trial.
• A prison door can be heard slamming on the record.
• A promotional film, based on *The Trials of Oscar Wilde* and directed by Peter Whitehead, was made for this song but banned by "Top of the Pops," a British rock TV show.
• Recorded at Olympic Studios.
• Produced by Andrew Loog Oldham.

"WE WANT THE STONES"
Written by: Nanker Phelge
Recorded by: The Rolling Stones
Release date: June 1965
Record label: Decca
Album: None
EP: GOT LIVE IF YOU WANT IT! (U.K. 6/65)
• This song consists of the audience chanting the above "title," and it was listed as a separate track so that the Stones could get publishing royalties for it.
• Recorded at the Manchester Palace Theatre, March 1965.

WEBSTER, GUY
Photographer of the AFTERMATH (U.K.), FLOWERS and BIG HITS (HIGH TIDE AND GREEN GRASS) album covers.

WEDGBURY, DAVID
Art director of SLOW ROLLERS.

WEEKS, WILLY
George Harrison's favorite bassist

(where's Paul McC.?), who plays on the original backing track of "It's Only Rock 'n' Roll."

WEIDENFELD, GEORGE
Publisher who bought the world rights to Mick's autobiography for close to £2 million in 1983, a record for a single book acquired by a U.K. publisher. His company, Weidenfeld & Nicholson, London, plans to publish the book in late spring of 1984. When asked in 1975 if he'd ever consider writing a book, Mick replied, "I'd *never* do that."

WELCH, BOB
Former Fleetwood Mac-er and current solo artist who plays guitar on STONE ALONE.

WELWYN GARDEN CITY, HERTFORDSHIRE, ENGLAND
Mick Taylor's birthplace.

WENTWORTH COUNTY PRIMARY SCHOOL
Alma mater to both Keith and Mick, who originally met there when they were about five. They were friends till Keith moved away, giving the two the opportunity to discover Chuck Berry independently.

"WE'RE WASTING TIME"
Written by: Jagger/Richards
Recorded by: The Rolling Stones
Release date: June 1975
Record label: Decca
Album: METAMORPHOSIS
• This is one of the two songs that do not appear on the American pressing of METAMORPHOSIS.

WEST, LESLIE
New York-born and bred guitarist (Vagrants, Mountain, West, Bruce & Laing) and one of rock's all-time

Mick and Andy Warhol.

heavyweights, who was a contender for Stoneship during the ''Great Guitarists Hunt'' of February 1975.

WEST SUSSEX QUARTER SESSIONS
Mick, Keith, and Robert Fraser were on trial here after the Redlands bust.

WESTHILL INFANTS SCHOOL
First school Keith attended.

WETHERBY ARMS
Kings Road club where the Stones rehearsed. Bill first saw them there, and auditioned for the band around Christmas 1962.

WEXLER, ANITA
Tape mixer of ''Apache Woman.''

''WHAT A BLOW''
Written by: Bill Wyman
Recorded by: Bill Wyman
Release date: May 1974
Record label: Rolling Stones Records
Album: MONKEY GRIP
• Byron Berline—country fiddle.
• Danny Kootch—guitar.
• Joe Lala—percussion.
• Mac Rebennack—organ and pedals.
• Dallas Taylor—drums.
• Boneroo Horn Section: Peter Graves, Mark Colby, Ken Faulk, Neal Bonsanti.

''WHAT A GUY''/''YOU WENT AWAY''
1965 Bobbie Miller single produced by Bill, who cowrote the flip side.

''WHAT A SHAME''
Written by: Jagger/Richards
Recorded by: The Rolling Stones
Release date: December 1964
Record label: Decca/London
Albums: THE ROLLING STONES NO. 2
THE ROLLING STONES, NOW!
Single: Flip of ''Heart of Stone''
(U.S. 12/64)
• Ian Stewart—piano.

''WHAT TO DO''
Written by: Jagger/Richards
Recorded by: The Rolling Stones
Release date: April 1966
Record label: Decca/London
Albums: AFTERMATH (U.K.)
MORE HOT ROCKS

''WHAT'S THE POINT''
Written by: Bill Wyman
Recorded by: Bill Wyman
Release date: February 1976
Album: STONE ALONE
• Dallas Taylor—drums.
• Joe Vitale—R.M.I.
• Van Morrison—guitar.
• Joe Walsh—slide guitar.

• John McFee—fiddles, pedal steel guitar.
• Ruth and Bonnie Pointer—backup vocals.

''WHEN SHE HELD ME TIGHT''
SOME GIRLS outtake.

''WHEN THE WHIP COMES DOWN''
Written by: Jagger/Richards
Recorded by: The Rolling Stones
Release date: June 1978
Record label: Rolling Stones Records
Albums: SOME GIRLS
SUCKING IN THE SEVENTIES (live)
Singles: Flip of ''Respectable'' (U.K. 9/78)
Flip of ''Beast of Burden''
(U.S. 11/78)

''WHERE THE BOYS GO''
Written by: Jagger/Richards
Recorded by: The Rolling Stones
Release date: June 1980
Record label: Rolling Stones Records
Album: EMOTIONAL RESCUE

WHIRLWIND, VINCE
Moniker Mick listed as ''professional name'' on an early Stones' fact sheet.

WHITE, BUKKA
Legendary blues artist whose guitar

tuning style Keith adopted.

WHITE, KEVIN
Mayor of Boston who bailed Mick, Keith, and company out of a Warwick, Rhode Island, jail after they were arrested during an airport scuffle, so they could make their date to play the Boston Garden in July 1972. He received a standing ovation at the show. Nine years later (still in office!), Mayor White refused to give the Stones a license to play at Boston's 2,800-seat Orpheum Theater because of the problems caused by their "small" gig at Sir Morgan's Cove.

"WHITE LIGHTNIN'"
Written by: Bill Wyman
Recorded by: Bill Wyman
Release date: May 1974
Record label: Rolling Stones Records
Album: MONKEY GRIP
Single: B/w "Pussy" (U.S./U.K. 11/74)
• Danny Kootch—twelve-string guitar.
• Joe Lala—percussion.
• John McCuen—dobro, mandolin.
• Dallas Taylor—drums.

WHITEHEAD, ANNIE
Horn player on "Jump Up."

WHITEHEAD, PETER
Producer and director of both *Charlie Is My Darling* and *Tonight Let's All Make Love in London*, he also directed the promo film for "We Love You."

WHITELEY'S
London department store where Brian worked in the sports section until he was caught stealing.

Patti Hansen and Paul Wasserman.

WHO, THE
British quartet who released "The Last Time" and "Under My Thumb" after Keith and Mick were found guilty during the Redlands trial, vowing to keep the Stones music alive until the band was able to record again. In 1982, Who leader Pete Townshend confessed to having not cared at all about this, releasing the record for its publicity value. The Who's segment in "The Rolling Stones' Rock and Roll Circus" can be seen in the Who documentary film, *The Kids Are Alright*.

"WHO BREAKS A BUTTERFLY ON A WHEEL?"
London Times editorial denouncing the sentencing of Mick and Keith after the Redlands trial. It was written by editor William E. Rees-Moog, who claimed that Mick was treated harshly because of his celebrity status.

"WHO'S BEEN SLEEPING HERE?"
Written by: Jagger/Richards
Recorded by: The Rolling Stones
Release date: January 1967
Record label: London/Decca
Albums: BETWEEN THE BUTTONS (U.S.)
          BETWEEN THE BUTTONS (U.K.)

"WHO'S DRIVING YOUR PLANE"
Written by: Jagger/Richards
Recorded by: The Rolling Stones
Release date: September 1966
Record label: Decca/London
Album: NO STONE UNTURNED
Single: Flip of "Have You Seen Your Mother, Baby, Standing in the Shadow?" (U.S./U.K. 9/66)

WICK
Ron and Krissie's house in Richmond, England. Ron had a recording studio there and worked on I'VE GOT MY OWN ALBUM TO DO with help from Keith and Mick.

WICZLING, BOB
Drummer on "Come Back Suzanne" and "Seventeen."

WIENER, JACK
Producer of *Green Ice*, the 1981 Ryan O'Neal/Omar Sharif film for which Bill scored the soundtrack.

"WILD COLONIAL BOY, THE"
Song performed by Mick on the *Ned Kelly* soundtrack LP.

"WILD HORSES"
Written by: Jagger/Richards
Recorded by: The Rolling Stones
Release date: April 1971
Record label: Rolling Stones Records
Albums: STICKY FINGERS
          HOT ROCKS
          MADE IN THE SHADE
Single: B/w "Sway" (U.S. 6/71)
• Pete Townshend and Ronnie Lane

are possibly singing backup vocals on this song.
• J. Dickinson—piano.
• This song is about:
A. Anita, written at the time when Mick and Marianne Faithfull were breaking up;
B. Marianne, when she was in a coma in a hospital in Australia;
C. Keith's reluctance to leave Anita and two-month-old Marlon to tour with the band;
D. Gram Parsons;
E. All of the above;
F. None of the above.

WILKES, TOM
Graphic designer of FLOWERS and BEGGARS BANQUET.

WILLIAMS, JERRY
Pianist on "Worry No More."

"WIND HOWLIN' THROUGH"
Written by: Ron Wood
Recorded by: Ron Wood
Release date: August 1981
Record label: Columbia
Album: 1 2 3 4
• Alan Myers—drums.
• Engineered by Tom Yuill.

"WINE & WIMMEN"
Written by: Bill Wyman
Recorded by: Bill Wyman
Release date: February 1976
Record label: Rolling Stones Records
Album: STONE ALONE
• Dallas Taylor—drums.
• Danny Kortchmar—guitars.
• Hubie Heard—organ.
• Guille Garcia—percussion.
• Rocki Dzidzornu—percussion.
• Terry Taylor—Leslie guitar.
• Albhy Galuten—synthesizer.
• Jackie Clark—guitar.
• Ruth and Bonnie Pointer—backup vocals.

WINGS OF ASH
Film Mick was scheduled to start shooting in September 1978. He was to play the part of Antonin Artaud, founder of the Theater of Cruelty, opposite Andrea Marcovicci, who would appear as Anaïs Nin.

"WINTER"
Written by: Jagger/Richards
Recorded by: The Rolling Stones
Release date: August 1973
Record label: Rolling Stones Records
Album: GOATS HEAD SOUP
• Nicky Hopkins—piano.
• Nicky Harrison—string arrangements.

WINTER, JOHNNY
Texas blues guitarist who Jagger/Richards wrote "Silver Train" for and who recorded it before the Stones.

"WISH A WOMAN"
EMOTIONAL RESCUE outtake.

WITH LOVE FROM...

Book published in 1980 by A & W Publishers, U.S., containing a collection of "lipographs." These were lipsticked lip-impressions on paper of celebrities from Mae West to Luciano Pavarotti which were originally done for the Save the Children Foundation. Auctioned at Sotheby's in London for the charity, the largest sum, $1,500, went for Mick's "lipograph."

WOHLIN, ANNA

Swedish woman who was living with Brian when he died. She pulled him from the pool.

WOLF, HOWLIN'

One of the Stones all-time American blues idols, whose songs made up much of the band's early repertoire and who attended one of Brian's famous rent parties in 1962. Bill and Charlie performed with him on his LP THE LONDON HOWLIN' WOLF SESSIONS, which was released on Rolling Stones Records in the U.K. The two also performed on Howlin' Wolf's LONDON REVISITED in 1974.

WOMACK, BOBBY

Co-composer of "It's All Over Now," which he performed as lead singer of the group the Valentinos. He played guitar and bass on "Fountain of Love," and opened for the Stones on some of the dates of their 1981 U.S. tour.

WOMEN AGAINST VIOLENCE AGAINST WOMEN

Group which called for a boycott of Warner Communications albums in 1976 because of the cover and promotional campaign for BLACK AND BLUE. Three years later, the boycott ended when Warners agreed that the group could meet with the art and marketing departments of Warner Bros. Records regarding future album and advertising art.

WOMEN'S WEAR DAILY

Fashion industry paper which, in 1972, named Mick on their "Cat Pack List," of the *ultimate* jet-setters, along with Henry Kissinger, Lord Snowdon, Truman Capote, and Ari and Jackie Onassis.

WONDER KNOB, LTD.

Chris Kimsey's production company.

WONDER, STEVIE

American superstar who opened for the Stones during their 1972 U.S. tour and often jammed with them during their finale, "Satisfaction."

WOOD, ART

Ron's older brother by ten years, Art sang with Alexis Korner's Blues Incorporated in the very early sixties, going on to form a band called the Artwoods, which contained Jon Lord. He is also an artist.

"Black and Blue." The Rolling Stones
ON ROLLING STONES RECORDS & TAPES
Distributed by Atlantic Records
PRODUCED BY THE GLIMMER TWINS

WOOD, JESSE JAMES

Ron's son, born in 1976.

WOOD, KRISSIE

The now ex-Mrs. Ron, Krissie and Ron met in the early sixties at—of all things—a Rolling Stones show at the Crawdaddy Club (she was a fan of Brian's). In April 1975, Krissie and a friend were arrested at Wick when police were looking for Keith (who'd been staying there) and heroin on the premises—and found the heroin but no Keith. Several years later, they were acquitted. Ron and Krissie were divorced in March 1978.

WOOD, LEAH

Ron and Jo Howard's daughter, born in 1978.

WOOD, MR.

Ron's father, who operated a tugboat and also had a harmonica band.

WOOD, MRS.

Ron's mother, who worked at tinting photographs by hand.

WOOD, TED

Ron's brother, who's eight years older than him and is also an artist and a musician. Ted was a member of the Temperance Seven, a sixties British band specializing in twenties jazz, and now owns the Red Lion, the pub next door to Olympic Studios in London.

WOOD, TYRONE

Ron's third child, born August 20, 1983 in New York City.

WORKERS PLAYTIME

1971 B. B. Blunder LP featuring Mick Taylor.

WORKMAN, GEOFF

Engineer on GIMME SOME NECK.

WOOD, RON

Born: June 1, 1947

"Honest" Ron Wood/Woody/Ronnie is the Stones' Stone—a favorite within and without the Rolling Stones, who has the distinction of being the only band member to be a rock star before being a Rolling Stone. Growing up with two musically motivated brothers, in a household where his father also was in a band, Ron started learning clarinet, drums, and washboard at an early age, making his debut on the last at the age of nine in his brothers' skiffle band. He studied art and briefly worked as a sign painter while playing guitar in his early- to mid-sixties band, the Birds. When they broke up, he joined the Jeff Beck Group on bass, and finally, in 1969, the Faces, where he found worldwide fame and fortune as lead guitarist. (See Birds, The; Beck, Jeff; Faces, The.)

Ron was the Stones' choice to replace guitarist Mick Taylor in 1975, but Ron was reluctant to leave the Faces, although he did accompany the Stones on their 1975 Tour of the Americas as a guest artist. In December 1975, upon Rod Stewart's leaving the Faces, Ron left too, becoming the seventh "official" Stone and taking over Keith's dreaded job as onstage foil to Mick.

Ron is the father of three children, and an accomplished artist, creating album covers for the Faces LPs, his own solo albums, and for other artists. He's an active rock 'n' roller, having recorded four solo LPs since 1974, doing his own tours while a member of the Faces, heading the New Barbarians while serving as a Rolling Stone, and posing as professor in lecture events to promote that good old rock 'n' roll.

"... Christ, it's not like you're hiring a cook or something."

—Mick Jagger

"Ron Wood had to please both me and Keith. I can sort of tell a good guitar player, but probably Keith can tell better than me. Remember, Keith used to be lead guitarist for the Rolling Stones."

—Mick Jagger

"He has an instinctive feel for what Brian and I originally worked out as far as guitars and the music go. Siamese twins—they both play. Look at it like this: there's one guy, he's just got four arms."

—Keith Richards

"Woody has made the band seem more human."

—Mick Jagger

"Woody's fabulous! He's made this band come back to life again!"

—Bill Wyman

Bill and Astrid.

"WORLD'S GREATEST ROCK 'N' ROLL BAND, THE"
The Rolling Stones.

WORMWOOD SCRUBS
Prison where Keith spent the night after his Redlands bust trial in 1967. Later that year, Brian also spent a night here after his first drug trial.

"WORRIED ABOUT YOU"
Written by: Jagger/Richards
Recorded by: The Rolling Stones
Release date: October 1981
Record label: Rolling Stones Records
Album: TATTOO YOU
• This song was originally recorded for BLACK AND BLUE.

"WORRY NO MORE"
Written by: Williams
Recorded by: Ron Wood
Release date: May 1979
Record label: CBS
Album: GIMME SOME NECK

• Charlie Watts—drums.
• "Pops" Popwell—bass.
• Jerry Williams—piano.

"WOULD YOU LET YOUR SISTER GO WITH A ROLLING STONE?"
Headline of a 1964 article written for the British music paper *Melody Maker* by Ray Coleman, this phrase was adopted and popularized by Andrew Oldham to further the Stones' outlaw image.

WREN, ANDY
Singer Brian took Ian Stewart to hear, with thoughts of starting a band with him after both Ian and Andy answered Brian's ad in *Jazz News*.

WRIGHT, BETTY
Backup vocalist on MONKEY GRIP.

WRIGHT, NICHOLAS
Photographer of the cover of ENGLAND'S NEWEST HIT MAKERS—THE ROLLING STONES.

WYMAN, ASTRID (LUNDSTROM)
Bill's constant companion since he divorced his wife in 1967 up until the summer of 1983. Although not legally married, Astrid used Bill's last name. She and Bill lived with his son, Stephen, in the south of France for many years, and it is rumored that their move back to England in 1982 was the cause of their reported break-up. Their movie, *Digital Dreams*, was the last project they worked on together.

WYMAN, STEPHEN
Bill and Diane's son, born in 1962. After his parents divorced, Stephen lived with Bill and Astrid Lundstrom in France, attending school there and majoring in economics. He plays synthesizer on "Ride On Baby" on his father's 1981 solo album, also helping dad with the LP jacket's photography.

(For all other Wyman relatives, see the surname Perks.)

WYMAN, BILL

Born: October 24, 1936
*The following is reprinted from a fact
sheet sent to American fans in spring
1964:*

BILL WYMAN
REAL NAME Bill Wyman. [Authors' note: liar.]
BIRTH DATE 24. 10. 41. [Authors' note: liar.]
BIRTH PLACE Lewisham.
HEIGHT 5'8".
WEIGHT 10st.
EYES Greeny/Brown.
HAIR Black.
PARENTS' NAMES William/Kathleen.
BROTHERS/SISTERS John, Paul, Judy, Anne.
HOME Beckenham.
INSTRUMENTS Guitar.
MUSICAL EDUCATION Piano lessons.
ENTERED SHOW BUSINESS AT: 21.
FIRST APPEARANCE Marquee Club.
BIGGEST BREAK IN CAREER Meeting Beatles.
TV DEBUT "Thank Your Lucky Stars".
RADIO DEBUT "Saturday Club".
HOBBIES Science fiction, records.
FAVOURITE SINGERS Les Paul, Chuck Berry.
FAVOURITE COLOUR Blue.
FAVOURITE FOOD Scampi, Pork chops.
FAVOURITE BAND Chuck Berry Combo.
FAVOURITE DRINK Orange squash.
FAVOURITE CLOTHES Modern, casual.
FAVOURITE COMPOSER Cole Porter.
MISC. LIKES Cashew nuts, poetry, girls.
MISC. DISLIKES Arguments, marmalade.
TASTES IN MUSIC R & B, Jazz, Classic, Pop.
PERSONAL AMBITION To meet Chuck Berry.
PROFESSIONAL AMBITION Top the hits.
WHERE EDUCATED Beckenham Grammar.

The stationary bassist of the Rolling Stones (born Bill Perks) began his musical career at the age of four, taking piano lessons, picking up the organ and clarinet, and singing in the church choir for ten years along the way. After school and a two-year stint in the Royal Air Force, Bill married, formed a band called the Cliftons, had a son, and answered an ad in *Melody Maker* to audition for the Rolling Stones, who needed a bassist. They *also* needed amplifiers. Bill had the biggest amp and got the job. Still, as a family man, he couldn't risk full-time Stoneship, keeping his clerical engineering job until "Come On," the band's first single, was released in June 1963. As Stonemania changed his life-style, Bill went "girl crazy," a condition leading to his divorce in 1967. Always upset that the Stones had no use for his material, Bill started releasing solo albums in 1974 and is now at work on his fourth. He is the only Stone with his own publicist and manager and had a major international hit with his song, "(Si Si) Je Suis Un Rock Star" in 1981. He is the official Stones historian, friend of famous painters and writers, an avid tennis player, fan of classical music, and poetry collector. In late 1982, he ended his self-imposed exile to France, returning to England to live.

"On stage I might look absent and lost but I'm totally thinking about the music. I just watch the audience. I dig all the audience."
—Bill Wyman

"When Charlie moves, I'll move."
—Bill Wyman

"Bill was seen to take three steps forward on this tour [1981]—never known to do that before."
—Alan Rogan

"You had me, Charlie, and Brian on the side like…well, not backup musicians, but almost. . . ."
—Bill Wyman

"I'd rather pack it in while we are up at the top. Another few years and we might be pushing it. . . ."
—Bill Wyman, 1980

"If Bill wants to leave the band, I mean, that's okay with me."
—Mick Jagger

"He's got this little mind that remembers everything."
—Keith Richards

"Bill was always the Rolling Stone that nobody ever knew."
—Brian Jones

"He's much better than we think."
—Keith Richards

"Things have been so good for me the last two years."
—Bill Wyman, 1982

X., MISS
Marianne Faithfull was referred to by this name in the court transcript of the Redlands bust.

X., MISTER
The vanishing Mr. Sneiderman was referred to by this name in the court transcript of the Redlands bust.

YAMAZAKI, KAZUHIDE
Artist who created the paintings which served as the stage backdrop for the Stones 1981 U.S. tour and the cover of STILL LIFE. The stage he designed for the Stones was the largest portable concert stage ever built, at a width of sixty-four feet, with two eighty-foot ramps.

YARDBIRDS, THE
British quintet most famous for giving the world Eric Clapton, Jeff Beck, and Jimmy Page (in that order), who opened for the Stones on their eighth British tour, fall 1966. In 1964, *very* pre-Stone Ron Wood performed with the band at the Marquee Club when vocalist/harmonica player Keith Relf was ill; guitarist Clapton asked if anyone in the audience knew how to play harp, and sixteen-year-old Woody's friends pushed him on the stage.

YARNHAM, LAURIE
Alias used by Chris Jagger when winning a Mick Jagger look-alike/ act-alike contest at Greenwich Town Hall, September 1964.

"YER BLUES"
Beatles song performed by A. N. Other at "The Rolling Stones' Rock and Roll Circus."

"YES SIR, THAT'S MY BABY"
Song that Jack Nitzsche was orchestrating at RCA Studios in Hollywood, July 1964, when the Stones and Oldham dropped by to visit him, meeting engineer Dave Hassinger for the first time.

"YESTERDAY'S PAPERS"
Written by: Jagger/Richards
Recorded by: The Rolling Stones
Release date: January 1967
Record label: Decca/London
Albums: BETWEEN THE BUTTONS (U.K.)
      BETWEEN THE BUTTONS (U.S.)
      MILESTONES
      ROLLED GOLD

• Chris Farlowe released this song as a single produced by Mick.

"YONDERS WALL"
Stones song recorded, with Allen Klein producing, for "The Rolling Stones' Rock and Roll Circus." It was never released.

"YOU BETTER MOVE ON"
Written by: Alexander
Recorded by: The Rolling Stones
Release date: January 1964
Albums: DECEMBER'S CHILDREN
      THROUGH THE PAST, DARKLY (U.K.)
      SLOW ROLLERS
EP: THE ROLLING STONES (U.K. 1/64)

"YOU CAN MAKE IT IF YOU TRY"
Written by: Jarrett
Recorded by: The Rolling Stones
Release date: April 1964
Record label: Decca/London
Albums: THE ROLLING STONES
      ENGLAND'S NEWEST HIT MAKERS
• Ian Stewart—organ.

"YOU CAN'T ALWAYS GET WHAT YOU WANT"
Written by: Jagger/Richards
Recorded by: The Rolling Stones
Release date: November 1969
Record label: Decca/London/Rolling Stones Records
Albums: LET IT BLEED
      HOT ROCKS
      LOVE YOU LIVE (live in Paris)
      SLOW ROLLERS
Single: Flip of "Honky Tonk Women" (U.S./U.K. 7/69)
      Flip of "Sad Day" (U.K. 4/73)
• Jimmy Miller—drums.
• Al Kooper—piano, french horn, organ.
• Rocky Dijon—percussion.
• Nanette Newman, Madelaine Bell, Doris Troy, and the London Bach Choir—vocals.
• Jack Nitzsche—choral arrangement.
• The album version of this song is over two minutes longer than the single version.
• The song was performed by the Stones at the "Rock and Roll Circus."

"YOU CAN'T CATCH ME"
Written by: Chuck Berry
Recorded by: The Rolling Stones
Release date: January 1965
Record label: Decca/London
Albums: THE ROLLING STONES NO. 2
      THE ROLLING STONES, NOW!

"YOU CAN'T JUDGE A BOOK"
Unreleased Bo Diddley song that Mick, Keith, Brian, Tony Chapman, and Ian Stewart recorded in October 1962.

"YOU GOT THE SILVER"
Written by: Jagger/Richards
Recorded by: The Rolling Stones
Lead singer: Keith
Release date: November 1969
Record label: Decca/London
Album: LET IT BLEED

• "You Got the Silver" marks Keith's lead singing debut!
• This song appears on the soundtrack of the film, *Zabriskie Point*.
• Nicky Hopkins—piano, organ.

"YOU GOTTA MOVE"
Written by: McDowell/Davis
Recorded by: The Rolling Stones
Release date: April 1971
Record label: Rolling Stones Records
Albums: STICKY FINGERS
      LOVE YOU LIVE (live in Paris)

"YOU KNOW MY NAME (LOOK UP THE NUMBER)"
Beatles song on which Brian plays tenor saxophone.

"YOU'RE SO VAIN"
Carly Simon song on which Mick sings harmony.

YOUNG, DOUG
Head of Doby Guitars and builder of Keith's two 1983-vintage custom hand-made solid-body guitars. One of these, a gift to Patti Hansen from Young, has Keith and Patti's names inlaid, with small diamond chips below each name and a mother-of-pearl skull and cross-bones which matches one of Keith's rings.

YUILL, TOM
Engineer on "Wind Howlin' Through."

ZZ TOP
Top U.S. rock act which opened for the Stones at their Texas shows in 1981.

ZABRISKIE POINT
1969 Michelangelo Antonioni film which includes "You Got the Silver" on its soundtrack.

ZAGANNO, JOE
Engineer on EXILE ON MAIN ST.

ZEMAITIS, TONY
Guitar maker, whose custom-made five-string is one of Keith's favorites. Woody started having his guitars made by Zemaitis after a rash of guitar thefts. He believed Zemaitis's guitars were so unique no one would dare to nick them.

ZOUZOU
French actress Brian dated with some difficulty—he knew no French; she knew no English. They somehow leaped the language barrier and planned in vain to make a film together. Without Brian, ZouZou later starred in *Chloe in the Afternoon*.

ZWERIN, CHARLOTTE
Codirector, along with the Maysles Brothers, of *Gimme Shelter*.

PHOTO CREDITS

Richard E. Aaron/Star File, pages 23; 78; 80 (right); 91 (left); 110 (lower right); 143. Bill Bastone/Star File, pages 48 (top left); 82 (left). Globe Photos, pages 26 (top right); 45 (lower right); 54 (top); 65; 131 (left); 132; 141. Bob Gruen/Star File, pages 31 (center); 57 (center); 61 (top right); 83 (right); 84 (right); 108; 127 (center); 147 (right). Steve Judit/Star File, page 44 (left). Keystone Press Agency, pages 4 (top); 6 (top); 25; 34 (left/right); 62; 70; 101; 107. Bob Leafe/Star File, page 131 (right). Virginia Lohle/Star File, page 30 (left). Bob Mendelsohn/Star File, page 47 (lower left). Neal Preston, cover; pages 11 (right); 13 (right); 16 (top/ bottom right); 17 (lower left); 32 (bottom); 35 (bottom center); 38 (top right); 43 (top left); 45 (top right); 48 (lower right); 49; 50; 53 (top left); 57 (top left); 60 (top); 64 (top right); 67 (center); 71 (right); 73 (bottom); 74; 79 (center/right); 80 (left); 81 (lower right); 82 (center); 84 (left); 85 (top right); 86; 89 (top center); 91 (right); 92 (right); 98 (left); 99 (left); 102 (right); 105; 106 (lower right); 111; 115 (right/ top center); 116 (center); 118 (left); 119 (left). Chuck Pulin/Star File, pages 36; 72; 128; 138. RDR Productions, pages 2 (top); 24; 59; 63 (left/ top right); 97 (right); 117; 119 (right); 120 (right); 137; 146. Phyllis Rosney / Star File, pages 17 (lower right); 20 (top right); 22; 31 (top); 71 (center); 73 (top); 81 (top right); 95 (left/right). Star File, page 63 (lower right). Joe Stevens, pages 46 (top left); 75 (bottom); 88; 102 (left); 124 (center); 125 (top right); 142; 145. The Private Collection of Gary Victor, pages 15 (center); 20 (top right); 35 (left); 44 (right); 45 (top left); 51 (top right); 55 (center); 56 (right); 58 (center); 60 (lower right); 77 (left); 90 (center); 92 (center); 96 (left); 97 (left); 100 (lower left); 115 (lower right); 116 (right); 120 (left); 124 (right); 129 (center); 134 (center/top right); 135. A. Frank Ziths/Star File, page 2 (top). Vinne Zuffante/Star File, pages 14; 46 (lower right); 51 (top left); 53 (center); 114 (right); 127 (top right). Various promotional pictures and album art courtesy of: Rolling Stones Records, London Records, Decca Records, ABKCO Records, EMI Records, Warner Bros. Records, CBS Records, A&M Records, Mercury Records, United Artists Records.